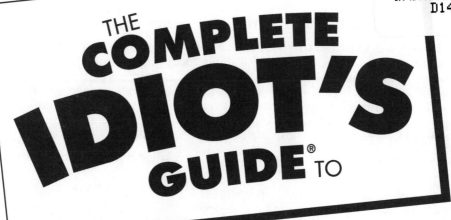

THE **COMPLETE IDIOT'S GUIDE**® TO

Surviving Bankruptcy

by Carol Costa and James R. Beaman, J.D.

ALPHA

A Pearson Education Company

Publisher
Marie Butler-Knight

Product Manager
Phil Kitchel

Managing Editor
Jennifer Chisholm

Acquisitions Editor
Mike Sanders

Development Editor
Deborah S. Romaine

Production Editor
Katherin Bidwell

Copy Editor
Amy Lepore

Illustrator
Jody Schaeffer

Cover Designers
Mike Freeland
Kevin Spear

Book Designers
Scott Cook and Amy Adams of DesignLab

Indexer
Brad Herriman

Layout/Proofreading
Svetlana Dominguez
Mark Walchle

Contents at a Glance

Contents

Foreword

Bad things can and do happen to good people. The proliferation of consumer bankruptcies in recent years is solid evidence of this fact. As a creditor's lawyer, I have been on the other side of numerous cases where good, responsible people have been forced to file bankruptcy because of circumstances beyond their control—death of the family's breadwinner, smothering medical expenses not covered by health insurance, loss of employment, and physical disability resulting in a loss of earning capacity.

At the same time, I have also seen a good number of cases where bankruptcy is the result of abusive credit practices on the part of undisciplined consumers. Bankruptcy, as a legal institution, is the system that is in place in response to the credit economy that has overtaken everyday business in our society. *The Complete Idiot's Guide to Surviving Bankruptcy* is written in an easy style to make what can be quite complex more understandable by those good people who find themselves in need of the help and protection that is obtainable only through the bankruptcy system.

The first four chapters of this work are devoted to bankruptcy avoidance. Excellent references are given to aid consumers in restructuring their monetary situations to deal positively with their delinquent debts. Debt counseling is a positive force in this country, helping debtors dig out from under crippling debts, and helping creditors to be treated fairly and equally by the debtors, ultimately to receive full payment, albeit somewhat tardily.

The remaining chapters of this work describe in understandable, but general, terms the various types of bankruptcy cases available to consumers who must seek the intervention of the bankruptcy court in dealing with their creditors. The author makes credible references to the proposed legislation pending in Congress that will change the Bankruptcy Code. While no one knows what changes will ultimately be enacted, if any, it is clear that all the proposed changes are such that bankruptcy will become even more complicated and more difficult for the average consumer.

The complexities of bankruptcy law are demonstrated by the hundreds of volumes of cases from across the United States that interpret the Bankruptcy Code. Bankruptcy proceedings are subject to their own complex rules and timelines that are prescribed for each bankruptcy court regardless of where the court might be located. In addition, individual bankruptcy courts are authorized to promulgate their own localized rules and timelines to supplement those pertaining generally to all bankruptcy courts. Only a bankruptcy lawyer is apt to have ready and timely knowledge of the general rules and timelines with the many regional variations pertaining to them.

Pre-petition planning, as the author points out, is critical; yet cases exist where courts have found pre-petition planning to be sometimes legitimate, and sometimes not. A seasoned bankruptcy lawyer is a necessity for a debtor who wishes to not only survive bankruptcy, but also to obtain all the benefits that the Bankruptcy Code was ordained to provide to those in need of its protection.

This work is not a "how-to" manual for filing one's own bankruptcy or shepherding one's own case through the complex bankruptcy court system. In fact, the title to this work gives a glimpse of the author's free-wheeling and sometimes lighthearted approach to a complex and not-so-humorous system. For instance, does the author mean that this work is intended only for "complete idiots" or does the author mean that this work is simply meant to be a "complete guide" to the intricacies of bankruptcy for the uninitiated? Rather, this book is a general guide that is intended to dispel some of the fear of the unknown attendant to the bankruptcy process, while at the same time affirming that a good person is still a good person, even if that good person has the misfortune to fall upon bad times and need the protection of the United States Bankruptcy Code. Sometimes bankruptcy must be endured, but it can always be survived.

—**Gerard R. O'Meara** is an attorney practicing with the law firm Bury, Moeller, O'Meara & Gage based in Tucson, Arizona.

Introduction

The decision to file bankruptcy is like jumping out of an airplane with engine trouble into a field of flowers. At first, your only thoughts are the necessity of escaping the confines of the plane that will surely crash and burn.

The plane is going into a nosedive because it is loaded down with debts, your debts. The staggering weight of all those bills is enough to bring down a commercial airliner, so what chance did the single engine you've been traveling through life in have to stay airborne?

The first hundred feet whiz by, and all you feel is relief at having found a way to get rid of all those bills. Your parachute opens and you begin to move more slowly, rocking and swaying with the gentle wind, gazing down at the empty field you are about to land in. That's when you start worrying about what you are actually going to find in that field.

There are lots of flowers, so it could be swarming with bees. Perhaps the field is actually a pasture where a big mean bull is waiting for you to land so he can gore you with his horns. Or maybe you're going to land in a tree, and the parachute lines will become entangled in the branches and cause you to be stuck there forever.

The purpose of this book is to help you land safely in the field of flowers that bankruptcy represents. The book will guide you through this unknown field and tell you exactly what you can expect to find there. There will be no bees, no trees, and pardon the pun, no bull.

Although filing bankruptcy is no laughing matter, it should not be viewed as a crash and burn. It is simply a way out that you may or may not choose to follow. Just as you wouldn't jump from that plane without a parachute, you should not enter into bankruptcy without getting all the information this book provides.

This book is divided into five parts:

➤ **Part 1, "The Credit Cards Are Stacked Against You"**—What began as a friendly game has turned into a nerve-shattering battle against rising interest rates and late fees. Although you may feel overwhelmed by the situation, you are not without choices. These chapters will guide you through the decision-making process by helping you explore all the options open to you. You will learn how to analyze your debt situation and take affirmative action.

➤ **Part 2, "How Do You Spell Relief? B-A-N-K-R-U-P-T-C-Y"**—Creditors refuse to deal, and Donald Trump hasn't returned your phone calls. Using the information and assessment methods you learned in Part 1, you are ready to study the bankruptcy laws and determine the type of bankruptcy that will best suit your individual needs. Advice and resources for finding an attorney in your area are included in this section.

➤ **Part 3, "You've Studied the Chapter, Now You're Buying the Book"**—You deserve a fresh start and the freedom to answer the phone without using that German accent. Careful planning is needed before filing bankruptcy. In this part, you learn how to organize and report your assets so you retain the things you need to get a fresh start.

➤ **Part 4, "Your Day in Court"**—After all the preparation, your lawyer files the bankruptcy petition, and the automatic stay goes into effect. The phone calls and late notices stop. With your personal plan in motion, you are now guided through the actual filing process. This section includes information that will help you effectively handle all the details and legal issues of your case.

➤ **Part 5, "Life After Bankruptcy"**—Your creditors have split up the $200 the trustee got for your old car with no windows. You have the chance to start over. This section tells you how to reestablish credit and avoid the pitfalls that can get you into trouble again. The last chapter in this section provides an overview of the pending legislation for bankruptcy reform and explains how it will affect the average consumer.

About This Book

This guide for the financially stretched and stressed explores alternatives to bankruptcy and explains the laws and procedures of the process of filing bankruptcy. The complexity of the federal bankruptcy code and the various types of bankruptcy are broken down and presented in a simple, easy-to-understand format. Advice and suggestions for rebuilding credit and financial security after a bankruptcy filing are also included. Information on rules and procedures is based on the current bankruptcy regulations with an overview of the pending legislation and the changes that may result if it is signed into law.

Using This Book

As you read through each section of this book, you will find a number of brief notations and illustrations that are designed to inform and entertain. Remember, one of the goals of this text is to help you relax and approach your financial problems with objectivity. With this in mind, the following boxes offer tips, definitions, and warnings.

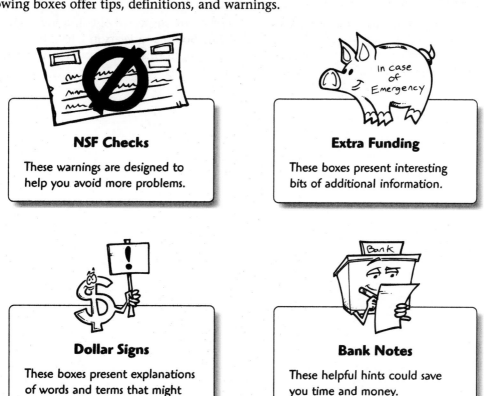

NSF Checks

These warnings are designed to help you avoid more problems.

Extra Funding

These boxes present interesting bits of additional information.

Dollar Signs

These boxes present explanations of words and terms that might be new to you.

Bank Notes

These helpful hints could save you time and money.

Each chapter of this book ends with a section called "The Least You Need to Know," a recap of the most important elements covered in the preceding text.

Acknowledgments

Thanks to our families, who are a constant source of encouragement and support.

Thanks to our agent, Andree Abecassis of Ann Elmo Agency, for her friendship and expert representation.

Thanks to Mike Sanders, Debbie Romaine, Amy Lepore, Katherin Bidwell, and the staff of Pearson Education who contributed their expertise to this book.

Thanks to Patty Cain, who cheerfully assisted us as we were gathering and processing the information for this book.

Thanks to all of James Beaman's clients who, through the years, have asked many of the questions we have attempted to answer in this book.

Trademarks

All terms mentioned in this book that are known to be or are suspected of being trademarks or service marks have been appropriately capitalized. Alpha Books and Pearson Education, Inc., cannot attest to the accuracy of this information. Use of a term in this book should not be regarded as affecting the validity of any trademark or service mark.

Part 1

The Credit Cards Are Stacked Against You

Although this book is about bankruptcy, Part 1 focuses on all the things you can do to help yourself and avoid bankruptcy.

Today, the world operates on something called revolving credit, and it is easy to get caught in its ever-spinning cycles. If you have credit, you don't have to wait for anything. You can get it instantly. This often causes you to buy things you don't really need, just because you can. The credit cards quickly stack up against you, threatening to topple over and smash your credit rating and your self-esteem.

It's too late to go back and undo things, but you can remain in control. In Part 1, you will have a chance to explore and examine all the options that are open to you.

You're Not a Loser

In This Chapter

➤ Maintain your self-esteem

➤ Take an objective look at your financial picture

➤ Determine the expenses to keep current

➤ Check your bankruptcy risk

It's amazing how quickly a company that was anxious and pleased to provide you with a generous line of credit can turn on you. It doesn't take much to fall out of favor with your creditors. Just miss a payment, and those unpleasant little notes appear on your statement. Miss another payment, and the phone calls start coming.

If you get too far behind, your account is turned over to collection, and then the unpleasant tone can become downright nasty. Bill collectors are often adept at intimidation, and a call from one of them can ruin your day faster than a frog can zap a fly.

Once you fall behind and your creditors begin to snap at your heels, your stress level is likely to rise. Stress can affect you in many different ways, and none of them are good for you or the people around you.

Whether your inability to meet your financial obligations is temporary or long term, there are solutions you can explore and choices you can make that will help relieve the stress.

Bankruptcy should be a last resort, and it should not be entered into lightly. It is a step that should be taken only after careful consideration and study. Don't let your creditors control your life. They have no personal interest in you or your family. Take your time and make sure the decisions you make are the right ones for you.

Hold Your Head High

One of the most important things you can do when you are in financial distress is keep a positive attitude. Getting down on yourself is not going to accomplish anything. Self-esteem governs the way you present yourself to the world at large. If you have a good opinion of yourself, others will view you as a competent, valuable person.

Maintaining a good self-image is vital, and that doesn't mean hiding your problems from friends and associates. It means you have the fortitude to admit you're in trouble and to seek the solutions you need to erase the problems and go on with your life. If you can keep your head up in the face of trouble, you will find that others will look at you with admiration rather than pity.

Feeling sorry for yourself will not make your problems disappear. A positive attitude about yourself and your situation will give you the clarity and resolve you need to put your problems in perspective and deal with them effectively. As you go through life, you are likely to encounter many obstacles. Money or the absence of it is often viewed as the primary cause of problems. However, a lack of funds is not the direct cause of the problems; it is the result of other more significant problems.

Take an objective look at your life and your lifestyle. Before you go any further, you must determine how you got into financial trouble. Before a viable solution can be reached, the real problem must be identified. Start with the fact that your expenses exceed your income. Now try to figure out why that is so. This is a personal challenge, and only you can provide the right answers to questions relating to health, education, economic problems in industry, or a simple case of spending too much on luxury items.

Extra Funding

The Federal Reserve estimates that the typical family owes more than one and a half times its annual income in short-term, high-interest debt.

Once you've determined the underlying cause of your current financial dilemma, you're on your way to recovery. If your problems are due to the poor health of yourself or a family member, there are a number of agencies that can help you. Almost every disease known to man has its own support group. These groups are there to offer assistance and information.

Go to the phone book, the computer, your doctor, or any other resource you can think of and ask for help. Organizations like the American Heart Association, the American Cancer Society, and Easter Seals can help or can refer you to the proper places in your area. Contact information for these organizations and others is listed in Appendix A, "Resource Directory," of this book.

If it's a lack of education that's kept your income lower than your expenses, there are programs that allow you to keep working while you train for a higher paying job. Unfortunately, new and better technology has had a large impact on our society's work force. Every day, people are being replaced by computers and automation. If you have lost your job for this reason or as a result of an economic slowdown in your industry, you may benefit from more education or retraining.

There are programs and agencies that can help you learn a new trade or enhance your current skills so you can increase your earning potential. The Employment and Trade Administration (ETA) is a government program that teaches job skills and provides placement services and assistance for dislocated workers.

If your current dilemma is due to overspending, the solution may appear simple: Stop doing it. Of course, you realize that's not all that easy. If it were, you would have done it before you landed in the middle of credit card hell.

There are groups that can show you how to channel your energies in new directions. Debtors Anonymous is one such group. This organization exists to help its members stay solvent and avoid compulsive spending. You will find contact information for this fellowship group in Appendix A of this book. Often, just finding a new interest that doesn't involve big expenditures is one way to curb impulse buying.

Now that you've pinpointed the source of your financial problems and are thinking of ways to eliminate that source, it's time to move on to the next step.

Bank Notes

For information on specific services of the ETA in your area, contact them through their Web site at www.doleta.gov/ or call 1-877-US-2JOBS.

Take a Long, Hard Look at Your Debts

There's no painless way to do this. You will have to open every bill, even the ones you might have thrown in the trash, and look at them. Take courage from the fact that this is something you will have to do anyway, even if you decide to file bankruptcy. Listing every creditor and the amount of the debt is required.

Initially, the person in the household who handles the finances and pays the monthly bills should do this. If you are that person, go to it. If you are not that person, get your partner, wife, brother, child, or whoever and ask him or her to do it. This is not a pleasant task, so you may have to do it together so you can give each other moral support.

Start by separating the usual household expenses from the installment payments. If you like, you can put the two categories in alphabetical order. It might make you feel better to organize them in a logical manner.

Begin by listing all your monthly household expenses. This includes rents, utilities, auto insurance, association and maintenance fees, cable television, estimated food costs, medicines, medical and life-insurance premiums, medical supplies, and anything else you pay out on a regular basis.

Don't worry about including a clothing allowance. Some of those credit card bills and department store accounts are probably for clothes that are still hanging in your closets. Right now, unless you're sitting there stark naked, new clothing is the least of your worries.

NSF Checks

Money issues are a leading cause of divorce in the United States. If you're married, avoid blaming your spouse for your financial problems. Instead, use your energies to work through the crisis.

After you've listed and totaled the household expenses, take a separate sheet of paper to list all the mortgages, auto loans, medical bills, credit card companies, banks, and finance companies where you have open accounts.

You can set up a simple worksheet to itemize each creditor and the amount of the debt. It should have columns to list the necessary information and can be formatted as in the Creditor Worksheet example:

Creditor Worksheet

Creditor	Total Amount	Monthly Payment	Secured By
ABC Bank	$150,000	$1,200	House
DEF Bank	$10,000	$425	Auto
Dr. Johnson	$850	$50	Unsecured
VISA	$4,100	$150	Unsecured
MasterCard	$5,200	$175	Unsecured

Dollar Signs

A loan that was obtained by allowing a creditor to put a lien on a piece of property is a **secured** debt. The loan amount is usually based on the value of the property, also called collateral. If the debtor defaults on the loan, the creditor can confiscate the property.

As you can see, some debts are *secured* and others are *unsecured*. It is important to identify and classify your debts in this way.

Although the amount you pay for rent and the amount you pay for the mortgage on a house serve the same purpose—keeping a roof over your head—they are actually quite different as far as your financial picture is concerned. So if you've included your mortgage payment in with the household expenses, move it to the creditor list instead.

This is because you could move out of rental property and no longer be liable for the monthly payment on that property. The mortgage on a house is a liability that continues whether you live in the property or not. In addition, a house, even one with a huge mortgage, is an asset. Assets are good. Assets are things you want to hang on to if at all possible.

The other reason a mortgage payment is not listed with the household expenses is because it is a secured loan. Secured loans are in a special category because if you don't make the payments on a secured loan, the property used for collateral can be confiscated or repossessed by the lender.

Losing the collateral you put up for a loan is to be avoided if at all possible. Not only do you lose the asset, you lose all the payments you have already made on that asset. Even worse, if the lender sells the asset and does not get enough money to satisfy the balance of the loan amount, you are liable for the difference.

This does not happen too often with real estate assets such as houses because they tend to appreciate in value as time goes on. It does happen frequently with vehicles, business equipment, and any property that lessens in value with use.

For example, you buy a car with no money down, financing it for $15,000 through a bank, credit union, or finance company. The term of the loan is five years. As soon as you drive that car off the dealer's lot, it begins to depreciate. Two years later, you still owe $10,000 on the car, but now the car's value is only $9,000.

If the lender were to repossess the car because you couldn't make the payments, the lender would try to sell it. Even if the car were sold for the full value of $9,000, there would still be an outstanding balance of $1,000 on the original auto loan. You would be liable for that amount even though you no longer have the car to drive. Adding insult to injury, because you have no car, you're now riding the bus to work—while the lender is still after you for the balance of the loan!

This is not to say that you can't make some type of arrangement with the lender if you find yourself in a situation in which you can't make your payments. Sometimes the lender will take the car or other property back and release you from all liability on the original loan. This is especially true if you decide to file bankruptcy. (You will find detailed information on this in later chapters.)

A house is generally worth more than you paid for it after two years, and the difference is your *equity* in the property. That is all the more reason you don't want the lender to take it away from you because you have fallen behind in the mortgage payments.

When a lender takes possession of a house for nonpayment of the mortgage, it is called a *foreclosure*. Remember that word, foreclosure. There is nothing that will hurt your credit standing more than a foreclosure. Ask mortgage lending professionals and they will tell you that they can work with a client who has filed bankruptcy, but it is very difficult to secure another mortgage loan for someone who has a foreclosure in his or her credit history.

> **Dollar Signs**
>
> **Equity** is the difference between the value of the property and the loan amount. If a piece of property is worth $100,000 and the mortgage is $80,000 the equity in the property is $20,000.

If you've ever seen a theater production called a melodrama, you know that the hero will risk his life to keep the villain from foreclosing on the heroine's family homestead. Although you should definitely not risk life or limb to keep a piece of property, you should take whatever other steps are necessary to avoid foreclosure.

There are legal means that can be used to save the homestead from foreclosure, and these will be explained in detail along with other actions relating to federal bankruptcy laws.

Now that all your expenses are listed and totaled, you will be able to compare this amount to your monthly income. If you're having trouble paying your bills, you already know that your expenses are bigger than your income. Actually putting this down on paper may give you the jolt you need to do something about it.

See What You Can Cut

No matter what your monthly deficit is, you can benefit from cutting expenses. At the very least, the money you save can be used to make payments on credit cards and loans. With this in mind, consider some of the following suggestions.

Reducing your monthly outgo begins by asking yourself what expenses must be kept current in order to keep house and health intact. Obviously, the rent or the mortgage payment is essential. Utilities are also necessary, but you may be able to cut a few corners with them.

For example, if you run the air conditioner at 68 degrees, try turning the thermostat up a few degrees to save a few dollars. The same applies to your heating bill. Turn the thermostat down and put on a sweater. Monitor your water use. Water conservation not only saves you money, it also is good for the environment.

How about that telephone bill? Are you paying extra for conveniences you could do without, such as caller ID and call waiting? Are you making long-distance phone calls in the middle of the day that could wait until the less expensive evening rates kick in? Have you talked to the phone company about discount or one-rate plans?

Cable television is another monthly expense that can be eliminated. You'll still have network programs to watch, and when those get too bad, you can read a book, play a game with the kids, or just sit and talk with someone you like. You could also surf the Internet, but make sure the Internet usage fees don't include extras you can live without. There are even Internet providers that offer free services.

Bank Notes

The public library is a wonderful resource for books, audiotapes, and videos. Most libraries also have computers and Internet connections you can use.

If you need a car to get to work, the car payment must be kept current. However, if the payment is high and you've been paying on the car for a year or more, you might be able to refinance the loan and lower that payment. However, refinancing a loan often means that you will pay out more in interest because it will take longer to satisfy the liability.

Gasoline, auto maintenance, and insurance go along with the car and are in the essential category, but you may be able to cut back there, too. If you have a good driving record, you can research the cost of insurance through a variety of companies. Rate quotes are available by telephone or the Internet.

Take a look at your food budget. Do you even have a food budget? A tried-and-true method is meal planning. Plan your weekly meals in advance and then purchase what you need for those meals. Cut down on those trips to the grocery store for one or two items. Try to get everything you need in one weekly or biweekly trip.

Use coupons for additional savings, but don't run yourself ragged chasing down specials from one store to the next. What you save in groceries, you'll spend in gasoline. Remember that your time is also a valuable commodity.

Over-the-counter drugs and even prescription medicines are another area where you can economize. If possible, buy store brands or generic equivalents of the medicines and remedies you use, including prescriptions. Check with your pharmacist or doctor to make sure the generic brand will work before changing.

Although you may not have included entertainment on your list of expenses, the amount you spend going to the movies, out to dinner, or to the theater can be substantial. Review the places you've gone and the things you've done over the last month and see how much you actually spent on entertainment.

Don't sit home and pout about giving up the latest slasher film. Instead, substitute something less expensive, such as a trip to an art gallery or museum. If you want to see a particular film, go when the rates are lower or wait until it's released on video. Instead of going to a Broadway show, go to an off-Broadway show. Some of them are just as good or better.

Another option is the possibility of adding a part-time job that pays enough to stay solvent, but keep in mind that working another job may also increase or add to your expenses. Working two jobs means more traveling, which necessitates bus fare or gas money. It also means you will be more tired than usual and may start leaning toward fast foods or other conveniences that cost more. You may also have to pay out additional funds for childcare.

Learning to live on a budget or restrict expenditures isn't easy, but it isn't life threatening and may even be good for you. Since your list of monthly expenses reflects your personal lifestyle, it is up to you to decide what can be cut or reduced.

Whatever money you manage to save by cutting expenses or increasing your income should be used to reduce some of the other payments you are making.

The whole idea is to keep what you have. Don't jeopardize an asset because another creditor is screaming at you to pay him first. You put everything down on paper to help you prioritize your liabilities. Keep your list and update it weekly or monthly.

NSF Checks

Payments to credit card companies go down as the balance goes down, but be sure to pay the bills on secured loans first. Your first priority is protecting your assets.

One of the things people tend to do is pay all the small bills first so that fewer creditors will be hounding them. That may not be the smartest method to follow. The first bills to be paid each month should be your mortgage or the rent on your house or apartment. Next is your auto loan and utilities and whatever else you need to keep working and earning some type of income. If at all possible, protect your assets and keep a roof over your head. Do that in the order that is most important to you and your family.

Review your list of expenses and debts. Highlight those bills that must be kept current and pay them first each month. The last thing you want to do is add to your financial worries by getting evicted from your apartment or having the bank start foreclosure proceedings on your house.

Bank Notes

Financial experts advise that your bills be prioritized and paid in the following order: mortgage or rent, utilities, secured debts, credit cards and unsecured debts, and then medical bills.

NSF Checks

Cash advances and the so-called convenience checks sent by credit card companies often trigger extra fees and higher interest rates.

Extra Funding

Credit professionals suggest that your nonmortgage debts, which include credit card payments, should be less than 15 percent of your net (take-home) salary.

Is Bankruptcy in Your Future?

Asking yourself the following questions may help you decide how close you are to having to declare bankruptcy:

1. **Are you normally late in paying your monthly bills?**

   Everyone runs into unexpected expenses such as medical bills or car repairs that throw the monthly budget off. However, if you are consistently late on most of your bills, you know you have a problem.

2. **Have you reached or exceeded the limit on all or most of your credit card accounts?**

   Running up credit card balances is easy to do, especially today when the companies are constantly sending you those "convenience checks" to cash and use. It can quickly become a vicious circle.

3. **Are you only able to pay the minimum payment on your credit card balances?**

   Credit cards are billed on a cycle that is less than 30 days. This increases the amount of interest charged to your account each month. This is one of the reasons why it is so hard to make a dent in the balance if you are only able to pay the minimum amount required.

4. **Do you have to dip into your savings to pay your bills each month?**

   Even if you are keeping up the minimum payments and are not incurring late fees, using your cash reserves to pay monthly bills can lead to trouble. If your income drops or unexpected expenses arise, you will have nothing to fall back on and will have to borrow money to survive.

5. **Do you use a credit line or cash advance to make your monthly payments?**

   If you are doing this on a regular basis, you know you are trapped in a financial whirlpool.

6. **Are you still making payments on items you no longer own?**

   This could be a television set that became too expensive to repair, a car that had to be towed away, or a household appliance that you donated to the church rummage sale. This is a common situation and can often be the result of simple bad luck.

7. **Have you been denied credit?**

   Regular financial institutions such as banks and credit unions use a percentage ratio that compares your expenses to your income, and they will deny credit to people deemed to be over the standard limits. Finance companies tend to have more liberal terms, but the interest rates they charge are much higher. To make a safer, more reasonable determination, base your answer on the criteria followed by banks and credit unions.

If you answered yes to all or most of these questions, you are in a high-risk situation. You are probably teetering on the edge between solvency and bankruptcy. This doesn't necessarily mean you've run out of choices, but it does mean you need to take action before things get any worse.

Taking Appropriate Action

Action is the key word in this situation. However, action doesn't mean doing things that will make your financial condition worse. Strange as it may seem, some people who are living on the edge financially have a tendency to accrue more debts. Perhaps they feel that their economic condition is like a fire raging out of control. Since the local fire department isn't likely to come to their rescue, they decide that throwing a few more logs on the inferno won't make a big difference.

It's like an overweight person who is discouraged with dieting. The dieter has been cutting calories and trying to exercise, but the scale isn't showing the desired results. So the dieter goes on an eating binge, and the scale shows another 10 pounds.

People who are having serious financial problems may feel just as discouraged as the dieter who is popping buttons and breaking zippers. They are working 40 hours a week, and everything they earn goes to pay bills. There is nothing left over for entertainment.

The temptation to give yourself a break and do something nice for yourself is often a strong motivator. What makes it worse is that you may still have some room on some of those credit cards.

Perhaps in the back of your mind, you're thinking that since you will be filing bankruptcy anyway, adding more dollars to your total debts is no big deal. You might even consider skipping a payment on one or more of your bills so you can spend the cash on something that will bring you pleasure.

Dinner at your favorite restaurant, a new outfit, electronic equipment, or anything else you might fancy might make you feel better or allow you to forget your problems for a short time, but like a mirage in the desert, the feeling will quickly fade away.

Extra Funding

Being nice to yourself in times of stress or trouble is a natural reaction, and there is nothing wrong with wanting to be distracted from your problems. However, there are ways to give yourself a break that will not add to your debt burden. One of the best stress relievers is exercise. A vigorous walk, swim, or aerobic workout may help you both physically and mentally.

In the long run, you may even feel worse for having spent money on something frivolous. And then there's the possibility that an emergency will arise and you will be out of cash and out of credit. If your car breaks down, it is unlikely that you would be able to find a mechanic who would be willing to fix it for free. Most dentists, doctors, and plumbers expect to be paid for their services.

No matter how bad your financial situation is, it can always get worse. If it deteriorates further because of circumstances you are unable to control, it is considered misfortune. If it worsens because of your own actions, it may be considered irresponsible and possibly even fraudulent. As you learn about bankruptcy and the laws that govern it, you will become more aware of how the actions you take before a case is filed can affect its outcome and your future.

The Least You Need to Know

➤ Don't let your bleak financial picture destroy your self-esteem.

➤ Give each new financial decision careful and serious consideration.

➤ Secured debts should be paid before unsecured debts to protect your assets.

➤ Prioritize your bills and pay them in that order.

➤ Having your car repossessed doesn't always satisfy the loan amount. You can still be held liable.

➤ A foreclosure on your credit history is more damaging than a bankruptcy.

Chapter 2

Don't Be Intimidated

In This Chapter

➤ Face creditors head on

➤ Open the mail

➤ Answer the phone

➤ Use a direct, honest approach

Dealing with creditors and collection agencies is difficult and frustrating. Their persistence in tracking you down at home and at work can become a real problem for you, your family, your employer, and your co-workers. It's no wonder that many people in financial trouble tend to refuse phone calls and dump late notices in the trash unopened. Unfortunately, these tactics don't stop the phone calls and late notices from coming.

Fantasizing about winning the lottery or getting some other wonderful windfall may be a nice temporary diversion and can even help you cope better, but the odds of it actually happening are astronomical.

While you are researching the options that will provide solutions to your financial problems, you must deal with your creditors.

Creditors Have Rules to Follow

A federal law, the Fair Debt Collection Practices Act, regulates how creditors and their agents must treat you, the consumer, when they are attempting to collect a debt or payment from you. Unfortunately, some creditors and many of the collectors they employ try to take advantage of the fact that you are in financial distress. They are aware that your situation may have you feeling panicky, confused, defensive, and vulnerable.

To deal effectively with creditors and collectors, you should know the rules and refuse to be intimidated. In general, it is illegal for a debt collector to do any of the following:

1. Contact your employer or neighbors about your debt
2. Call you late at night or too early in the morning
3. Telephone you repeatedly
4. Make threats or use profane or obscene language
5. Continue to contact you after you have sent a cease letter

Each of these general rules has specific explanations and examples that are intended to protect you from harassment and unfair practices. Be aware of what collectors can and cannot do so you can deal with them accordingly.

Many employers don't like employees to get personal phone calls on the job. If this is the case, tell collectors that they are jeopardizing your employment by calling you at work. By law, they are required to honor your request to call you only at home. They are also prohibited from calling you at inappropriate places such as a friend's house or a hospital.

Of course, some collectors are adept at getting information about you and may very well use it to make contact with you. If it happens, remind the collector that he or she is violating the law. Most are usually so surprised that you know what the law is that they apologize and hang up quickly.

Creditors may call a friend or a relative if you have given them permission to do so. Although you may think you would never give such permission, take a look at the credit application you signed. Often there is a space on the form for personal references or a place to list your closest relative.

The form asks you to list the name, address, and phone number of a relative who does not live with you. The fine print on the application or contract states that the creditor may contact that relative using the information you have provided. When you sign the contract, you are agreeing to that particular clause or stipulation.

Bank Notes

If you are having problems making your payments, you should contact your creditors, explain the situation, and try to work out a plan that will keep your account from being turned over to a collection agency. Some creditors will work with you and some will not, but it's worth a try.

The creditor is also allowed to contact your relatives and friends if that communication is solely for the purpose of locating you and if the creditor does not reveal why contacting you is necessary. For example, a friend might get a phone call stating that you have applied for a loan and that the caller needs more information to process the paperwork. The collector makes it sound like your friend would be doing you a favor to provide a phone number or alternative way of contacting you. Although this might seem misleading or deceptive, it is not against the law.

If you are having credit problems, advise your relatives that they may get a phone call from a collector. This may be embarrassing for you, but it is better to bring the problem out in the open and discuss it. Chances are good that your relatives already know you're in trouble, and if they know in advance that they may be getting calls from your creditors, you can both decide on the best way to handle the calls.

Extra Funding

People who work for collection agencies are trained to track you down and know how to word third-party inquiries so that they are not in violation of the law.

The time of day when collectors are allowed to call you is restricted to the hours between 8 A.M. and 9 P.M. in the time zone where you live. If you get a call earlier or later than that, simply tell the collector what time it is and hang up.

Although this may seem like a diversionary tactic, it is not. You are protecting your privacy and your rights as prescribed by law. It is just one of the ways you control your financial dilemma. Since the collector is not supposed to call you repeatedly, once you've ended the call, your phone should not ring again that day or evening.

If you are represented by an attorney, the collector must communicate with you through the attorney unless your lawyer gave the collector permission to contact you directly. If you have an attorney who does that without consulting you first, get a new attorney.

Don't let any creditor or collector insult, threaten, or harass you. Creditors are expressly forbidden to use obscene or profane language or threaten you. They can advise you of certain consequences that failure to pay your bill might trigger, such as legal action. However, these consequences must be true. For instance, they can't tell you that they are going to put up a billboard proclaiming that you are a deadbeat.

The law requires that a collection agency send you a written notice of the debt and all information relating to it. This notice may be the first communication you receive from the agency. If a phone call comes first, the written notice must be sent within five days of that contact. If you are disputing the amount of a loan or other account balance, you must do so in writing. That written notification stops collection proceedings until the discrepancy is corrected.

Bank Notes

You do not admit liability when you fail to dispute a debt. In a court action, the creditor would still have to prove that you owed the debt.

Don't try to put off creditors with disputes that have no basis. It may stop collection actions for a time, but a false dispute could be considered fraudulent and make your situation worse. When a claim is disputed, the creditor must provide written proof that it is valid. If the creditor's claim is verified, collection actions resume.

Last but not least is the regulation that prohibits a creditor or collector from contacting you after you sent a written request to stop. Although the written request, known as a cease letter, sounds great, there is a loophole. The creditor is allowed to contact you one more time to acknowledge the cease letter and to advise you of other actions the creditor may pursue under the law. The usual remedy under the law is a court action. This could mean anything from a lawsuit to a judgment that will result in garnishment of your wages.

The rules that the creditors must follow during the collection process do not in any way relieve you of the liability of the debt. Knowing your rights under the Fair Debt Collection Practices Act gives you a means of handling creditors so they don't take advantage of you or jeopardize your job. The purpose of these laws is to help you deal with creditors, not ignore them.

Late Notices Aren't Hate Mail

As bad as they make you feel, the late notices you receive in the mail are not really a personal attack on your character. Most of these notices are generated by a computer, a piece of equipment with no feelings about you.

What is a late notice, anyway? It's just a piece of paper with a printed message, a series of sentences made up of ordinary words. The late notice doesn't convey a nice thought or a humorous line. It's not a greeting card. It's a business communication and should be treated as such.

Resist the urge to throw the communications from your creditors into the nearest trash receptacle. Throwing the notices away won't make the problem disappear. It may help you ignore the problem, but that's not wise.

Open every piece of mail that your creditors send. If the notice is the same one you got yesterday or last week, throw the last one away and keep this current one. Even if you think you know what the notice is going to say, open it anyway and read it.

There are three reasons for opening, reading, and keeping the most current bill or late notice. First, and most important, you need to know if the creditor is going file suit against you or try to *garnish* your wages.

You don't want a process server showing up at your front door or, worse yet, at your place of business. A process server is a messenger who personally delivers the official notice that a lawsuit or other legal

Dollar Signs

Garnishment is a court order that requires your employer to deduct funds from your wages to pay a creditor.

action has been filed against you. If you know your creditors are getting to that point in the collection process, you can take action to protect yourself and your assets and possibly avoid a costly court action.

Second, if you decide to file bankruptcy, you will have to provide this information to your attorney. The bills and late notices provide an accessible record of the amount of each debt. They also have information like the address of the creditor and your account number. You'll need that information as well.

Third, forcing yourself to do something you don't want to do is an accomplishment. It is also one of the ways you can monitor your situation and exercise some control.

Opening the mail is like winning a small battle. You are taking the fear of the unknown out of the picture. If you don't know exactly what you owe or what your creditor's next move is, you are in danger of losing both the battle and the war.

For Whom the Bell Tolls

The bell in this case is the telephone. When you're in financial trouble, every time the telephone rings, your first thought is that a bill collector is on the other end of the line.

You can answer the phone with a German accent so that the caller will think she's reached the wrong number. You can answer the phone and tell the caller that you're not home, that you've moved and left no forwarding address, or that the house is on fire and you can't talk. Any of these pretenses will work once or twice, but of course, the collectors will just keep calling.

Actually, some creditors and collectors are pretty ingenious when it comes to tracking you down and getting you to talk to them. In the long run, it is really easier to accept the call and deal with it. Just remember what you've learned about the rules and regulations that govern creditors and their agents during the collection process. If necessary, jot down the key points and post the list next to your telephone.

Remember that old childhood rhyme, "Sticks and stones may break my bones, but words can never hurt me." Words cannot cause you physical harm. If they could, phone solicitors would all be on life support.

Keep in mind that the person calling you is just doing his or her job. Like the computer that sends out late notices, the collector doesn't know anything about you. You are just a name on a list of people that he or she has been instructed to call.

Take the sting out of the collector's call by reminding yourself that this person has one of the worst jobs in the world. No one is ever happy to hear from a collector. Many people the collector contacts are rude and even verbally abusive. When you think about it, you should feel sorry for this poor person who is doing this thankless, unrewarding work to pay his or her own bills.

In case of Emergency

Extra Funding

Under the law, a collector is prohibited from using any type of language or symbol on envelopes or postcards that indicates that the communication is from a debt collector.

If you put things in their proper perspective, you remain in control. If you let apprehension and fear take over, you are being managed by the situation. Don't let that happen. Good decisions are made when you remain in charge. So answer the phone and maintain your composure. If the collector violates the rules or won't listen to your side of the story, you can always hang up.

Promises, Promises

Creditors and collectors have one goal: to get you to send money. They really don't care what you have to do to accomplish this; they just want to be able to make a notation next to your name that says you agreed to send a payment.

The temptation to promise them a payment is great. "The check is in the mail" is probably the most overused sentence in the English language. Don't use it unless it's true. The best answer is an honest answer. Don't promise what you know you can't deliver. Don't make excuses. Collectors have already heard them all. If you can't make a payment, say so.

Sometimes a creditor will tell you that you can avoid a lawsuit or some other dire consequence by sending a payment by a certain time. Don't be pressured into making a payment on an unsecured debt that will jeopardize your home mortgage payment, rent, or utilities.

NSF Checks

Banks sometimes close the accounts of customers who write bad checks on a regular basis and report these closures to other banks, making it difficult to open an account elsewhere.

The other big temptation that must be strictly avoided is sending a check when you don't have enough funds in the bank to cover it. In today's high-tech world, everything is done electronically. Checks clear your bank account in a very short amount of time. Some companies have been known to take customers' checks directly to the banks on which they are drawn to collect their money the same day the check is received.

Writing a bad check can trigger several consequences, none of which are beneficial to you. The bank returns the check to the company that tried to collect the funds marked "NSF," which means "nonsufficient funds," and promptly charges you a hefty fee.

Bank fees for NSF checks are currently about $25 for each transaction. This amount is immediately charged to your checking account and is deducted from the balance. This jeopardizes other checks you may have written and causes them to be returned as NSF, resulting in even more NSF fees being charged against your account.

The other side of the road, the side your creditor is on, can become even more dangerous. You still owe the original payment, and the creditor will most likely add more fees to your account balance because your check didn't clear. The creditor also has the option of prosecuting you since writing a bad check is a criminal offense. You don't have to be an accountant or a math whiz to understand how sending out checks without the funds in the bank to cover them can turn a shaky financial situation into a true disaster.

Writing a postdated check is just as risky. A postdated check is one that is written in advance of the date on the check and is not intended to be cashed before that date. For example, you write a check on June 1 but date it for June 15. The recipient of a postdated check is supposed to hold the check until June 15 before trying to cash it. Many collectors try to talk debtors into sending postdated checks, promising to hold the checks until the date specified on it. Some creditors will actually hold the check until the date specified, but you should never rely on that happening. Most will just add it in with the other checks and send it on to the bank.

You might think that a bank would refuse to cash a check before the date that is written on it. If a single check were taken to a real live bank teller who actually looked at the date, that would be true. The teller would tell the person trying to cash the check that the check was postdated and not legal. However, most checks are part of deposits that contain several checks.

Even if the deposit is carried into the bank and given to a teller, chances are more than good that the postdated check wouldn't be noticed and would be accepted and run through the bank's computer. The electronic equipment would process the postdated check, and it would be charged to your account and be treated like any other check. If the funds weren't in the bank to cover it, the check would be stamped "NSF" and be treated as such.

There is only one sure way to guard against the additional charges and consequences of an NSF or postdated checks. Never write a check, postdated or otherwise, if you don't have the funds in the bank to cover it.

As you talk to creditors, you will find some who will try to convince you to send in a postdated check. Don't do it. You're the one who will suffer the consequences if the check goes to the bank before it is intended. Tell the creditor you will send the check when you have the funds to cover it.

The direct, honest approach is the only sensible way to deal with creditors. It is the only approach that protects you. You're already in trouble financially; don't complicate it and make it worse.

Extra Funding

If a collector succeeds in getting a consumer to make a payment with a postdated check, the collector is required to give the consumer at least three days' notice but not more than ten days' notice before depositing the postdated check. Also, if the bank funds are not sufficient to cover the postdated check, it can be used to file criminal charges against the consumer.

Leave the Juggling to the Circus Acts

Everyone should keep a close eye on his or her bank balance. People who are in financial trouble must be even more cautious. You may hate to look at your bank statement because it reminds you of how broke you are, but it's another thing that must be monitored and controlled. Every deposit and check should be recorded and your balance updated with each entry. It only takes a few minutes to add the deposits and subtract the checks from your account balance.

If there is a question about a check or deposit, call your bank right away to get it resolved. Many banks have electronic systems that allow you to check your account balance. You can also see if a deposit has been credited to your account and verify that a check you wrote has been cashed. The electronic systems are good and the information reliable, but remember that the electronic system doesn't know what checks you've written that haven't yet gotten to the bank.

Meager funds require closer scrutiny. Service charges for NSF checks or errors in your bank balance are a waste of money. The $25 you pay for an NSF check could buy groceries or pay the phone bill.

The other advantage of keeping your bank account updated is that doing so enables you to accurately track all your income and expenses. It helps you see where you can cut back and occasionally enables you to find money you didn't realize you had. When a creditor calls and asks if a payment has been mailed, you may be able to say, "The check's in the mail," and know that it's true.

For some people, writing checks is like using credit cards. As long as the credit card isn't refused, they keep on charging things. As long as there are checks left in the checkbook, they keep on writing checks. They never keep a running balance in the check register—heck, they usually don't even record the checks they write.

Bank Notes

Be sure you deduct any outstanding checks in your check register from the balance your bank reports on any given date. It is your responsibility to verify your bank balance.

If you are not one of these people, you are excused and may go on to the next chapter. If you are one of these people, you need to take a simple bookkeeping course, find a friend who can show you how to balance your checking account or figure out how to do it yourself. It's really not that difficult. All you need is a little practice and a bit of self-discipline.

One of the envelopes that arrives in the mail from the bank every month contains a statement. The statement will tell you everything you need to know about your account, including all the money that was deposited in the account, all the checks that have cleared the account, and any other charges that have been deducted. All the account activity for the previous month is laid out on the statement for your review.

As a matter of fact, if you look on the back of a bank statement, you will usually find instructions to follow for balancing your account. Wealthy people have management companies or accountants who handle their checking accounts and balance them each month. However, even millionaires should keep tabs on their bank accounts. Consider how many times you've read about a celebrity who discovered that he or she was in financial trouble because an unscrupulous accountant or manager was mishandling the celebrity's funds.

Bank Notes

Most financial institutions have customer service representatives who will be happy to help you balance your account or find a discrepancy.

The point is that knowing exactly what you have and how it is being spent is crucial to your economic status. You might be thinking that you don't have enough money to keep track of or worry about, and that may be true at this moment in time. However, this is a temporary situation, one you can and will improve. Whether you are riding in a chauffeur-driven limousine or scrounging pennies to buy gas for an old car with dents, you should know how to monitor your income and expenses.

The bank makes it easy by sending you that statement each month. Take advantage of this service and sit down and review the information the statement contains. Then make sure your personal records agree with the bank's records. If they don't agree, find out why.

Knowing how to balance your bank account and how to manage the money you have are skills that will help you achieve and maintain financial stability.

The Least You Need to Know

➤ Creditors and collectors must follow the rules set forth by the Fair Debt Collection Practices Act.

➤ Ignoring late notices and collection calls may make the situation worse.

➤ Never write a check without the funds to cover it.

➤ Postdated checks are a bad idea.

➤ Monitoring your bank account and scrutinizing all expenditures are required for recovery.

I suppose fleeing to a cabin in the Northern Territories is outta the question...

Chapter 3

Consider Some Options

In This Chapter

➤ Reducing monthly payments

➤ Student loans

➤ Refinancing

➤ Barter plans

➤ Another way to increase your take-home pay

If you were marooned on a deserted island, you would have to devise ways to maintain your body, mind, and spirit. Because you are an intelligent being, adapting to a new lifestyle on the island would be not only possible but challenging.

Resourcefulness would replace complacency. Necessity would force you to use alternatives: coconuts instead of microwave dinners, a stream and a sturdy rock instead of a laundromat, the comfort and shade of palm branches instead of a water bed in a luxury apartment. In place of a sitcom with canned laughter, you would contemplate the wonders of the universe.

When you are in financial trouble, there are times when you wish you could escape to the simplicity and solitude of a deserted island. You probably can't do that, but you can dig down and summon up the resourcefulness you need to improve your situation.

Don't Stay in Debtors' Prison

It's time to get out your list of monthly payments. These include credit card accounts, loans, medical bills, department store accounts, and whatever else you have that requires a monthly payment. Review your financial picture and see if there are debts that can be consolidated to reduce your overall monthly payments. One larger loan that will allow you to pay off a number of existing accounts is often feasible.

If you own a house, consider a home-equity loan. A *home-equity loan* is a second mortgage. The amount of the loan is based on the equity in your house, the difference between the value of the property and the existing first mortgage.

A home-equity loan is a step that should be taken only if it will solve your financial crisis. Partial relief is not enough. Risking the equity in your home for another liability is not wise unless it equals a long-term, permanent answer for your problems.

Dollar Signs

A **home-equity loan** is an additional mortgage, often referred to as a second mortgage. The loan amount is determined by taking the appraised value of the home and deducting the amount remaining on the first mortgage. A home-equity loan places an additional lien against your property.

Most banks and mortgage companies will loan you 80 to 85 percent of the amount of equity you have in your house. The following calculation will explain how this works:

Property value: $150,000

Existing 1st mortgage: $100,000

———————————————

Total Equity: $50,000

× .80

———————————————

2nd mortgage loan $40,000

Some banks and mortgage lenders will loan you up to 100 percent of the equity in your house. However, these lenders may charge a higher interest rate on the loan. A home-equity loan can be used to pay off many of your smaller monthly obligations and therefore eliminate those debts and the monthly payments that go along with them.

The payments on the home-equity loan are spread over a longer period of time than other types of loans, usually 12 to 15 years. The length of time you are given to repay the loan makes the payments lower and may significantly reduce the amount of money you pay out each month.

The interest rate on a home-equity loan is usually a set rate. Unlike credit card rates that can rise substantially over a period of time, this interest rate stays the same for the term of the loan.

There is, of course, a downside to using the equity in your house to pay off charge accounts and other bills. The biggest drawback is the temptation to use the charge accounts again. If you're not careful, you could end up with more monthly payments than you had in the first place. You have also tapped into the equity in your house and have reduced the amount you would realize if you had to sell the property. Also, home mortgages are secured loans. That means if you default on either the first mortgage or the home-equity loan you run the risk of foreclosure, and could lose your house.

The only way you benefit from a home-equity loan is if you have the discipline to cut up the credit cards and only make purchases you can afford. In other words, like the person marooned on a deserted island, you must adapt to a different lifestyle.

If you don't own a house, there are other types of loans you may be able to get to consolidate your debts and lower your total monthly payments. There again, this option could put you further in debt if you are not willing to modify the spending habits that made the consolidation loan necessary.

> **Bank Notes**
>
> One advantage of a home-equity loan is that the interest may be tax deductible, saving you more money at the end of each year.

Avoid working with finance companies. Their rates and terms are much higher. You are better off providing a bank or credit union with collateral because you will receive better terms and rates that will help your financial picture, not threaten to make it worse.

Another option you may want to consider is selling assets to pay off some of your debts. Stocks, bonds, jewelry, antiques, automobiles, your baseball card collection, and anything else of value that you own can be sold. This option requires very serious contemplation.

Obviously, you don't want to part with possessions that have great sentimental value or things that you planned to pass down to your children. As you are thinking about this option, remember that some of these items may be lost anyway if you decided to file bankruptcy.

If you decide you can't physically part with the asset, you may be able to use it as collateral for a consolidation loan. Keep in mind that doing so puts the asset at risk. In the event that you fail to make the loan payments, you could forfeit the collateral.

Are You Still Paying for Your Education?

One debt that cannot be discharged, even by filing bankruptcy, is a student loan. This is an obligation connected to the federal government, and like tax liabilities, it must be paid in full. If you fail to make payments on your student loan and it falls into default, you will be penalized and charged late fees. In addition, if you have a federal income tax refund coming to you at the end of the year, that refund can be confiscated and applied to your loan amount.

A student loan can be deferred. You can go back to school and get more education, and the payments on your prior loans will be deferred while you are taking more classes. Of course, if you have to take out new loans to continue or add to your education, you will be incurring more debt. This is not necessarily bad, if the additional education will enable you to get a higher paying job. For example, a teacher with a Master's degree usually earns more than a teacher with Bachelor's degree. A person with an MBA earns more than someone with a four-year business degree.

NSF Checks

Keep copies of all student loan documents, correspondence, and payment records so that the information is readily available and easily accessible when needed.

If you do decide to go back to school, remember that it is not an easy road, especially if you are out of the habit of studying and living like a student. On the other hand, education is one of the keys to success and financial stability. Student loans can be consolidated and refinanced. Doing so requires some research. One disadvantage is that lowering your monthly payment may increase the term of the loan and the interest rate. You will be starting over again as a new borrower.

For more information on refinancing, consolidation, and student loans in general, contact the U.S. Department of Education. Information on this government resource and other student loan organizations can be found in Appendix A, "Resource Directory."

Other Loans and Groans

Depending on the length and amount, most loans can be refinanced. There are instances when refinancing not only will help reduce your monthly payments, it also will afford you a better interest rate. Of course, the types of loans you have and the interest rate you are paying on them was determined by your financial status at the time you requested the loan. People with no credit history or a poor credit history are often charged high interest rates on auto loans. Unless they have substantial collateral, they can't even get personal loans.

If you have a loan with a high interest rate and have been making the payments, you can probably refinance the loan for a longer term and a better interest rate. Although this won't save you anything on the principle amount of the loan, it will reduce your monthly payment and improve your financial condition by making more cash available to you each month.

Trade and Save

Although banks and credit card companies will not accept trades in lieu of cash payments, many businesses and individuals barter for merchandise and services every day. There are organizations that register and connect people who want to engage in trades. If you have a marketable skill or a garage full of merchandise from a failed business venture, this is worth exploring.

No one is going to make your monthly payments for you, but you can barter for services and merchandise that you would otherwise have to pay cash for or purchase with a credit card. This will free up some cash or credit that you can then use for monthly payments.

There are direct trades you can make. This method exchanges one service for another. A restaurant may give you complimentary meals in exchange for your accounting skills. A clothing store may give you merchandise in exchange for creating a Web site for its business. The possibilities are endless. Just be sure that you are getting full value for the services you are providing and that the time you put into this trade doesn't jeopardize your regular paycheck.

Membership organizations that assist traders provide lists of businesses that want to barter. Even if you don't consider yourself a small business, your particular skills may allow you to become one and start bartering. The good thing about belonging to a barter organization is that many of them operate on a credit voucher basis. That means instead of just trading one service for another, you accumulate credits that will be honored by any of the members.

For example, an artist provides a painting of a landscape to a framing studio. The artist then receives 1,000 credits for the painting. The artist can then use those credits for any service in the bartering system. If the artist needs a haircut, he can use some of the credits at a barbershop that belongs to the organization. If he needs his tax return prepared, he can use his credits to pay an accountant who belongs to the organization to do the return.

The bartering organization establishes an account for each member and keeps track of the credits and debits used. Monthly statements and a current list of all the members and what they offer are provided for a small fee or percentage.

The following is a list of commonly bartered goods and services: accounting, advertising, airline flights, architect services, art work, brochures, catering, computers, delivery or courier, entertainment, furnishings, graphic design, interior design, legal services, marketing, maintenance, materials, office space, office equipment, printers, public relations, restaurants, staff training, video production, and writers.

The National Association of Trade Exchanges is a national organization that can provide information on exchange groups in your area. Contact information for this organization can be found in Appendix A.

Extra Funding

Bartering usually allows the trader to access goods and services for less than the equivalent cash price of these goods and services.

Bank Notes

Although trades may not be the solution to your immediate financial dilemma, they can help ease the situation by improving your cash flow.

The IRS Doesn't Pay Interest

Many people are so afraid of owing the IRS money at the end of the tax year that they go to the other extreme. They give the IRS extra money each payday and let this money accumulate all year long. Finally, at the end of the calendar year, they file a return and ask for a refund. Some of these taxpayers say that this is their way of saving money, and they like getting a nice lump sum at the end of the year.

The problem with this logic is twofold. First of all, the IRS doesn't pay interest on the extra taxes you pay during the year. The only time the IRS pays interest on your money is when it has collected or held it in error. If you are claiming less withholding allowances than you are entitled to claim, the error is yours.

Would you open a savings account at a bank that didn't pay interest? Probably not. In fact, you would probably shop around and find out which bank pays the highest interest rate before you even open an account.

Second, the interest-free funds that you voluntarily give to the IRS during the year are funds you could be using to pay your bills. This tax money could and should be included in your net paycheck so you can decide where it will do the most good.

If you have trouble saving money and feel it is better to have funds deducted from your paycheck in advance, you can do so by setting up a savings account that accepts direct deposits from your employer. Instead of depositing your money with the IRS, put those funds in a savings account. You will still have extra money at the end of the year, and what's more, you will have earned some interest on that money as well. If you are in financial distress, you will have access to those funds. The IRS doesn't let you withdraw excess tax money in the middle of the year to pay an unexpected expense.

When you were hired by your employer, you were asked to fill out a form called a W-4. On this form, you indicated your marital status and the number of withholding allowances you were claiming. The information you provided on your W-4 determines the amount of federal income tax your employer deducts from your paycheck.

Federal withholding tax is just one of the taxes deducted from your paycheck. Don't confuse federal withholding tax with other taxes that your employer deducts such as *Social Security tax* and *Medicare tax*. There is no way to control or adjust Social Security tax and Medicare tax; they are percentages of your gross wages that are determined each year by federal regulations.

If you are receiving federal tax refunds in excess of $500 each year, you may be claiming two few withholding allowances on your W-4. Consider that a refund of $600 at the end of the year translates to $50 per month in additional cash that could be in your pocket. $1,200 at the end of the year means an extra $100 in your take-home pay each month.

A person with a spouse and two children is entitled to claim four withholding allowances, one allowance for each member of the family including himself or herself. If this person earns gross wages of $500 per week, the standard tax deduction table specifies that the employer should withhold $23 from his or her paycheck for federal withholding tax. However, if the person is only claiming three allowances instead of the four that are entitled, the employer is taking out $31, or an additional $8 per week.

Dollar Signs

Social Security tax and **Medicare tax** are used to fund the Federal Insurance Contributions Act (FICA) that provides for a government-administered system of benefits related to old age, survivors, disability, and hospitalization insurance.

This amount continues to increase as the withholding allowances decrease. If the person is claiming no allowances, withholding for taxes goes to $56 per week instead of $23, a difference of $33 per week or $132 per month. That equals more than $1,700 in a year. You can see that these taxes add up, and the more you earn, the higher the tax for each unclaimed withholding allowance.

Adjusting the number of withholding allowances on your W-4 is a simple procedure. Your employer has extra copies of this form, and all you have to do is fill out a new one to replace the old one. The employer cannot go back and adjust the taxes already paid in under the old W-4 allowances, but it will begin adjusting the taxes with your next paycheck in accordance with the allowances claimed on the new W-4 you submit.

In addition to the number of people in your household, you can add withholding allowances to take itemized deductions into account. For example, if you purchase a new home during the tax year, you will have additional deductions for interest on the mortgage and property taxes. These deductions may be substantial and put you into another income tax bracket, so it is reasonable to increase your withholding allowances accordingly.

This is perfectly legal. All you are doing is adjusting the amount of tax deducted from your paycheck to correspond to your final tax liability at the end of the year. The trick to determining the number of withholding allowances that will balance the amount you pay in with the amount you owe at the end of the year is to use common sense and practicality. It won't do you any good to put extra money in your pocket each week if, in doing so, you incur a tax liability that you won't be able to pay.

Most income tax liabilities cannot be discharged by bankruptcy, so while you shouldn't hesitate to keep whatever you're entitled to keep, don't go overboard and claim six allowances when your household consists of you and your pet turtle. Also, keep in mind that your employer is required to send the IRS a W-4 that claims 10 or more allowances or one that claims an exemption from taxes. Workers who expect to pay no income tax during the year may be considered exempt.

Increasing your withholding allowances is just another way to increase your cash flow. A lump-sum tax refund may be nice to have at the end of the year, but you may appreciate it more in weekly or monthly installments that will pay for groceries or utility bills.

For more information you can get the IRS publication 505, *Tax Withholding and Estimated Tax*, which provides detailed instructions for completing your W-4, and IRS publication 919, *How Do I Adjust My Withholding*. As you review these publications, remember that you must consider all the tax deductions you are entitled to claim in order to estimate your tax liability at the end of the year. Last year's tax return will help you determine the amount you should pay for the current year.

NSF Checks

Only students or people with a very low income may be exempt from taxes. Do not claim this status unless it is true. Underpayment of taxes may result in penalties and interest.

Keep Your Eye on the Ball

All the suggestions in this chapter are designed to help you monitor and control your finances. Dealing with creditors and finding ways to reduce your payouts, increase your income, and increase your cash flow may all be necessary to improve your financial picture. However, you may be in so far over your head that these actions are as effective as throwing a bucket of water on a raging forest fire. You may need a lot more, a lot faster to make any headway or see any results.

All the information you have read so far is basic. It is presented to help you focus and remain in control. If you are going to come out of this financial dilemma without getting burned, you have to keep your head and develop a good plan. Proposed legislation regarding the bankruptcy laws makes it more important than ever to explore all your options and learn as much as you can about financial matters, especially your own.

Analyzing your financial condition and looking for ways to improve it may seem like an exercise in futility right now, but whatever insights or knowledge you acquire will help you in a number of other ways. Any action you take to reduce expenses or improve your cash flow is positive and therefore valuable to you.

Whether you work with your student loan lender to revise the terms or payments on your loan, become more aware of your tax bracket and status, or learn how to trade materials and services, you will be storing information and acquiring experience. The more things you know and understand about your economic situation the better. These are the keys to obtaining and maintaining financial security.

If you are able to make even the tiniest dent in that mountain of bills, you will have taken an important step forward. You will also be more aware of how and why you landed in the middle of financial hell, and you can start thinking of avenues to follow that will lead you in a more secure direction in the future. Having the tenacity to look for solutions rather than allowing yourself to shuffle along, hoping for a miracle that will save you from financial ruin, is a healthy response to your dilemma.

Fairy tales are built around the knight in shining armor who charges in at the last minute to save the kingdom from falling into the hands of the enemy. Your own kingdom and everything in it is under your control. It is up to you to charge in and save it and to protect the material things you need for your own health and well-being. Discovering how you got into financial trouble is an important part of the process that will get you back on the right track again. There will be a lot of decisions to make, and you are the only one who knows your situation well enough to make them.

In the coming chapters, you will find more roads to explore. These roads may all lead to the same place, but some are longer and more difficult to travel. There are no short cuts, but there may be a few detours.

No one can tell you exactly what road is the best one for you to follow. Suggestions, advice, and information will be presented to you. Hopefully, you will take the time to absorb all of this before making a decision so that the path you choose to follow will be the right one for you and your family.

Sometimes the journey is more important and more rewarding than the actual destination. Getting out of financial hot water is a lot more difficult than getting into it. Therefore, every lesson you encounter on your journey back to financial security should be studied carefully and stored in your memory bank.

Once these lessons are a part of your life's experience, you can draw on what you have learned and use the knowledge whenever needed to keep yourself stable and economically sound. The one thing you never want to do is turn your financial future over to someone else to handle. It may seem like a good escape route, but like the celebrities with dishonest advisors and accountants, it can lead you into deeper trouble.

The Least You Need to Know

➤ Reducing expenses requires discipline and determination.

➤ Government-backed student loans cannot be discharged through bankruptcy.

➤ Trading marketable skills is one way to improve cash flow.

➤ Don't let the IRS hold on to cash you need for everyday expenses.

Chapter 4

Examine Your Options

In This Chapter

➤ Good lenders

➤ Avoiding disreputable lenders

➤ Debt counselors

➤ Settlements with creditors

Even though your credit rating may be falling faster than a skydiving elephant, you must exercise caution when borrowing money or looking for ways out of your financial difficulties. Beware of any company that has a slogan or an ad such as "Credit problems? No problem!" or something similar. These companies rely on your desperation and take advantage of your already precarious perch on the edge of disaster.

There are still other companies that say they can repair your credit. The Federal Trade Commission warns that such companies can't do anything for you that you can't do for yourself. Most simply vanish with your money. Only time and a conscientious effort to repay your debts will improve your credit status.

You have explored a number of smaller options that can help you gain control of your finances and change your spending habits. Now it's time to concentrate on the three major choices that have the potential to erase your debts or get them into a manageable state. Depending on your level of debt and the amount of discipline you can muster, you have three main options: debt consolidation, debt counseling, or bankruptcy.

Lenders Come in All Shapes and Sizes

Debt consolidation is an option that was introduced in earlier chapters. Now you will examine it in depth to make sure you understand all that it entails and what the long-term consequences of this option are.

A debt-consolidation loan allows you to pay off the balances of some or all of your bills, thereby eliminating the monthly payments for those accounts. Then you are left with one payment to make that should be considerably lower than the total of the payments you have eliminated.

These loans work well if you have the discipline to cut up your credit cards and change your spending habits. If your credit rating is already trashed, you will need some sort of collateral to obtain a debt-consolidation loan from a reputable lender.

There are always going to be lenders promising to give you a quick, easy loan, but dealing with one of these companies may only get you into more trouble. Exorbitant interest rates combined with impossible terms are hidden under appealing ads designed to attract desperate borrowers. These lenders may offer loans based on the amount of equity in your house or the value of the asset used for collateral. A responsible, reputable lender will help you tailor the terms and payments to fit your budget.

Remember, you may be financially tapped, but you are still in control and can only improve your situation by making careful, sensible decisions. The following are warning signs that a lender may not be reputable:

1. The lender tells you to falsify information on the application.
2. The lender pressures you into applying for a loan or applying for more money than you need.
3. The lender suggests payments that are more than you can afford or terms that will be hard to live with.
4. The lender fails to provide required loan disclosures and legal documentation.
5. The lender promises one set of terms and gives you a different set of terms to sign.
6. The lender tells you to sign blank forms that will be filled in later.
7. The lender fails to give you copies of documents you have signed.

Before accepting any loan, make sure you know and understand all the terms of that loan. This is especially true if you are putting up some type of collateral for the loan.

The annual percentage rate (APR) is probably the most important thing to compare when looking for a loan. You should look for a loan with a fixed rate, meaning one that stays constant for the term of the loan.

Many lenders offer adjustable-rate loans. An adjustable rate means that early in the loan, the interest rate may be two or three percentage points lower than normal. In exchange for the initial low rate, the interest rate begins to rise and your payments increase over a specified time.

This type of loan is good for a lender because it can raise the rate over the term of the loan, and each time the interest rate rises, your payment increases. If you are considering this type of loan, make sure you know how much and how often the interest rate will increase. All the terms should be clearly spelled out in the documents before you sign.

You must also find out if the interest rate on the loan can be increased if you miss a payment or are late with a payment. This is a common practice used to accelerate the rate on credit card balances and can be applied to any loan.

If you are getting a home-equity loan or a second mortgage, you will have to find out what the points and other costs will be on the loan. Each point equals 1 percent of the loan amount. A $20,000 loan with two points will cost you $400 ($20,000 × .02).

Most loans that involve real property have fees that the borrower is expected to pay. Before signing any papers, have the lender give you a statement outlining all the costs. This is called a *good faith estimate*.

Points can be added into the principle amount of the loan, but that, of course, means you are borrowing more and paying interest on the higher amount.

Find out how many years you will make payments on the loan. A bill-consolidation loan to pay off credit card accounts may mean that your payments are spread over a longer period of time. This is fine as long as you can easily manage the payments over that time period.

Find out if there is a balloon payment on the loan. A balloon payment is a large payment usually at the end of the loan term. Some lenders will offer you nice low payments for a specified term, say five years, and then expect the entire balance to be paid in full. If you don't have the money to make the balloon payment, you will default on the loan and lose your collateral. At the very least, you may need to take out another loan to make the balloon payment.

Is there a prepayment penalty on loan? A prepayment penalty is a fee charged to a borrower when a loan is paid off early. Sometimes the prepayment penalty is a percentage of the loan balance; sometimes it is a set fee.

Some prepayment penalties decrease over the life the loan and disappear entirely after a certain time. Prepayment penalties are negotiable, so you should try to get them eliminated from the loan agreement.

All lenders try to talk you into taking their insurance and adding the premiums into your loan payments. This can be costly, and

Bank Notes

An adjustable-rate loan may work for you if there is a ceiling on the interest rate. In other words, there must be a limit placed on the rate that determines how much it can increase over the life the loan.

Dollar Signs

A **good faith estimate** lists all charges and fees the borrower must pay to obtain the loan. This should include points, document preparation fees, and recording fees.

Extra Funding

Prepayment penalties run from 2 to 4 percent of the loan amount being paid off. On a loan with a large balance, this can be quite costly.

chances are you already have life insurance and disability insurance through your employer or your personal policies. You don't have to take this additional insurance, and refusing it should not affect your eligibility for the loan. There is usually a place on the loan application that states you have declined the insurance, and that is where you should put your signature or initials.

Before signing any loan document, be sure you understand any dollar amount, term, or condition. If you don't understand, ask questions until you do understand. Don't sign any document if the terms differ from what you originally thought they would be. Be prepared to walk away.

NSF Checks

If you are uncomfortable with any aspect of the loan, don't cash the loan proceeds check. That will prevent complications in the event you decide to rescind the loan acceptance.

Make sure you get a copy of all the documents. They contain important information and must be retained for your records. After you've signed the papers and accepted the funds, you can still cancel the loan if you feel uncomfortable with any of the terms or conditions. Under the Truth in Lending Act, you have three business days after closing to cancel the loan. This is known as your right of rescission.

To exercise your right of rescission, you must notify the creditor in writing. Send the notice by certified mail so you get a return receipt proving that the notice was delivered in a timely manner. After you rescind, the lender has 20 days to return your collateral or release claims to it. You, of course, must return the loan funds.

If you feel that a lender or a creditor has violated your rights, you may file a complaint with your state's attorney general's office, banking regulatory commission, or the Federal Trade Commission.

"The customer decided to rescind the loan."

Debt Counselors Work for You

If you are unable to settle your own debts through a consolidation loan or negotiations with your creditors, there are a number of organizations and individuals that you can go to for help.

The best time to contact your creditors and talk about settlements or payment plans is before you fall too far behind and have been turned over to collection. Unfortunately, most people do not follow that timeline. They keep thinking that things will get better and that they will be able to catch up on the delinquent bills. Once your accounts have been turned over to collection, your creditors may refuse to talk to you directly. At this point, you may be thinking that bankruptcy is the only option you have left, but you still have another choice.

Professional debt counselors can serve as a buffer between you and your creditors. They can often strike deals and reach settlements with creditors that you could not accomplish on your own. The main reason a debt counselor can accomplish more than you can on your own is because the very fact that you have gone to a counselor for help demonstrates to the creditor your willingness to work out a debt repayment plan.

There are many nonprofit organizations that you can contact for free, confidential information and guidance. Once you've met with a counselor, you will be advised of the fees charged for the service. These fees are usually nominal because many services are partially funded by contributions. Be cautious and check out individuals and companies with your local consumer protection agency or the Better Business Bureau in your area.

The following list is a sampling of the agencies that can help you or refer you to qualified individuals and organizations:

➤ National Foundation for Credit Counseling

➤ American Consumer Credit Counseling

➤ Association of Independent Consumer Credit Counseling Agencies

More information on each of these agencies can be found in Appendix A of this book.

Most attorneys that handle bankruptcy filings also offer credit-counseling services. A good attorney will try to help you work out settlements and payment plans with your creditors as an alternative to filing a bankruptcy petition with the court.

An attorney or debt counselor approaches the creditor in a businesslike, unemotional way and discusses ways to settle the delinquent accounts. Of course, before the counselor can contact creditors on your behalf, you must sit down and work out a plan and a course of action.

The plan you devise with your counselor will be structured to repay your debts based on your current income. It will take into consideration your individual needs and living expenses. Often the plan will depend on the creditors' willingness to reduce interest rates and forgive late fees and penalties. Sometimes the counselors will convince a creditor to settle for an amount less than the current liability balance.

Once a monthly payment amount has been established, you will pay that amount to the credit counselor, who will then spread it out among your creditors. The amount each creditor will receive will have been negotiated and predetermined under the plan. A successful plan requires your full cooperation and participation.

Bank Notes

The debt repayment plan will relieve the stress of dealing with creditors and overdue bills, but like the other solutions you have considered, it, too, requires a change in your lifestyle and spending habits.

The plan is not an instant solution or a quick fix to your financial problems. It is a commitment that you must honor and fulfill over several months or years. The length of the plan will be determined by you and your counselor. During the course of the plan, if your circumstances change, you will have to go back to the counselor and devise a new plan.

You will still be responsible for reviewing monthly statements to make sure your payments are correctly recorded. If your plan requires that late fees and other charges be waived, you will have to monitor that and make sure the credits are applied to your accounts.

In addition, you will have to continue to make regular payments on any debts not covered by the plan. Most debt repayment plans cover unsecured debts such as credit card and department store accounts. Secured loans on homes, autos, or other property will continue to be paid monthly according to the terms of the original note (loan agreement). In some cases, the debt counselor may be able to help you renegotiate a mortgage or auto loan to adjust the payments to a more manageable amount.

Your credit history will not be wiped clean by a repayment plan. Nothing will do that, not even bankruptcy. Creditors continue to report information about accounts under a debt repayment plan. Under the Fair Credit Reporting Act, information on your debts can stay on your credit report for up to seven years. A bankruptcy stays on your credit report for that long or longer, up to 10 years.

Creditors may even report that your account balances were revised by waiving late fees or other adjustments made under a counseling repayment plan. However, once you have begun to pay your accounts in a steady, timely way, your credit report will reflect that and will help you obtain new credit in the future.

By this time, you have surmised that there is no easy way out of financial trouble. No matter what course of action you follow, you will be making a number of decisions and concessions to resolve the problems.

Although credit card companies may be too persistent and too aggressive in the marketing tactics that prompted you to open accounts, the ultimate decision to accept the account and use it remains with the consumer. Once the bills start coming, you must open them and deal with the balances and payments. However, you don't have to open the solicitations that arrive on a daily basis. You can avoid temptation by throwing all of those special offers directly into the trash.

You are intelligent, creative, and resourceful. Whatever your financial problems, if you remain in control, you can focus on the information you need to make the decisions that are right for you.

The Least You Need to Know

➤ Investigate lenders before entering into loan agreements.

➤ Make sure you understand all the terms and conditions of a consolidation or home-equity loan.

➤ You have three days to rescind any loan agreement you are having second thoughts about.

➤ Debt counselors work for you and can help you settle with creditors.

➤ A debt repayment plan is tailored to suit your individual needs.

➤ All solutions and options depend on you and your willingness to participate and cooperate.

Part 2

How Do You Spell Relief?
B-A-N-K-R-U-P-T-C-Y

Now that you have researched all your other options, it is time to take a close look at the last resort. Bankruptcy offers relief and a fresh start, but it is a legal action that requires study and planning.

In Part 2, you will learn about the different types of bankruptcy, called chapters. Each chapter will be explained in detail to help you determine which one is best for you and your financial situation.

Chapter 5

Understanding Bankruptcy Laws

In This Chapter

➤ Bankruptcy—a federal case

➤ Automatic stay

➤ Chapter 7 bankruptcy

➤ Nondischargeable debts

With knowledge comes power. This may be a little dramatic, but it's appropriate for anyone who is under attack from creditors and feeling off balance and vulnerable. It is always better to know exactly what you are getting into before you actually make the leap. It is even better to take the time to study all the elements of a particular move, especially one that has long-range effects.

Bankruptcy will remain on your credit report for up to 10 years, but if you've been wrestling with financial problems for any length of time, your credit report may already look worse than the Florida coastline after a hurricane. Your bills are piled up like debris on the beach, and bankruptcy will restore order or, at the very least, sweep away much of the debris.

You Must Make a Federal Case Out of This

The rules that govern bankruptcy can be found in Title 11 of the United States Code. In other words, bankruptcy is a federal case, overseen and administered through the federal court system.

A bankruptcy petition asks the court to review the financial condition of the petitioner and to reduce or eliminate the debts that are dischargeable or help the debtor deal with creditors through court-ordered settlements or repayment plans.

When a debt is discharged through the bankruptcy courts, the debtor is relieved of liability. The debt is eliminated, and the creditor must settle for whatever payment the court issues to the creditor. In many cases, especially when the debt is unsecured, the creditor receives nothing and must write off the liability in full.

Credit card debt is usually unsecured debt. For some time now, credit card companies have been lobbying Congress to effect changes in the federal bankruptcy laws. The main complaint of the credit card companies is that many debtors run up charges with the idea that they will be able to discharge the debt in bankruptcy court. However, studies show that the percentage of people who abuse the system is small. Most people who file bankruptcy are forced into it by circumstances beyond their control.

If a creditor holds a secured liability against you (a mortgage or an auto loan, for example), the court can still discharge the debt. You will not have to pay the creditor, but you most likely will lose the *collateral* that secures the debt.

This is why you and your lawyer need to sit down before the bankruptcy petition is filed and decide which chapter is right for you. That is, which type of bankruptcy will allow you to get the fresh start you need without stripping you of the things you need to sustain you and your family.

The first thing you must be aware of is that some debts cannot be discharged through bankruptcy. The debts that cannot be discharged are as follows:

➤ Most federal and state tax liabilities

➤ Child support and alimony

➤ Student loans

➤ Court fines

➤ Liabilities resulting from criminal activity

➤ Liabilities for personal injuries caused by drunk driving or driving under the influence of drugs

➤ Liabilities based on *punitive damages* arising out of a court action

In addition, if the judge determined that you obtained money or property by fraudulent means, any debt connected with that money or

Dollar Signs

Collateral is property that is subject to a lien. The measure of the lien or the security for the debt is the value of the collateral that secures the claim.

Dollar Signs

Punitive damages are damages (a dollar amount) awarded in excess of normal compensation to a plaintiff in a court case to punish a defendant for a serious wrong.

property would not be discharged. The court will also scrutinize your financial records to make sure you have not done anything dishonest in connection with your bankruptcy case. Illegal tactics include destroying or hiding property, falsifying records, or disobeying a court order and can result in your bankruptcy petition being denied.

For example, you cannot sell a car with a fair market value of $5,000 to your cousin for $100 with the intention of buying it back after the bankruptcy is resolved. You can't hide the family heirlooms at a friend's house. All of these conditions are covered under the federal bankruptcy code, and you will be required to supply documentation to support the schedules and claims that are part of your bankruptcy petition.

Creditors Must Cease and Desist

The filing of a bankruptcy petition automatically stops most actions against the debtor or the debtor's property. This is called an *automatic stay*.

The automatic stay is the reason most people file bankruptcy. It halts the creditors in their tracks. Foreclosures, lawsuits, and garnishments are brought to an end, at least for the moment. The idea behind the automatic stay is to give debtors a break in the action, a time out, in which to sort things out and reorganize their life and their financial affairs.

From the court's point of view, the automatic stay preserves all the assets of the debtor so that they can be examined and the bankruptcy case can be administered in an orderly fashion. It keeps lien holders from seizing or foreclosing on property before the court determines whether such action should be allowed.

Special rules apply to certain ongoing expenses such as utility services. If you have overdue utility bills, the automatic stay prevents the utility company from continuing collection efforts regarding that bill. In addition, the utility company may not cut off your service for a period of 20 days after the filing date of your bankruptcy. When this grace period ends, however, the utility company can require you to pay a deposit and can cut off your existing service if you fail to provide that deposit.

There is another exception to the automatic stay that can take place if you have money on deposit in a financial institution where you also have a loan. The bank, savings and loan, or credit union may take the funds you have on deposit and apply them to your loan balance. To avoid this, your attorney will advise you to remove funds that could be confiscated prior to the bankruptcy filing.

Also, keep in mind that the creditors are notified through the court, and it may take up to 10 days for them to receive a notification of your bankruptcy filing. In the meantime, if creditors call, you should tell them that you have filed a bankruptcy petition. You will have a case number that you can provide, and this should put an end to calls from creditors who haven't yet received the court's notice.

Extra Funding

Federal bankruptcy laws, with the exception of exemptions, are the same in every state. When federal laws conflict with state law, federal law takes precedence.

Dollar Signs

An **automatic stay** is a court injunction issued automatically upon the filing of a bankruptcy petition. It prohibits collection actions against the debtor and the debtor's property.

NSF Checks

If bankruptcy is the option you choose, don't delay. Contact an attorney and get the paperwork started immediately. The sooner you start, the quicker the process will move along and afford you the relief you are seeking.

In rare instances, a creditor may continue collection efforts after the notification. If that happens, contact your attorney so that appropriate measures can be taken to enforce the automatic stay. A creditor who violates the automatic stay will be dealt with by the federal court.

For the most part, the late notices and letters stop, the phone stops ringing, and any legal action your creditors are pursuing is put on hold. Although the automatic stay is a powerful tool, don't wait until the sheriff is at the door with a summons, or the tow truck is rounding the corner to take your car away, to file your bankruptcy petition.

In Chapter 1, "You're Not a Loser," you assessed your bankruptcy risk. This gave you an opportunity to determine if you were in danger of losing any property used as a collateral for a loan.

Study the Chapters

The chapter of bankruptcy most often filed by individual debtors is Chapter 7. Under Chapter 7, a debtor's nonexempt assets are sold and the proceeds distributed among the creditors. With some exceptions, the remaining balances on the debts are then discharged by the court, and the petitioner walks away free and clear of his creditors.

Dollar Signs

The **means test** is also known as the "ability to pay" test. Your attorney will analyze your financial situation, and together you will determine whether you qualify for a Chapter 7 bankruptcy filing.

Sounds great—and it is great for many people who are suffering from severe financial distress and have no hope of ever catching up on their bills and becoming solvent on their own. Chapter 7 allows these individuals to wipe the slate clean and get a fresh start. Granted, the bankruptcy will stay on their credit report for a long time, but as you have already learned, their credit rating is most likely beyond saving anyway.

Because the majority of debtors file under Chapter 7 and are able to eliminate unsecured debts, such as credit card accounts, the credit card companies have been lobbying Congress to change the existing bankruptcy laws. Most of the proposed changes to the bankruptcy laws are directed at Chapter 7 filers. Sponsors of the bill want to make it more difficult for people to qualify for a Chapter 7 bankruptcy.

The federal bankruptcy code already contains provisions designed to keep people from taking unfair advantage of their creditors by filing Chapter 7. If the current legislation passes, it will in effect tighten those provisions and make fewer people eligible to file Chapter 7 based on what is called a *means test*.

All your income and assets will be reviewed and compared to your liabilities. If you have sufficient income to pay your creditors over the next three to five years, you may not qualify to file Chapter 7.

Another circumstance that could prevent a debtor from filing under Chapter 7 is the time factor. If liabilities were incurred at a time when the debtor was unemployed or in another situation in which it was apparent that repaying the debts would be difficult or impossible, it indicates possible abuse of the bankruptcy code. Sometimes this is called "credit card load up," and it includes the practice of running up credit card debt in anticipation of getting those debts discharged by filing a Chapter 7 bankruptcy petition.

The United States bankruptcy code also addresses loans, including credit card cash advances, and the purchase of luxury items within the two months preceding the bankruptcy filing. These debts may be deemed nondischargeable, and you will have to pay the creditor.

These are critical issues that should be honestly examined and discussed with your attorney. You will be asked to provide written information pertaining to your income, assets, and debts.

After reviewing all the aspects of your current financial condition, your attorney will be able to tell whether you qualify for a Chapter 7 bankruptcy and if that chapter will be the most beneficial and appropriate for your situation. The process of filing a Chapter 7 bankruptcy will last for several months. The automatic stay goes into effect immediately, but the actual discharge of debts will not occur that quickly.

NSF Checks

A judge can deny your discharge of debts if it is determined that you have done something dishonest in connection with your bankruptcy case.

A New Estate and State of Mind

The bankruptcy code refers to a Chapter 7 filing as a liquidation. A less harsh definition of liquidation is "to melt." When something melts, it spreads and becomes larger. This is a good way to think of Chapter 7. Under this type of bankruptcy, you will be spreading a little of what you have over the large area occupied by your creditors.

Chapter 7 is a viable option for individuals or couples who don't have many assets and have an abundance of unsecured debts. It calls for a liquidation of assets, and if you don't have many assets to liquidate, there's not much your creditors can get from you. Even if you do have assets, certain items such as your home may be exempt from liquidation. More information on the specific *exemptions* of assets under all the bankruptcy chapters will be discussed in subsequent chapters.

Dollar Signs

Exemptions are the types and values of property that are removed from the bankruptcy estate and therefore not available to satisfy the claims of creditors. Exemptions vary from state to state.

When you file a Chapter 7 bankruptcy petition, a new entity, called the "bankruptcy estate," is formed. The bankruptcy estate covers all that you own as of the date you filed the petition. It will also encompass anything you inherit within six months after the filing date. Anything else obtained or earned after the filing date will not become a part of the bankruptcy estate.

The exception to this is a tax refund. Since this refund presumably is based on income earned before the bankruptcy petition was filed, it would become a part of the bankruptcy estate. When you are planning a bankruptcy filing, you may want to wait until after you receive the tax refund and use it for immediate expenses to avoid it being put into the bankruptcy estate and doled out to your creditors.

The Role of the Bankruptcy Trustee

The court will assign a Trustee to oversee and administer the bankruptcy estate. Each state has a panel of Trustees, and they are appointed to cases on a rotating and random basis. One of the Trustee's responsibilities is to determine which of your assets should be liquidated or sold. The Trustee then manages the sale of those assets and distributes the money generated by the sale to your creditors.

In examining your financial reports and records, the Trustee will check to see if you have made payments to creditors that may be considered preferential. A preferential payment is one that is more than $600 and was made within 90 days of the bankruptcy filing. For example, if you owe money to a friend or relative and don't want that person to have to get in line with the rest of your creditors, you pay the debt off. However, if the Trustee decides that you have given a particular creditor a preferential payment, that creditor will be contacted by the Trustee and ordered to return the payment.

The Trustee has the option of going back one year to retrieve preferential payments in a Chapter 7 filing and will do so if the creditor is determined to be an insider (that is, a relative or friend of the debtor). Any funds returned to the bankruptcy estate will then become part of the proceeds distributed to all the creditors. Depending on the state statues, the Trustee can go back as far as four years if there is reason to think any transfer of property or cash was fraudulent.

Obviously, the Trustee is checking to make sure your prebankruptcy planning was honest and above board.

Most Chapter 7 filers will not have extra cash to make preferential payments, nor will they have valuable property to transfer or hide. Many are fortunate to have a decent roof over their heads. Nonetheless, the Trustee scrutinizes the particulars of each case to ensure that all the creditors receive the same unbiased treatment.

Bank Notes

Any property that is not exempt goes into the bankruptcy estate. In addition, preferential payments and property that was fraudulently transferred can be returned to the bankruptcy estate by order of the court.

Chapter 7 Is a Rescue from Hard Times

Although significant changes may occur in the bankruptcy laws relating to Chapter 7, the average person will still be seeking relief under this type of bankruptcy. No matter what the legislators or credit card companies believe, most people who file Chapter 7 are people who have exhausted all other alternatives. They have fallen on hard times through health issues, employment problems, accidents, or a number of other circumstances that have made it impossible to maintain their credit obligations.

Under current law, Chapter 7 bankruptcy can be filed once during a six-year time period. The majority of people who file Chapter 7 do it only once in their lifetime. It is not an enjoyable experience. It is a legal maneuver that exists and that should be used to resolve crushing financial problems. When you file Chapter 7, you are in effect throwing yourself on the mercy of the court. It takes courage to do that.

The court-appointed Trustee will take charge of all you own and will decide what you can keep and what you must give up. No one comes out of a bankruptcy unscathed. Everyone loses something, but a good attorney and careful planning can ensure that you only lose the things you can live without.

An irresponsible person does not file bankruptcy. An irresponsible person simply walks away from it all, leaving all the unsecured creditors holding the bag. Chapter 7 is a positive step taken by a responsible person. When you file a Chapter 7 bankruptcy, you begin a long process that requires honest, deliberate preparation. You are putting yourself and some of your assets at risk because you want to settle your debts.

Your financial records are examined and scrutinized, but when it's over, you have earned the legal right to begin again. Chapter 7 is the simplest form of bankruptcy, and it affords permanent relief from creditors once the debts have been discharged. During the course of the Chapter 7 process, if your circumstances change, you still have the option of converting to one of the other bankruptcy types.

Extra Funding

Personal bankruptcy filings in the United States have dropped from a record 1.4 million in 1998 to l.2 million in 2000.

This confirms the idea that has been stressed throughout this book; you are always in control of your financial future. Even if you decide that a Chapter 7 bankruptcy filing is right for you and then begin the process, you still have the option of changing your mind. You can drop the case or convert your case to another type of bankruptcy filing.

Why would you want to change directions once you have chosen your course of action? Because the plan you are implanting is based on your current circumstances. If those circumstances change, you are free to make a new plan that will accommodate those changes.

For example, a person who has filed for Chapter 7 bankruptcy because of a long period of unemployment may suddenly get a good job offer with a substantial salary. The new job would enable this person to start paying the bills and get out of debt in a reasonable amount of time. In such an instance, converting the bankruptcy case to another type of bankruptcy in which a payment plan could be developed to satisfy the debts might be considered.

Bank Notes

An unexpected windfall, such as an inheritance, would generally become part of the bankruptcy estate created in a Chapter 7 bankruptcy filing.

Or perhaps the Chapter 7 filer who has been collecting cans and recycling them to buy burgers at the local fast-food place inherits millions from a long-lost uncle. Good-bye fast-food burgers, hello filet mignon.

Due to the fact that life and circumstances are constantly changing, you should be aware of all the different types of bankruptcy. The other thing you should be mindful of is that although situations in your life can be instantly transformed for better or worse, the decisions you make based on those changes require a little more time and consideration. A new job or an inheritance may provide a stable source of income, but before you abandon your Chapter 7 case or convert to another type of bankruptcy, seek competent legal and financial advice.

The fees you may pay for an attorney or an accountant will usually come back to you in the long run in one way or another. A competent adviser can save you both time and money no matter what your situation or circumstances.

The Least You Need to Know

➤ Certain debts, such as child support payments and most tax liabilities, cannot be discharged in a bankruptcy case.

➤ An automatic stay has an exception for utility companies.

➤ A financial institution that is one of your creditors may confiscate deposit funds and apply them to the loan.

➤ Chapter 7 is for people who have many debts and few assets.

➤ Bankruptcy petitions are supported by documented reports of your financial records.

➤ A Chapter 7 bankruptcy liquidates assets and distributes funds to creditors before discharging debts.

Chapter 6

Other Types of Bankruptcy

In This Chapter

➤ Chapter 11

➤ Self-liquidation

➤ Chapter 13

➤ Chapter 20

➤ Chapter 12

Chapter 7 bankruptcy works well for individuals with few assets and with personal, unsecured debts that are out of control. The provisions of Chapter 11 and Chapter 13 are usually better for small businesses, entrepreneurs, or individuals with more assets to protect.

These chapters are more complex and include a court-approved plan for repaying creditors. These bankruptcies are designed to give the troubled business or individual relief from creditors while reorganizing income and assets and developing a plan to settle the debts. Although creditors may only receive a percentage of the note receivable held, they usually realize a lot more than they would receive under a Chapter 7 filing, in which the debts may be totally discharged.

Chapter 11—A New Opportunity

Chapter 11 bankruptcy is for businesses in financial trouble. It provides the debtor with the opportunity to continue a business enterprise by getting the creditors to halt collection actions. In return, the debtor must submit a plan of reorganization that outlines payments and a time period during which the creditors will be paid.

Under Chapter 11, the debtor also has the option of choosing a liquidating plan of reorganization that provides for the sale of certain assets to fund the repayment plan. A plan of reorganization should be structured based on the amount of funding required to implement it.

A bankruptcy estate is formed when a Chapter 11 bankruptcy is filed, but in most cases, a Trustee is not appointed. However, the reorganization plan must be approved by the court and the creditors. If the court decides that a Trustee is needed, the Trustee will then take control of the business and the property.

Dollar Signs

Under **Chapter 11** bankruptcy, a court-confirmed plan of reorganization details a payment plan for each creditor and stipulates whether each debt will be paid in full or in part.

The bankruptcy court appoints a committee of creditors to review and vote on the debtor's plan of reorganization. These committees are entitled to seek their own legal counsel and financial advisors to protect their interests and have the fees paid through the bankruptcy estate. The creditors are not expected to unanimously approve the debtor's plan, but the court will set guidelines for the number of creditors that must approve it.

A Chapter 11 bankruptcy case can continue for some time and result in more attorney fees and costs than the other types of bankruptcy. However, there are advantages that may make the extra time and expense worthwhile.

Under Chapter 11, the debtor can restructure the business using the reorganization plan because it can include provisions that accomplish the following:

➤ Restructuring payment terms on a secured debt resulting in lower payments spread out over a longer period of time

➤ Reducing the principle amount of a debt if the value of the property is less than the liability amount owing on it

➤ Extending repayment of past-due taxes such as federal and state income taxes and real-estate property taxes

➤ Terminating unprofitable leases or contracts

➤ Paying unsecured creditors less than 100 percent of each dollar owed

The debtor remains in control provided a plan is filed in a timely manner. If not, the creditors have the option of devising their own plan that will most likely call for liquidating the business assets to pay the debts.

Once the reorganization plan is approved, it becomes a binding contract for the debtor and the creditors. The rights of all the parties are spelled out in the plan. Any debts eliminated or reduced by the plan are discharged. There are no debts that are considered to be nondischargeable under a Chapter 11 bankruptcy.

Prebankruptcy planning is crucial to the success of a Chapter 11 filing. An entrepreneur or small business owner needs expert advice to decide whether Chapter 11 will work or if the business assets should be liquidated under a Chapter 7.

Do It Yourself or Leave It to the Court

Closing down a small, insolvent business venture can be a financial nightmare. The owner may be torn between the responsibilities of honoring the legal rights of the creditors and minimizing the damage to personal assets. A bankruptcy filing should solve or alleviate the financial problems, but sadly, it does not always do that. Companies can go out of business without filing bankruptcy, and the possibility of liquidating assets and settling with creditors outside of court should be considered.

Rather than filing Chapter 7 or trying to reorganize under Chapter 11, an owner can sell the business assets and distribute the proceeds from those sales to the creditors. Some of the advantages of doing this are as follows:

➤ An owner may be able to get a better price for merchandise and/or equipment because of his or her knowledge of the market and the value of these items. This may substantially increase the proceeds realized from the sales.

➤ The owner can control which creditors get paid without fear that some payments will be deemed preferential and set aside by the court.

➤ An owner can act more quickly than a court-appointed Trustee in returning leased equipment and subletting business property, thus ending the financial distress sooner.

➤ Intellectual property, work in development, customer lists, and other business property can be transferred to investors or other insiders.

The prime disadvantage of dissolving a business entity without filing a bankruptcy petition is that creditors can continue collection actions; they will not be stopped by the automatic stay that bankruptcy affords.

If you do decide to dissolve a business enterprise and dispose of the assets yourself, it is prudent to seek legal advice before you proceed. Also, all transactions must be documented and the records retained in good order.

Bank Notes

A business with nondischargeable debts, such as tax liabilities, may fare better with a Chapter 11 payment plan rather than a Chapter 7 filing.

NSF Checks

Without the benefit of an automatic stay, creditors can foreclose or seize property that may be needed to keep the business operating.

Chapter 13—A Plan for Wage Earners

Chapter 13 of the federal bankruptcy code gives wage earners a chance to reorganize and restructure their financial affairs. Like Chapter 11, which typically is used by business owners, Chapter 13 requires the formation of a plan for debt adjustment and repayment. This chapter is for people who currently have and are expected to continue to collect a regular income. The other requirements for filing Chapter 13 are based on the amount of debt and the value of the debtor's assets.

Dollar Signs

A **noncontingent debt** is one that will not be affected by future events, such as pending legal actions. The dollar amount of the liability will not change.

Dollar Signs

A **liquidated debt** is one in which the exact monetary liability is known. This is opposed to a debt that has an unknown amount of liability, such as damages pending under a lawsuit.

Dollar Signs

Arrearages are scheduled payments including additional interest and late fees that a debtor failed to make on a loan or other liability.

The federal codes provides that an individual with regular income who owes less than $269,250 in *noncontingent, liquidated*, unsecured debts and noncontingent, liquidated, secured debts of less than $807,950 may be eligible to file a Chapter 13 bankruptcy petition.

Noncontingent debt means that all actions that resulted in the formation of the debt have already occurred. In other words, there are no pending lawsuits or other claims that might change the nature or amount of the debt. Under the bankruptcy code, the term liquidated means that the debt is one that can be determined by mathematical calculation.

These adjectives are obviously inserted into the code in an attempt to clarify and simplify the types of debts that can be included and discharged under a Chapter 13 filing. This makes sense because this filing is dependent on a plan that outlines the reduction and repayment of debts. Liabilities that are subject to change would interfere with the composition and implementation of the plan.

The terms of the reorganization and repayment plan extend over a period of three to five years. Payments are structured based on the estimated future income of the debtor. Under Chapter 13, creditors can expect to receive more than they would under a straight Chapter 7.

This is the reason credit card companies have been lobbying for new bankruptcy legislation designed to push some of the Chapter 7 filers into Chapter 13 instead. By requiring some debtors to use Chapter 13, this proposed change to the bankruptcy laws would ensure that some portion of unsecured claims would be paid to the creditors.

For the regular wage earner, Chapter 13 may be preferable for a number of reasons. Under Chapter 13, debtors are allowed to keep their property. Even nonexempt property that would be turned over to the Trustee in a Chapter 7 filing can be retained by the debtor. However, the debtor is required to pay the creditor an amount that equals the value of the property retained.

The value of any item is determined as of the filing date of the bankruptcy. For example, an auto loan has a balance of $8,000, but the vehicle has depreciated to a value of only $5,000. The Chapter 13 filer can opt to keep the vehicle and pay the creditor the $5,000 that the vehicle is currently worth. The creditor still gets interest on that amount but usually at a reduced rate from the original loan.

This benefit of bankruptcy is called a "cramdown" because the lien holder is forced to take the lesser amount through the court-approved plan. In a Chapter 13 bankruptcy, the creditors do not have the option of approving the plan and must abide by the decision of the federal bankruptcy court. In the case of a mortgage loan, back payments and late fees can be covered in the reorganization plan provided it includes regular payments in the future. Any *arrearages* that occur after the repayment plan is in progress would not be covered.

Other types of debts that might be nondischargeable under Chapter 7 bankruptcy filings may be discharged under a Chapter 13 provided certain criteria are met. Competent legal advice is necessary to make a determination on issues such as this.

A Trustee is appointed to Chapter 13 cases. Once your plan is approved, the Trustee will collect the payments you agreed to make under the plan and will distribute the funds to the creditors. Overall, the Trustee will make sure you live up to the terms of your repayment plan.

Your debts are not discharged under Chapter 13 until you have made the payments required by the reorganization plan. The exception to this is the *hardship discharge*. A hardship discharge may be granted provided the creditors have received the same amount that they would have gotten under a Chapter 7 filing.

If you are employed with a stable base salary—that is, a set amount you can count on each payday rather than a salary based on commission that can fluctuate from month to month—and you meet the other criteria in regard to your debts, Chapter 13 may be a viable option for you.

Chapter 13 is for regular wage earners with valuable nonexempt property that would become a part of the bankruptcy estate in a Chapter 7 and would be sold by the Trustee to pay creditors. That property can be retained in a Chapter 13 filing. This type of bankruptcy also provides relief for those who are dangerously behind on secured debts such as mortgages and auto loans.

The repayment plan allows you to catch up and save assets from foreclosure and repossession. With the help of an attorney, you can devise a debt-reduction and repayment plan that will enable you to become solvent over the next few years. In addition, even though you have filed a bankruptcy that will be reported to the various credit bureaus, if you honor your repayment plan and make regular payments to your creditors, those payments will be reflected on your credit report also. This will demonstrate your stability and improve your credit rating.

Bank Notes

Property that depreciates or that is depleted by use may actually be worth less than the liens against that property.

Dollar Signs

A **hardship discharge** is a court order that discharges the debts of a person who has fallen into circumstances, such as illness or job loss, which make it impossible to pay any portion of those debts. The court will require verification that the hardship is legitimate.

Chapter 20—7 + 13 = 20

It is possible that after filing a Chapter 13, a person's circumstances may change to the point that he or she no longer is able to honor the repayment plan. Health problems, unexpected job loss, and a number of other factors can alter a person's financial situation. Therefore, if you file a Chapter 13 and find you cannot live up to the repayment plan, you may have the option of converting your bankruptcy case to Chapter 7.

At the same time, a Chapter 7 filer who does not get all debts discharged because of the restrictions of the law may be eligible to file a Chapter 13 and form a reorganization plan under which the nondischargeable debts are paid over a three- to five-year period. In legal circles, this is known as a *Chapter 20*. Some courts have held

NSF Checks

In some cases, depending on the amount of the arrears, the delinquent amount will become part of the debts paid over time in the plan of reorganization.

that a Chapter 13 petition filed to cover debts not discharged in a Chapter 7 filing should be dismissed. However, the court will examine the circumstances surrounding each case before dismissing it.

Chapter 20 is not a type of filing, but results from the provisions of the bankruptcy code that allow a debtor to change from one type of bankruptcy petition to another. It combines the benefits of both Chapter 7 and Chapter 13 and must be carefully planned.

When debts are too large to meet the limitations of a Chapter 13 filing, you may be able to file a Chapter 7 to eliminate some of the debts so that you will then qualify for a Chapter 13. There are many issues that figure into a Chapter 20, and all must be given careful consideration before attempting this combination of filings.

Your legal advisor can help you make the proper decisions based on your particular situation and circumstances.

A Special Chapter for Family Farmers

Chapter 12 is a bankruptcy filing used specifically for family farmers. It calls for a simple reorganization plan for farmers whose debts fall within certain limits. Chapter 12 is for people whose primary source of income comes from farming. Currently, the provisions for Chapter 12 are not a permanent part of the bankruptcy code, but expire and must be reinstated every few years.

Choosing the Right Chapter

The federal laws governing bankruptcy are complicated and require a lot of study. Lawyers are constantly attending educational seminars on these laws. With every case that is filed, new issues arise and new interpretations are presented to the courts. Each case is documented and recorded. The legal profession can then draw on that information and use it to help the clients who are seeking relief under the bankruptcy laws.

You are not going to learn everything about bankruptcy from this book or any other written on this subject. The best you can do is become familiar with the various bankruptcy chapters and begin to form your plan. Even if you read this book three times, even if you commit the whole text to memory, if you are going to file bankruptcy, you need the help of an attorney.

As with any legal procedure, you use bankruptcy to achieve an end or solve a problem. The more information you gather, the better equipped you will be to make decisions about your case. This information will enable you to work effectively with your attorney.

If and when new legislation is passed that revises the current bankruptcy laws, it is believed that attorneys who handle bankruptcy cases will have greater burdens placed on them. As it stands now, attorneys ascertain the financial status of an individual client and, based on the clients assets, liabilities, income, and expenses, advise the client to file one type of bankruptcy or another. While attorneys will still be required to determine the type of bankruptcy a client should file, the criteria by which they make this determination will be more involved and will necessitate closer inspection and scrutiny.

Dollar Signs

Chapter 20 is not actually a chapter under the bankruptcy code; rather, it's a term used to indicate the combination of filing both Chapter 7 and Chapter 13 (7 + 13 = 20).

Dollar Signs

Nonexempt property is any property that will become a part of the bankruptcy estate and fall under the control of the Trustee and be sold to satisfy the claims of creditors.

You have reviewed the basic structure of each of the bankruptcy chapters and have learned how they are used. Therefore, you already know that Chapter 7 and Chapter 13 are the two types of bankruptcy filed by individual debtors.

Business owners and farmers usually file Chapter 11 and Chapter 12, respectively. While there are some proposed changes to these chapters, they are not as extensive and will not have as drastic an effect as the ones being considered for the individuals seeking relief under Chapters 7 or 13. For example, the main change for Chapter 12 is that it would be made a permanent part of the bankruptcy code; it would not expire and have to be renewed and reinstated every few years as it is now.

NSF Checks

You should never enter into any legal action without seeking professional counsel.

The pending legislation for the bankruptcy chapters used by individuals is based in part on the premise that some debtors who file Chapter 7 and have all their debts discharged are actually capable of paying a portion of those debts. In those cases, the debtors would be required to file a Chapter 13 instead.

This information is presented here to make you aware of the importance that the federal court and our country's legislators place on bankruptcy attorneys and their part in the process. A more in-depth look at the proposed changes in the bankruptcy laws and how lawyers will be required to examine the financial situations of clients can be found in the last chapter of this book.

The Least You Need to Know

➤ Chapter 7 is for people with limited or no income and few assets.

➤ Chapter 11 allows a business to continue to operate under a reorganization plan.

➤ Chapter 13 allows filers to retain their assets and prepare a plan to reduce debts and repay creditors.

➤ Expert legal advice is necessary before a final decision on filing is made.

Getting It All Together

In This Chapter

➤ Review your assets

➤ Review your liabilities

➤ Estimate your income

➤ Determine day-to-day expenses

Now that you have taken a look at each type of bankruptcy, it's time to go back to your personal situation and examine it closely. This is the first step in bankruptcy planning. You should not make a final decision until you have met with an attorney. Before that initial meeting, you need to dig through all your financial records and gather as much information as possible.

You may be thinking that you already know enough. You can't pay your bills, and the creditors are driving you crazy. You need that automatic stay to go into effect as soon as possible. While all of that may be true, you need to gather all your records and information to answer the questions your attorney will ask.

You will be given a number of forms and schedules to complete. If you have the foresight to assemble most of the information in advance, the process of filing for bankruptcy will move faster and smoother. The sooner you file, the sooner you get the much-longed-for automatic stay.

What Is Truly Yours?

You may have a houseful of furniture and several vehicles, but consider what you actually own outright. That is, what possessions do you have that you don't owe money on? Get a legal pad or something else to write on and start making a list. The easiest way to do this is to start at one end of your house or apartment and move methodically from room to room. If you have a spouse or partner that will be joining you in the bankruptcy filing, that person should work with you on the exercises in this chapter.

Some states, such as Arizona and California, are community property states. That means whatever belongs to the community formed by marriage belongs to both parties. This is an important consideration when you are preparing to file bankruptcy because it is possible that some valuable assets were obtained by one party or the other before the community was formed and may be excluded from the bankruptcy proceedings if only one party in the community files the petition. However, remember that both parties may be responsible for debts incurred by the community.

Your legal advisor will examine this issue, but you must supply the initial information. With this in mind, start a list for each spouse that notes which possessions you consider to be the sole property of one or the other. To help you go through this procedure, you will follow a fictional couple, Jack and Jill, as they go through their dwelling and gather the information they will need to bring to their attorney for their initial consultation.

Just for the record, Jack recovered from his head injury and he and Jill got married. Both of them are employed. Jack is an auto mechanic, and Jill is a secretary at an insurance agency. Jill has better handwriting, so she is handling the pencil and paper while Jack opens cabinets, drawers, and closets and calls out the items he finds there.

Jack and Jill start in the kitchen and list the major appliances because they live in a house they purchased together. If you rent a house or an apartment, the appliances may belong to your landlord. As each item is listed, an estimated value is noted next to it. If the item is financed, a notation is made to that effect so that when the liabilities are gathered, they can be matched up to the assets to form a complete financial picture.

In the kitchen, Jill lists the following items:

> Electric range $200
>
> Refrigerator $500, ABC Appliance Store
>
> Microwave oven $100

Jill does not list the dishwasher since it is built-in and therefore is considered to be part of the real estate or house. Her list continues as follows:

> Small appliances (can opener, mixer, etc.) $100
>
> Everyday dishes and glasses $100
>
> Silverware $50
>
> Assorted pots and pans $150
>
> Miscellaneous utensils $75

Food processor $100

Kitchen table and chairs $300

Jill has a set of china that she inherited from her grandmother before she married Jack. She lists it on a separate page under her name and estimates that the china is worth $500.

In the living room, the following items are noted:

Sofa $700, Designer Furniture Store

Two arm chairs $500, Designer Furniture Store

Three lamps $150

End tables $500, Designer Furniture Store

Television $1,500, Big Screen City

Stereo system $500, Stereo City

Music collection $300

Bank Notes

A Chapter 7 debtor is required to turn over nonexempt assets to the bankruptcy Trustee. Therefore, it is important for the attorney to identify and analyze all assets owned by the debtor.

The living room also contains a cabinet with Jack's collection of antique pistols. Jack received the collection from his uncle's estate a few years before he met Jill. The collection, which is worth approximately $6,000, is listed on the separate sheet reserved for Jack.

Moving on to the master bedroom, Jill lists the furniture, clothing, and other accessories. The most valuable items in the bedroom are pieces of jewelry:

Bedroom set $600

Clothing (Jill) $500

Clothing (Jack) $400

Clock radio $20

Two lamps $60

Wedding ring set (Jill) $800

Wedding ring (Jack) $200

Gold signet ring $250

Diamond pendant $200

Pearls $150

Gold cuff links $100

Assorted costume jewelry $150

In the second bedroom, Jack and Jill have some assorted furniture and their computer. These items are listed as follows:

Computer $1,500, Computer City

Desk $200

Bed $50

Bookcase $50

Books $100

Desk chair $75

File cabinet $100

In the third bedroom, occupied by their twin boys, there are bunk beds and dressers valued at approximately $500. No notation is made for the children's clothing or toys because these items have little or no resale value.

Most of the wall hangings in the house are family photos in inexpensive frames. Since the photos' value is purely sentimental, they are not listed. However, Jack and Jill do have two oil paintings that they received as wedding gifts, and those have been appraised at $500 each.

In the storage room off the kitchen, the following items are added to the list:

Washer $200

Dryer $250

Power lawnmower $200

Two 10-speed bikes $650

Assorted tools $100

Extra Funding

Pending legislation may end the requirement in some states for the names of minor children to be listed on bankruptcy applications.

Like any mechanic, Jack has an abundance of tools. Most of them are kept at the shop where he works, and the total value of all the tools is listed on Jack's sheet as $4,100. These are listed separately because they are considered to be tools of trade, or tools needed to earn a living, which may be exempted from the bankruptcy estate.

With the listing of personal and household goods and furnishings completed, the couple moves back to the second bedroom, where the bills and other financial records are stored. To their list of assets, Jill and Jack add the following entries:

Cash in savings account $187, First Mechanics Bank

Cash in checking account $29, First Mechanics Bank

Personal residence $125,000, Mid-Atlantic Mortgage Co.

1999 Ford pickup truck $18,000, First Mechanics Bank

1992 Dodge station wagon $6,000

Savings bonds $1,000

IRA (Jack) $8,000

Dollar Signs

A **patent** is a government grant of the exclusive right to make, use, and sell an invention and to authorize others to make, use, and sell that invention. A U.S. patent is valid for 17 years.

Six years ago, shortly after he married Jill, Jack designed and constructed a tool for working on automobile engines. He obtained a U.S. *patent* on the tool but has never tried to market it to the auto industry.

The patent cost approximately $5,000 and is good for another 15 years. The cost of obtaining the patent is added to the couple's list of assets.

Putting their lists of assets aside, Jack and Jill take out the list they made a month or so ago of all their household bills and their outstanding loans, medical bills, and credit card accounts.

Determine Your Net Worth

What started Jack and Jill on the road to bankruptcy was an abundance of medical bills for their twin sons. Four years ago, the boys were born prematurely and had to remain in the pediatric intensive care unit of the hospital for more than a month. Although they had medical insurance through Jack's place of employment, the coverage was limited.

By the time the twins were big enough and healthy enough to come home, the hospital and doctor bills had exceeded Jack's insurance coverage by $82,000. With two babies to care for, Jill was not able to work, and because the couple had not expected twins, one more of everything had to be purchased.

For the four years since the twins' births, the family has been going along living on Jack's paycheck, which simply did not cover all their daily expenses much less the payments on the medical bills. Before they had the twins, the couple had an excellent credit rating, so the credit card offers and convenience checks were delivered to their mailbox two and three times a week.

Soon Jack and Jill were caught in the credit card maze. So much was going out to satisfy the monthly payments on credit cards that there was never any extra cash for emergencies, so the couple continued to charge clothing, shoes, Christmas gifts, family vacations, and so on. Then Jack's company went out of business, and he was out of work for almost a month. Even though he collected unemployment benefits during that time, it was a fraction of his normal wages, and the couple began to fall behind in their payments.

Extra Funding

Collectively, credit card companies contributed more than $40 million to political campaigns and candidates and are now lobbying for the passage of the pending bankruptcy reform laws.

Jack got another job with a good salary, but by then the late fees and additional interest were mounting up on the credit card accounts, and the hospital had turned them over to collection. They were constantly late on the mortgage payments and their auto loan. With their finances out of control, Jill went back to work a few months ago, but much of her salary is absorbed by childcare expenses.

Combining the list of liabilities with the list of assets, Jack and Jill are able to develop a balance sheet showing their current net worth. It is as follows:

Assets

> Cash in banks $216
>
> Savings bonds (gift to twins) $1,000
>
> Personal residence $125,000
>
> 1999 Ford truck $18,000
>
> 1992 Dodge station wagon $6,000

IRA $8,000

U.S. patent $5,000

Washer and dryer $450

Stove $200

Refrigerator $500

Microwave $100

Miscellaneous dishes, glasses, utensils $575

Furniture $3,330

Big screen TV $1,500

Stereo system and music $800

Clothing $900

Jewelry $1,850

Computer $1,500

Books $100

Oil paintings $1,000

Office equipment $475

Power lawnmower $200

Two 10-speed bikes $650

Assorted household tools $100

Mechanic's tools $4,100

Total Assets $181,546

Jill's china $500

Jack's gun collection $6,000

Total Assets $188,046

Liabilities

Mid-Atlantic Mortgage Co. (first mortgage) $81,500

First Mechanics Bank (second mortgage) $30,000

First Mechanics Bank (truck loan) $21,001

Atlantic Medical Center $24,000

Dr. Richard Brown $600

ABC Appliance Store (refrigerator) $350

Designer Furniture (living room) $2,400

Big Screen City (television) $1,000

Stereo City (stereo) $550

Computer City (computer) $800

Visa $7,800

MasterCard $9,100

Discover $4,200

Citibank $2,700

Student loans $8,600

Total Liabilities $194,601

Net Worth ($6,555)

As you can see, even if Jack and Jill throw their individual assets into the asset section, they still have a negative *net worth*. If their individual assets were not added in, their net worth would be ($13,055).

This balance sheet calculation of assets versus liabilities should be done by anyone contemplating bankruptcy. It presents an overview of your financial condition and allows you to see how that picture could change by eliminating some of the debts. Of course, a bankruptcy filing could cause you to lose some assets also, depending on the type of bankruptcy you choose to file.

In this fictional case, you have learned that the medical bills began the financial problems. The second mortgage that the couple took on their personal residence was used to pay down some of the medical bills and to negotiate a payment plan with the hospital.

With the equity in their house reduced, the credit cards became a source of money that could be drawn on, and as long as Jack was earning enough to pay the bills, they felt secure. However, when Jack lost his job, even though it was temporary, they fell behind in their payments. This caused them to run up more credit card debts, and now Jack and Jill are finding it impossible to catch up.

Jack and Jill's story is not an unusual one. With rising medical costs and insurance premiums, many people do not have adequate coverage for catastrophic events or illnesses. It only takes one serious incident to throw you into financial distress, and once the downward spiral begins, it is hard to catch up. Add a little more bad luck, such as a temporary job loss, and you could find yourself drowning in a sea of bills.

Bankruptcy offers relief to people like Jack and Jill. Perhaps they should have filed when the medical bills first occurred, but like you, they are responsible people who wanted to pay the bills. Now, after four years of trying, they are deeper in debt than ever and need help.

Dollar Signs

The difference between your assets and liabilities is your **net worth.**

Extra Funding

Unexpected medical expenses are one of the primary reasons cited for bankruptcy filings in the United States.

Based on the sample presented for this fictional couple, you should be able to work on your own balance sheet of assets and liabilities and determine your own net worth.

Look at Your Bottom Line

Once you've established your net worth, either positive or negative, you will need to go back to your list of payments for debts and normal household expenses and compare that to your net income. Your bottom line is going to be either positive or negative, just as the financial statements issued for businesses reflect either a profit or a loss. This is another area that will have to be reviewed with an attorney to determine which chapter of bankruptcy will be most beneficial for you and your financial situation.

Dollar Signs

Net income is the amount of a payroll check after all deductions have been subtracted.

To give you an example of how this information is reported, let's again examine the financial resources of Jack and Jill. Jack earns a weekly gross salary of $1,200. After taxes and a deduction for hospitalization insurance, Jack takes home $3,947 each month. Jill's employment brings in considerably less. Her gross monthly earnings are $1,500. After taxes, her *net monthly income* is $1,312.

The following list itemizes all of the monthly payments required to satisfy the loans, credit card accounts, and other debts that Jack and Jill have incurred over the last few years.

Creditor	Balance Due	Payment	Secured By
Mid-Atlantic Mortgage	$81,500	$580	House
First Mechanics Bank	$30,000	$250	House
First Mechanics Bank	$21,001	$467	Truck
Atlantic Medical Center	$24,000	$500	
Dr. Richard Brown	$600	$50	
ABC Appliance Store	$350	$25	
Designer Furniture Store	$2,400	$60	
Big Screen City	$1,000	$40	
Stereo City	$550	$25	
Computer City	$800	$40	
Visa	$7,800	$234	
MasterCard	$9,100	$273	
Discover	$4,200	$135	
Citibank	$2,700	$81	
USA Bank-student loan	$8,600	$200	
Totals	**$194,601**	**$2,960**	

Jack and Jill have a lot of debt, and almost 70 percent of their debt is in secured loans. However, the payments on the secured debts amount to less than 50 percent of the total monthly payouts (actually approximately 43 percent). Moving on to the second part of this task, Jack and Jill review the list of their normal household expenses. The following is the list of expenses paid out on a monthly basis.

Expense	Average Amount Spent
Food	$1,000
Utilities (electric, gas, water)	$200
Telephone	$30
Auto insurance	$100
Cable television	$30
Gasoline	$100
Life insurance premiums	$50
Dental insurance premiums	$25
Daycare for twins	$688
Total cash expenditures	**$2,223**

No listing was made for clothing or miscellaneous expenses because Jack and Jill are using their credit cards to purchase these items.

Based on these two lists, Jack and Jill's bottom line is as follows:

Monthly income, Jack	$3,947
Monthly income, Jill	$1,312
Total income	**$5,259**
Monthly debt payments	($2,960)
Monthly cash expenditures	($2,223)
Total payouts	**($5,183)**
Net cash over/short	$76 over

Since Jill went to work, the couple's bottom line is now showing an overage, or a profit, of $76 each month. However, as you know, an excess of $76 disappears in a blink of an eye. A doctor's visit, a prescription, a few trips to a fast-food restaurant, or any other type of family outing wipes out the extra dollars.

Once the few extra dollars are gone, any other expenses must be added to the mounting credit card bills. Also, consider the fact that children get sick, and parents are faced with the dilemma of finding someone to take care of them or losing time at work. Losing time at work often means losing a portion of the family's monthly income.

Add that to the fact that this fictional couple has already fallen behind in their payments due to Jack's temporary unemployment,

Bank Notes

Reviewing your check register or canceled checks can help you identify all your normal monthly expenses.

Extra Funding

Gathering essential information before your initial consultation with an attorney will help the attorney make appropriate determinations and suggestions as to the type of bankruptcy that may be most beneficial for you.

and with a meager bottom line of less than $100 per month, they are finding it impossible to catch up again. It is safe to say that Jack and Jill feel like they are tumbling down that hill again, falling faster and farther with each passing day.

You may be feeling the same way. Therefore, using the examples in this chapter, you can organize your financial information to prepare yourself for an initial consultation with a bankruptcy attorney. Armed with all the financial data that makes up your particular situation, an attorney will be able to assess your economic status and advise you properly.

Together you will work out a plan designed to improve your monetary condition and reverse the tide that is threatening to sweep away your assets and your sanity.

The Least You Need to Know

➤ If you are married, assets may be considered community property, regardless of the state you reside in.

➤ Organizing all your financial records will save you time and money in legal fees.

➤ Your net worth and bottom line are important determinations and will affect the type of bankruptcy you file.

➤ Your legal advisor will depend on you to supply complete information on your assets, liabilities, income, and expenses.

Chapter 8

Which Chapter Is Right for You?

In This Chapter

➤ Finding a good attorney

➤ Assets vs. liabilities

➤ Income vs. expenses

➤ Community property

➤ Choosing a chapter

With all your financial information organized and ready, you are anxious to get on with the process. The automatic stay that goes into effect with a bankruptcy filing sounds like heaven on earth.

You are already rehearsing the speech you will give to any creditors who might call after the petition is filed. "I was going to send you the entire balance due, but I decided to file bankruptcy instead. My case number is ...."

Although you are well on the way toward being able to cut the collector short with that speech, you still have decisions to make and work to do before it becomes a reality.

A Fool for a Client

Based on the information you already have digested about bankruptcy and its various chapters, you know that you cannot navigate these churning waters on your own. There's an old adage that says, "A lawyer who represents himself has a fool for a client." The underlying meaning is that even a professional attorney would not be objective enough to handle his own case.

In bankruptcy, objectivity is one of many things your attorney will bring to the table. Although you may think you are cool and detached, when your personal finances are thrown open to public scrutiny and examination, there are bound to be some emotional reactions. Your attorney will be your representative and will protect your interests and make the procedure as painless as possible for you.

Of course, the attorney's knowledge and experience in bankruptcy filings is even more valuable to you and your case. Some law firms specialize in bankruptcy cases, but don't start going down the listings in the Yellow Pages. You may already have an attorney, so start by talking to that person. Even if he or she doesn't handle bankruptcy cases, your lawyer will know someone else in the legal profession who does.

NSF Checks

Legal fees and practices vary from state to state and attorney to attorney. Find out if the attorney you are considering charges for the initial consultation and ask for an estimate of the legal fees you will have to pay for the attorney to handle your bankruptcy filing.

For many people who file bankruptcy, their bankruptcy case is their first legal experience. Personal recommendations are the best way to find a competent lawyer. Ask your family and friends to suggest a lawyer who has done legal work for them.

If you don't know anyone who can steer you in the right direction, a number of organizations can help you locate a competent attorney. The legal aid society in your community or the state bar association can help. If you have access to the Internet, you can visit the American Bar Association site, where you will find a directory of lawyers listed by state. The Web address for the American Bar Association is: www.abanet.org.

Many attorneys do not charge for the initial consultation. This gives you a chance to discuss your case and determine whether this lawyer is the one to represent your bankruptcy filing.

It is important to develop a good working relationship with your attorney. You should feel comfortable and confident in the person who is handling your case. It is a process that will continue for a number of months or, in the event you file a Chapter 11 or 13, a number of years.

Advice Based on Your Overall Financial Picture

Licensed legal practitioners are governed by a code of ethics that covers their obligations to their clients and their duties to work within the federal laws as well as the laws of their state. As your advisor, a lawyer will examine your financial records and explain which bankruptcy chapter you should file and why. Part of the attorney's duty is to make sure you fully understand all the points of law and the consequences of the potential bankruptcy filing.

In the initial consultation, your attorney will look over the materials you have gathered and give you advice. The fact that you have had the foresight to prepare a list of assets and liabilities and a list of income and expenses will give you a head start on the preliminary bankruptcy process.

Your assets will be compared to your liabilities. The attorney will determine which bankruptcy chapter will allow you to retain the majority of your assets while eliminating the most liabilities. Remember that there are certain debts that cannot be discharged through a Chapter 7 filing, and that will be another factor your attorney will take into consideration.

Your income will be compared to your expenses. You may recall that one of the provisions of the new bankruptcy legislation is a process called *means-testing*. Means-testing exists now, but this legislation would reinforce and emphasize it as a way of identifying debtors who have sufficient income to enable them to repay at least a portion of their unsecured debts. This would force some people to file a Chapter 13 reorganization rather than a straight Chapter 7 bankruptcy.

Although this law has not yet been passed, everyone in the legal profession is aware of it. Attorneys are therefore giving each client's case extra thought and analysis to avoid possible complications. The attorney will also determine whether any of the income of the debtor is exempt under the current bankruptcy laws. Examples of income exempt from creditors' claims are disability income and Social Security benefits.

Disability payments made under a disability insurance policy or an employer's benefit programs are exempt except for child support and spousal maintenance claims. Social Security payments to disabled persons under 62 years of age are also exempt, as are Social Security payments to persons over the age of 62.

Your attorney's expertise makes it possible for him or her to review your financial information and establish a preliminary plan for relief that conforms to the intricate provisions of the law.

Community Property

If you live in a community property state, you are familiar with the term and the provisions of the law as it applies to married couples.

The federal bankruptcy code has a framework of requirements that addresses community property. The purpose of these provisions of the law is to provide a balance between bankruptcy relief and the interests of creditors and other interested parties. Other interested parties include anyone such as a spouse who would be affected by the inclusion of certain property in a bankruptcy filing.

In the case of a married couple, if both spouses file jointly the bankruptcy estate that is formed obviously includes all the community property as well as the individual property of each of them.

If just one spouse files, the bankruptcy estate includes that spouse's separate property and the community property defined as follows: all interests of the debtor and the debtor's spouse in community property as of the commencement of the case that is:

➤ Under the sole, equal, or joint management and control of the debtor, and

➤ Liable for an allowable claim against the debtor, or for both an allowable claim against the debtor and an allowable claim against the debtor's spouse.

Bank Notes

The law protects the incomes of disabled or elderly persons from claims by creditors.

NSF Checks

Competent legal advice is needed to unravel all the complexities and interpretations of community property laws under the federal bankruptcy code.

In simpler terms, even if only one spouse files bankruptcy, community property may still be considered part of the bankruptcy estate. This is especially true if the community property has been used as security for a loan by the spouse who is filing the bankruptcy petition.

For example, if a man retains an interest in a house in which he no longer resides after a divorce and his ex-wife files bankruptcy, that house may become part of the bankruptcy estate because the ex-wife has control of the property. In a community property state, the income of an ex-spouse or a nonfiling spouse can also be included in the bankruptcy estate.

The most common filing, whether the state of residence is a community property state or not, is one in which the husband and wife file together as debtors. It is covered under the vows they made when they got married, "For better or worse, for richer or poorer."

Deciding on a Chapter

As an example of how an attorney analyzes a client's financial condition and renders a recommendation on the type of bankruptcy that will work best for that particular client, you will go along with Jack and Jill as they meet with an attorney.

Equipped with the financial statements they prepared, Jack and Jill have their initial consultation with their lawyer. After reviewing the information they presented, the attorney offers the following advice and information:

➤ The equity in their house falls within the exemption for homesteads or the principle residence and would not be lost in a bankruptcy filing.

➤ Jack's IRA funds are exempt unless they are the result of a recent deposit.

   This means you can't take money from a savings account and put it into an IRA account to protect the funds from becoming part of the bankruptcy estate. The IRA funds must have been in the account for a reasonable amount of time.

➤ The values assigned to the household furnishings and other items may be too high.

   Regardless of the cost of the items initially, you must be realistic in setting a resale value for them. Used appliances and furniture are not easy to sell. The fact that Jack and Jill have everything listed makes it easy for them to go over the items and reset values that are closer to what the used household items could realistically be sold for in the marketplace. The china Jill inherited is considered part of the household furnishings, and when she checks with some dealers, she finds that the value placed on the china should also be lower.

   This same advice applies to Jack's tools. The lawyer advises them to have someone who is knowledgeable about the resale value of tools estimate the value. The tool vendor who sells to the employees at the garage where Jack works would be a good person to help Jack set a realistic value on his tools.

➤ Jack and Jill live in a community property state, so all nonexempt property may be absorbed into the bankruptcy estate.

➤ Art work, jewelry other than wedding rings, the gun collection, and the patent would not be exempt and could be placed into the bankruptcy estate in a Chapter 7 filing.

Extra Funding

Funds in individual retirement accounts (IRAs) are exempt from the bankruptcy estate in most states.

There are legal procedures that may benefit Jack and Jill in regard to the loss of these items. This will depend on the prebankruptcy planning that will be done before a petition is actually filed.

➤ The debts owed on the appliances, furniture, and office equipment purchased at specific retail stores are secured debts.

When specific items are financed through an account at a retail store, the seller of the merchandise is protected by a purchase money security interest under the law. This means if Jack and Jill want to keep or redeem this merchandise, they will have to settle with the creditors and reaffirm the debts. Again, the specifics of this process will be explained and handled in the prebankruptcy planning.

A purchase money security interest does not apply to merchandise purchased with a credit card such as Visa or MasterCard.

➤ The savings bonds and everything belonging to the minor children are exempt from the bankruptcy estate provided they were not transferred into the children's names to take advantage of this provision.

The cash that Jack and Jill have on hand is less than the $150-per-person exemption in their state, so no action will have be taken on those bank accounts.

Based on the information reviewed and discussed with Jack and Jill, their attorney feels that a Chapter 7 bankruptcy filing would be best for them. Under a Chapter 7, their large, unsecured debts for medical bills and credit cards can be discharged. With careful planning, they will be able to retain the assets they really need and get a fresh start.

Jack and Jill have fallen behind in some of their payments, but they have kept their mortgages and auto loans current, and that is one of the key factors in advising a Chapter 7 rather than a Chapter 13 reorganization plan for them.

If Jack and Jill were in arrears on their house payments, a Chapter 13 would be suggested. This is because the house, their largest asset, is a secured loan. Under a Chapter 13, they would continue to make their mortgage payments, and the amount of the arrears would be included in the plan of reorganization and be set up to be repaid over the next three to five years.

Jack and Jill leave the attorney's office with a lot to think about. Even though the attorney advised them to file a Chapter 7, they are still also considering a Chapter 13 reorganization instead. The final decision is, of course, up to them.

Using this fictional couple and their financial information, you will learn about planning for both types of individual bankruptcy in the next chapters of this book. You will also learn about reaffirmations and redemptions for mortgages and any other debts that are secured by property or merchandise.

Keep in mind that under current bankruptcy laws, a Chapter 7 filing for Jack and Jill would be no problem based on their financial status. Their attorney has suggested Chapter 7 because this chapter of

Bank Notes

The amount of cash on hand that is exempt from the bankruptcy estate varies depending on the state where the bankruptcy is filed.

Extra Funding

The Chapter 13 reorganization plan would prevent the mortgage companies from foreclosing on the loans.

bankruptcy will provide the best relief from their debts and creditors. A Chapter 13 reorganization plan will also provide relief but not as quickly or effectively.

If the new legislation that is pending passes and is signed into law, Jack and Jill might have no choice but to file a Chapter 13 reorganization plan. This is because they have regular income. A plan could be structured that would enable them to reduce the amounts of their liabilities and pay back at least a portion of their unsecured debts over a five-year period.

Regardless of whether the new legislation is enacted into law, the basics of planning and filing for bankruptcy will stay the same. The proposed enforcement of more stringent means-testing will only affect certain wage earners seeking relief under the bankruptcy laws. People who have no assets and no disposable income should still qualify for Chapter 7 bankruptcy filings.

Also, all laws are subject to interpretation, and there is no way of knowing how new legislation will work or how effective it will be until it is actually put to the test. Based on the information you have absorbed so far, which chapter of bankruptcy would you choose for Jack and Jill? How does this fictional financial picture compare with your own situation?

Take the Time to Devise a Strategy

At this point, you have processed a lot of information about bankruptcy and the relief it affords. As you move on in this text, you will build on that information and learn some planning strategies that enable debtors to make financial adjustments that will improve their postbankruptcy situation and lifestyle.

Some strategies used by bankruptcy attorneys to mold a client's case are determined by the laws of the state where the bankruptcy is filed. In a subsequent chapter, you will learn more about the laws of various states and how they impact the residents of that state in a bankruptcy filing.

Bankruptcy attorneys are well versed in the laws of the states where they practice. Your attorney will rely on the information you supply to make his determinations and suggestions. You will only hurt your case and yourself by holding back information or being haphazard or careless in reporting it.

Take as much time as you need to list your assets, liabilities, income, and expenses. Then, instead of rushing off to present the information, let it sit for a few days. You'd be surprised at how many things may come to mind that you've forgotten to report or may not have reported accurately.

Writers generally put an article or manuscript aside for a certain amount of time before they attempt to edit it. This timeout from the work allows them to look at it with a fresh perspective. It also enables them to think about the piece objectively and make decisions about the information it contains without being influenced by the creative juices that flowed while the story was being written.

The information you write down about your financial condition may seem as horrific as the storyline of a Stephen King novel. However, the only connection between what you have written and King's work is the editing process that must take place.

Like a writer, allow yourself a little time and space. You may suddenly wake up in the middle of the night, remembering that Aunt Sophie left you a valuable first edition that is gathering dust in your mother's attic. You expend the time and effort to make your information as complete and accurate as possible because disclosure is very important in a bankruptcy filing.

As you move into the next part of this book, you will learn about planning, the legal process that takes place when a bankruptcy petition is filed, and the importance of honest and accurate disclosures and reports.

The Least You Need to Know

➤ There are organizations, such as the American Bar Association, that can help you find a good attorney.

➤ Your attorney will base his recommendations on the information you supply.

➤ If you reside in a community property state, the property of both spouses may become a part of the bankruptcy estate.

➤ Everything belonging to minor children is exempt from the bankruptcy estate.

Part 3

You've Studied the Chapter, Now You're Buying the Book

All the preliminary decisions have been made. You know which bankruptcy chapter will afford you the greatest relief. This is the time for careful planning. In this part of the book, you will move through the actual process of preparing and filing a bankruptcy petition. Although you will be doing this with an attorney, your participation is required.

Your financial future will be determined by the way the bankruptcy is handled. Your attorney will guide you and ask you a multitude of questions regarding your money, property, and debts.

You will also learn how certain assets are protected so that they don't become a part of the bankruptcy estate. This part will explain in detail the legal procedures that allow a debtor to work with creditors to avoid foreclosures and forfeits of property used to secure loans.

Chapter 9

Beginning the Bankruptcy Process

In This Chapter

➤ Bankruptcy worksheet

➤ Important questions

➤ Important answers

➤ Losses and other legal issues

Regardless of the type of bankruptcy chapter that has been deemed right for you, you will have forms to complete with lots of questions to answer. All of the information gathered during this beginning process will be used to prepare the actual bankruptcy petition that will be filed with the court.

It will also be used to determine the steps you may have to take before the petition is prepared and filed. This is where you begin to formulate the plan that will take you through the process with a minimum of effort. This is the plan that will enable you and your attorney to minimize the effects of the bankruptcy on your life and lifestyle.

Work It Out on Paper

At your initial consultation, your attorney will give you papers to take home and fill out. If you have made up your lists in accordance with the samples supplied in previous chapters, you will be able to attach those lists or easily transfer the information in them to these forms. Although the worksheets you are asked to complete may vary slightly from state to state and attorney to attorney, the questions and information required will be fairly uniform. The following guidelines will take you through the standard questions you will find on these forms.

Take care to print or type the information on the forms so that it can be easily read. If you are uncertain about how to answer any of the questions on the forms you are given, make a notation and discuss them with your attorney by telephone or at your next meeting.

Obviously, the first thing you will fill in on the form is your name. There will be space on the forms for your spouse's or partner's information. If the bankruptcy is to be a joint filing, all the questions that are asked must be answered for all parties to the bankruptcy.

If you have a middle name, write it out in full. This is for identification purposes and to cover the possibility that your name may be listed in different ways on some of the documents you will have to provide. You will also have to fill in your social security number, again for identification purposes and to track your tax reports, bank accounts, and other financial records.

For divorced filers, there is a space on the form to enter the name of the ex-spouse and the date the divorce decree was issued. Be sure to include any other pertinent information pertaining to the divorce. For example, if the divorce was obtained in a state or country other than the one in which you currently reside, include that information.

Much of the background information you are required to supply is used for verification. It is also used to determine whether you have lawsuits or judgments pending under other names that may affect your bankruptcy filing. For example, a divorced person may have incurred debts with an ex-spouse that he or she is still required to pay.

NSF Checks

When filling out the bankruptcy forms, provide as much information as possible. It is better to give too many details than to leave out facts that could affect your case. Your attorney will be able to sift through the information and pick out what is needed.

The form will also ask if you or your spouse or partner have been known by any other names within the last six years. This covers a multitude of situations, such as writers with pen names, actors with stage names, women who have married or remarried, and anyone who has used an alias or changed his or her name within that time period.

Your current address or place of residence will be listed next, and then, if applicable, you will have to supply information about former places where you have resided over the last six years.

Some states allow better exemptions for bankruptcy filers, but as a rule, you will have to be a resident of the state where you file for the greater portion of 180 days, or at least 91 days. In other words, you can't just pick up and move to another state to take advantage of more lenient bankruptcy laws. You must reside in the state where you are filing the bankruptcy petition for more than 90 days. If you're a legitimate bankruptcy filer, you probably couldn't afford to move anyway.

Several questions regarding your occupation and income will be included on the forms. These will cover things like the name and address of your current employer, how long you have been employed there, information on other employment over the last few years, gross and net wages, and the frequency of paydays. Again, the same questions apply to you and any other parties to the pending bankruptcy.

The only payroll deductions you will subtract from gross wages are taxes. Other deductions for insurance, savings plans, and other payments are considered income and must be added back into your net wages. Some of these amounts, such as those for insurance premiums, will be offset on the report of expenses you will complete. If you are self-employed, you will provide all the details of your business enterprise. Partnerships and any other business interests you have held over the last six years must also be reported.

To make sure you have included all of your income, you will be required to list the adjusted gross income for your last two income tax returns. Your spouse or partner's income should be listed here as well but separate from yours. Gross wages used in the preparation of the tax return are also itemized. The sources of the income for each year should be identified, too.

Finally, the form will ask if you have received income from any other sources during those years. This would cover nontaxable income such as inheritances and insurance proceeds. If this question applies to you, you will have to name the sources and amounts received.

To substantiate the facts and figures you have provided on wages and your adjusted gross income for the last two years, you will end this section of the questionnaire by listing additional information on the tax returns you filed for that time period. At some point, you will have to provide copies of the actual tax returns.

In the event that you failed to file timely tax returns, you have opened up a complication that needs to be addressed before a bankruptcy petition can be completed. A tax refund due to you must be received and disposed of before the bankruptcy is filed. Otherwise, the refund is considered a nonexempt asset and becomes a part of the bankruptcy estate. If you owe tax, remember that in a bankruptcy, many tax liabilities are nondischargeable debts, so you will still have to pay the taxes due. If you are filing a Chapter 13, you can include the taxes in your plan of reorganization and can pay the liabilities over the term of the plan.

Bank Notes

Include information about other names and places of residence that were reported on federal and state tax returns.

So Many Questions

There are a number of questions you must answer regarding your bank accounts and record keeping. This section does not ask for amounts on hand or on deposit; rather, it has you itemize all the financial institutions where you have accounts. The cash on hand and on deposit will be reported elsewhere on the forms. You will list the name, address, and account number for any and all checking or savings accounts in which you have an interest. For example, elderly or disabled relatives may have your name on an account so you can help them with their banking errands.

NSF Checks

You must report any account on which your name appears, even if it is not primarily your account.

Your attorney will tell you how to handle accounts that bear your name but that contain funds belonging to minor children or elderly parents so that these funds will not be included in the bankruptcy estate.

If you have a safe-deposit box, you will be instructed to list the name of the bank and the location of the box. You will also have to describe the contents and indicate who has access to the box and its contents. If the box has been surrendered or transferred, you will have to explain the details of such transactions.

Extra Funding

Currently, a Chapter 7 bankruptcy can be filed only once in a six-year period. There are no such limitations on reorganization plans for individuals (Chapter 13) or businesses (Chapter 11).

An important question on the attorney's prefiling forms is whether you have kept a set of books or any other records relating to your financial affairs within the last two years. If so, you will be asked to give the particulars regarding the possession and location of those records. An explanation will be required if these records are not available. Your attorney will need to know why the records are no longer accessible. If the records were disposed of or destroyed by fire, flood, or human error, the loss will have to be examined and substantiated. Although this may sound a little extreme, it is a provision of the bankruptcy laws that ensures that all transfers of property and money are documented and reported.

You will have to describe any property you are holding for another person and report the value of that property. If this applies to you, it would be better to give any such property back to its owner before your bankruptcy planning begins. If for some reason it is impossible to return the property you have been entrusted with, be very specific when listing it on the forms and carefully note the owner's information as well. Also be sure to discuss this situation with your attorney. You don't want to be responsible for someone else's property being lumped into your bankruptcy estate.

Any prior bankruptcy must be disclosed in detail on the form. Your lawyer will need to know all the particulars of that case. You will be required to state the location of the bankruptcy court, the nature and number of each case, the date when it was filed, and whether a discharge was granted or refused. If the case was dismissed or a composition, arrangement, or plan was confirmed, you will have to spell out the details.

Transfers, Losses, and Lawsuits

Receiverships, assignments, and other types of liquidation are the subjects of the next few questions on the bankruptcy forms. Many of these queries are to verify that you have not been a party to anything that would cause complications in your bankruptcy planning and filing. If any of your property is in the hands of a receiver, trustee, or other liquidating agent, you will have to give a brief description of the property and the name and address of the receiver, trustee, or other agent. If the agent was appointed by a court, the name and location of the court, the title and number of the case, and the nature of the court action must be specified.

The following questions are asked to determine whether you made any payments to creditors over that last year that could be deemed preferential by a bankruptcy Trustee. They also address the issue of property transfers that might be considered fraudulent by the Trustee. Remember that the Trustee can go back one year and require the creditor, relative, or insider to return the money or property so it can become a part of the bankruptcy estate in a Chapter 7 filing:

➤ Have you made any assignments of your property for the benefit of your creditors, or any general settlement with your creditors, within the last year? (If so, give dates, the name and address of the assignee, and a brief statement of the terms of assignment or settlement.)

➤ Is any other person holding anything of value in which you have an interest? (If so, give the name and address, location, and description of the property and the circumstances relating to the transfer of this property.)

➤ What repayments on loans in whole or in part have you made during the last year? (Give the name and address of the lender, the amount of the loan and when received, the amounts and dates of payments, and whether the lender is a relative, insider, or other relationship.)

➤ Have you made any gifts, other than ordinary and usual presents to family members and charitable donations, during the last year? (If so, give names and addresses of those who received the gifts and the dates the gifts were given. Also include a description and the value of the gifts.)

Bank Notes

In some cases, it may be prudent to delay the bankruptcy filing long enough to prevent certain payments from being set aside by the Trustee as preferential.

➤ Have you made any other transfer, absolute or for the purpose of security, of real or tangible personal property during the last year? (Give a description of the property, the date of the transfer or disposition, to whom it was transferred or how it was disposed of, and if the transferee is a relative or insider, the relationship, the consideration if any received, and the disposition of such consideration.)

➤ Has any of your property been attached, garnished, or seized under any legal or equitable process within the last year? (If so, describe the property seized or the person garnished and give details of the actions that resulted in these attachments, garnishments, or seizures.)

➤ Has any property been returned to or repossessed by the seller or by a secured party during the last year? (If so, give particulars, including the name and address of the party getting the property and a description of the property and its value.)

In addition, you will be asked whether any of your property was lost as a result of fire, theft, or gambling during the last year. If so, you will have to give specific details regarding the loss. This will include dates, names, places, the value, and a general description of the property that was lost. Property in this case also means cash, bonds, or securities.

The second part of the inquiry will relate to any insurance coverage you may have that covered the loss in whole or in part. If that is the case, you will, of course, have to provide the name of the insurance carrier and all the details of the claim.

Your attorney will also need to know whether you are or have been involved in any lawsuits within the last year. This refers to any lawsuit to which you were a party, regardless of whether it has anything to do with your financial situation or any property in which you may have an interest. One of the reasons this information has to be disclosed is because a lawsuit, especially one that has not been settled, is a potential source of income or liability and may affect your future finances.

Also, your bankruptcy attorney will want to make sure he or she does not have a conflict of interest in representing your bankruptcy case. Although the possibility may be remote, your attorney could have a connection to someone else who is a party to the lawsuit in which you are involved. If you have been a party to any type of lawsuit, you will have to provide the name and location of the court and the title and nature of the court proceedings. This would include information on any settlements or other actions.

In connection with the previous questions, your bankruptcy attorney will ask if you have consulted any other attorneys during the past year. Again, if the answer is yes, you will have to supply the name and address of the attorney and when and why you contacted this attorney or law firm.

Last but not least is the following question: Have you, during the last year, paid any money or transferred any property to an attorney or to any other person on his behalf? (If so, give particulars, including the amount paid or the value of the property transferred and the date of payment or transfer.)

NSF Checks

Pending lawsuits may present a variety of complications to your bankruptcy filing.

Bank Notes

Checks and double-checks of your answers and your financial information are done to protect you and your lawyer.

The purpose of this question is to determine whether you have sought legal advice or made any legal arrangements to hide or dispose of property that you don't want included in the bankruptcy filing.

If it appears that the same information is asked for in a number of different ways, it is because that is true. The idea behind it is to cover all the bases and make sure any information that could affect your bankruptcy filing has been revealed.

Once the bankruptcy is filed, the Trustee is going to examine all your records again and may ask for verification of anything that is not absolutely clear. Although this may seem like a long, complicated ordeal, it is for your benefit. Also, it is likely that most of these questions and situations will not be applicable to you and your finances and property.

If you haven't transferred any property, given preferential payments to a creditor, or been involved in losses or law suits, you can probably answer "no" or "n/a" (not applicable) to most of the questions and be done with the forms in short order. On the other hand, if these questions do apply to you and your affairs, they serve as reminders of matters that need to be discussed with your attorney.

Overall, the forms and all the questions are a necessary part of the planning that will ensure that your bankruptcy filing provides the relief you need and the means to begin again. The main purpose of a bankruptcy filing is to sweep away all the old debts that have been dragging you down and keeping you from moving forward in your life. Filling out the forms and answering a multitude of questions are tasks that may be more difficult for some debtors than for others.

Organizing Your Records

Obviously, a person who has kept good records can easily access the information needed for this part of the bankruptcy process. If you are one of those people who has to tear the house apart looking for lost paperwork, perhaps having to gather all this information for the bankruptcy court will help you be more organized in the future.

Being organized doesn't necessarily mean keeping every receipt and piece of paper that passes through your hands. In fact, keeping too much is often more of a hindrance than a help because it gives you that many more papers to look through when you are trying to find something.

The best way to ensure that you will be able to find important papers or information when you need it is to keep it all in one designated place. That designated place can be a box, a drawer, or a file cabinet. If you don't want to take the time to sort it out, just pile it in the box or drawer as it is received. By doing that, you will know that the most recent paperwork is on the top and older documents are closer to the bottom.

The important thing is that when you have to come up with a document, you should only have one place to go to find it. That is generally easier than having to organize a search party and scour the house from top to bottom because you don't remember which special cubbyhole you put it in.

If you don't have a desk or a file cabinet, you can purchase a storage box from any office-supply store. The cardboard file boxes that stack and that have a place on the outside to note the contents work well. You may want to get really serious about the business of organization, and if so, you can get file folders that fit nicely inside the boxes to separate different types of documents.

For example, your folders could be labeled Insurance Policies, Warranties, Sales Receipts, Autos, Bank Statements, and Recipes (to try when you're feeling brave). It may take some extra effort to label the folders and sort the papers, but it's a one-time chore. Once it's done, it will save you many minutes and possibly hours the next time you have to put your hands on something specific, like the warranty for the car battery.

One word of warning: The file boxes are easy to store and work with, but they are not fireproof. Anything of significant value that cannot be replaced should be retained in a fireproof metal box or a safe-deposit box at the bank. If you have valuable documents and other items locked up in a safe-deposit box, prepare a list of the contents of the box and keep it in your home file for a quick and easy reference tool.

A bankruptcy filing is the perfect time to get organized because it is a new beginning for you. Start out fresh with all your records and documents in good order.

NSF Checks

If you keep important records on your computer, don't store the back-up disks next to the computer. If there's a fire, both will be destroyed.

The Least You Need to Know

➤ Standard questions are asked of all debtors going into a bankruptcy filing.

➤ The success of the bankruptcy plan depends on your ability to be open and honest with your attorney.

➤ Preferential payments and certain transfers of property can be voided by a bankruptcy trustee.

➤ Your attorney will ask the same questions a number of different ways to make sure all pertinent information is revealed.

Chapter 10

Continuing the Bankruptcy Process

In This Chapter

➤ Real and personal property

➤ Tangible and intangible property

➤ Tax returns

➤ Schedules and other forms

➤ Verifying statements

As the preplanning process continues, you will have to delve more deeply into your financial information. Bankruptcy is a legal proceeding. For people who have never experienced any type of court action, it may seem daunting.

Don't think that your honesty and integrity are being challenged. As mentioned before, all the questions and probing into your affairs is simply a way to verify that all the elements of your case are brought to light. The whole purpose of bankruptcy is to discharge or reduce all your debts. If you failed to reveal a lawsuit to which you were a party and that lawsuit resulted in a monetary judgment against you, it would not be discharged in a Chapter 7 filing if it was not presented in the bankruptcy petition.

Your Forms Are Taking Shape

The rest of the forms your attorney will ask you to complete deal with your property, assets, and liabilities. Much of this information can be transferred from the lists you had the foresight to complete before the first consultation with your bankruptcy attorney.

The following is a sample of the questions you will find on the standard worksheet from your bankruptcy attorney, along with explanations of the information you will be expected to provide:

➤ **Real property.** Do you own any real estate? If yes, give the value, amount owed, and *lien holder*'s name and address. In the event that you own more than one piece of real estate, you will complete this information separately for each house or parcel of land.

➤ **Cash on hand.** List any deposits of money with banking institutions, savings and loan associations, credit unions, public utility companies, landlords, and others. This means security deposits paid to rental companies, deposits required by the utility companies before connecting service, and any other funds you gave to a person or company that are expected to be returned to you at some time in the future. The amount of the deposit and the name and address of the person or institution holding the deposit must be listed. If there is an account number assigned, indicate that, also.

Although money on deposit at banks and other financial institutions may become a part of the bankruptcy estate, it is unlikely that security deposits for partments or utilities would be withdrawn from the holders of those funds. However, those types of deposits must still be reported.

➤ **Personal property.** List all personal property and estimate the wholesale value (garage sale value) of the items listed. If you do not own anything in this category, enter "-0-" or "n/a." Note the use of the term "garage sale value." As you may recall, Jack and Jill's attorney advised them to revise the values assigned to their personal property. This is a good standard to apply to your own possessions. Ask yourself how much you could expect to get for each item if you were selling it at a garage sale.

Dollar Signs

Lien holders are mortgage companies, banks, or any other company or individual that may have a claim against your property.

Schedules or lists will be required for the following:

➤ All household goods, supplies, and furnishings and their estimated market value.

➤ Books, pictures, and other art objects; stamp, coin, and other collections.

➤ Apparel, jewelry, firearms, sports equipment, and other personal possessions.

➤ Descriptions of the makes and models of automobiles, trucks, trailers, and other vehicles. (Include information on financing and loan amounts and the lien holders on each vehicle.)

➤ Boats, motors, and their accessories.

➤ Livestock, poultry, and other animals.

➤ Farming supplies and implements.

➤ Office equipment, furnishings, and supplies.

➤ Machinery, fixtures, equipment, and supplies (other than those listed elsewhere for use in business).

➤ *Inventory.*

➤ Patents, copyrights, franchises, and other general intangibles.

Dollar Signs

Inventory is a very broad category and includes any merchandise, goods, or supplies used in a trade or business.

This last item is an area that can lead to a great deal of discussion. Tangible assets or properties are defined as those that can be touched. They can be easily appraised and assigned an actual or approximate value. An intangible article is one that's value is hard to determine. Patents and copyrights are the best examples of intangible properties. Either of these things could bring in millions of dollars to the owner, or they could result in no income at all.

If the intangible property is in the marketplace, an estimate of future earnings might be possible. For example, a patent on a medical device could be licensed to a company that is actively manufacturing and selling the device, and the patent holder would be receiving a portion of the profits. The value of the patent could therefore be linked to past sales and the revenue realized from those sales. However, demand for the device could end at any time, causing sales to slump and earnings to plummet.

If you hold a patent or a copyright on a product that is not currently in the marketplace and has no basis on which to predict income, it will take some groundwork and research to try and determine its value.

As you may recall, Jack holds a patent on a mechanic's tool. In the planning stage of this fictional bankruptcy, you will see how the value of Jack's patent was determined and whether he was able to retain the patent (because it is considered to be a nonexempt property).

Moving on to more tangible holdings, your attorney will ask for information on the following:

➤ Government and corporate bonds and other negotiable and nonnegotiable instruments.

➤ Money due to you from other parties. If someone owes you money for any reason, list the amount and the name and address of the person who owes you that amount.

➤ Claims or *counterclaims* against anyone else. This would be anything pending that might result in the transfer of rights, money, or property. Provide the name, address, and details of the claims or counterclaims.

Dollar Signs

A **counterclaim** is a legal action filed to answer or defend against the claim of another.

➤ Interests in insurance policies. Itemize the policies by number and carrier and indicate the surrender or refund value of each.

➤ Annuities (stock and interest in incorporated and unincorporated companies). Stock issued by a private company is usually assigned a par value, but it could bring a higher price if it were sold. If the stock is from a public company, it will be more marketable, and the value will most likely be determined by the price of the stock at the time the bankruptcy is filed.

➤ Interest in partnerships. This could be another intangible asset unless the partnership is in a business with a proven track record with earnings that can be substantiated.

➤ Life estates or trusts.

➤ Any other property not previously listed. This is, of course, a catch-all category for anything that might not be covered or listed in another place.

Checking with Uncle Sam

You will be required to provide copies of your last two tax returns. This is to verify the wages you reported, the taxes paid, and any tax liabilities.

If you don't have copies of the tax returns, your attorney will have you fill out the Department of the Treasury's Request for Copy or Transcript of Tax form (Form 4506) and, if applicable, a similar one for the state in which you reside. You may also have to sign a Power of Attorney and Declaration of Representative form (U.S. Treasury Form 2848). These forms together authorize your attorney access to your tax records, which would otherwise be confidential.

Other Verifying Documents

In connection with assets and property reported and listed on the attorney's bankruptcy planning forms, you will have to produce copies of the following documents:

Extra Funding

The law prohibits the IRS from disclosing your tax information to a third party without your written permission.

1. Deeds, mortgages, homesteads, and title insurance policies for your home or any other real estate you own
2. Any motor vehicle or mobile home titles in your name
3. All of your insurance polices
4. Any papers pertaining to a lawsuit of any kind within the last 12 months
5. All unpaid bills, collection agency notices, and any other papers that have been sent to you by any of the persons or companies to which you owe money
6. Bank statements for any and all accounts
7. Any other papers that you feel are important

NSF Checks

Trustees often request bank statements for the current month as well as statements for the two or three months before the bankruptcy filing.

As you can see, this list of required documents along with tax returns is pretty inclusive and will verify the information you presented on the worksheets. You will also have to sign a statement certifying that the information you provided is true, complete, and accurate to the best of your knowledge.

Your attorney will use the worksheets and lists you prepared to complete schedules that will become a part of your bankruptcy petition. There will be a schedule for your debts and creditors. Schedules for your personal finances will include one that sets forth all your income and one that sets forth all your normal expenditures or day-to-day living expenses.

Now that you have a good idea of the questions and forms you will have to wade through to get your bankruptcy started, you may want to forget the whole thing and go hide in a cave.

Before you cut yourself off from society, consider that with each stroke of your pen, you are moving closer to freedom from your debts and a brand new tomorrow. There may be some bankruptcy attorneys that wouldn't have you complete this type of paperwork and provide documentation to verify the information. That is an attorney you don't want to represent you.

This preliminary work is done so that when your Chapter 7 case is assigned to a Trustee or your Chapter 13 reorganization plan is filed with the court, all the necessary information is included and in good order. This will ensure that your bankruptcy filing goes smoothly without any sudden stops or glitches in the process.

The Least You Need to Know

➤ Under the bankruptcy code, a statement of your income and expenses is required to determine whether you have the capability to reorganize your debts in a Chapter 13 filing.

➤ Intangible properties, such as patents and copyrights, are not exempt from the bankruptcy estate.

➤ All the financial information you provide will be verified by bank statements and other documents.

➤ Copies of your last two federal income tax returns will be needed for your bankruptcy filing.

Chapter 11

Planning Your Bankruptcy Case

In This Chapter

➤ Bank accounts and other assets

➤ Sales and transfers

➤ Special strategies

➤ Chapter 13 plans

Once you and your attorney have settled on the chapter of bankruptcy that will afford you the greatest amount of relief, the preplanning begins.

Remember that no matter how dire your financial outlook may seem, you are still in control. You still maintain the right and the ability to make choices. One of those choices was to hire an experienced attorney who will guide you through the decisions and actions that will make your particular bankruptcy case go smoothly.

Using the sample financial information for our fictional couple, Jack and Jill, you will see how a plan was formulated that enabled them to protect certain assets and have the court discharge most of their bills by filing a Chapter 7 bankruptcy petition.

Depending on the state where you reside, your bankruptcy case will be tailored to fit the exemptions of that state. Jack and Jill reside in the state of Arizona, so their prebankruptcy planning takes into consideration the exemptions allowed under Arizona law.

More specific information on exemptions in various states will be covered in Chapter 14, "Filing a Chapter 7 Bankruptcy Petition."

Spend Any Excess Cash

Since cash or lack of it is a primary concern of any debtor, the first item explained to Jack and Jill is how to handle their bank accounts and cash flow. Because many of their debts will be discharged under Chapter 7, their attorney advises them not to make any more payments on any of these debts. This enables them to pay their mortgage payment on time and avoid more late fees.

The couple reported the current balance in their checking account as $187 with an additional $29 in their savings account, a total of $216. Under the laws of their state, the couple is allowed an exemption of $300 for cash on hand. At the time the forms were completed, they were safely under that exemption limit. However, in the time it takes to prepare and file the bankruptcy petition, their checking account will remain active. Payroll checks will be deposited and normal living expenses will be paid out.

For this reason, the actual filing of the bankruptcy petition is scheduled to coincide with the time of the month when the checking account holds the least amount of funds. When bills are paid with conventional checks from a checking account, there is always a period of transition. With electronic banking, the time between mailing the check and having it clear one's bank account is usually pretty short; however, to avoid any complications, Jack and Jill are advised to cash their paychecks and purchase cashier's checks to pay bills in the weeks immediately preceding the filing of their petition.

The cashier's checks are paid for at the time they are issued, and these transactions do not go through the couple's bank account. This ensures that the bank balance will remain as reported in the bankruptcy papers. Trustees assigned to Chapter 7 cases sometimes ask for all debtor bank account statements covering the month of the filing and two or three months prior to filing.

If you report that you have $100 in your bank account, the statement must verify that amount. Outstanding checks (those that have not yet cleared your account) can make your balance appear greater. The Trustee can request that you turn over the additional funds that appear to be in your account to the court for the bankruptcy estate.

The safest way to handle any excess cash on hand or in your accounts is to spend it on daily living necessities such as utility bills, food, or gasoline for your car. Withdraw any extra funds and spend it before your filing date so that your account balance reflects what is reported on the bankruptcy schedules that accompany your petition.

Bank Notes

In most states, exempted property includes the equity in your home, household goods, and tools of the trade.

NSF Checks

Monitor your bank accounts closely to ensure that balances do not exceed the amount exempted in your state.

The Best Laid Plans

Based on the advice Jack and Jill received at their initial consultation, they have gone back over all their household items and revised the estimates of resale value so that the total of all household items now falls within the exemption guidelines of their state.

This includes Jack's mechanic tools. Working with the vendor who sells tools and equipment to the garage and the other mechanics he works with, a more realistic fair market value has been placed on the tools Jack needs for his job.

The estimated value of the tools has been set and verified by the vendor to be approximately $2,000. Since the computer owned by Jack and Jill is last year's model, its value has been reduced to $500. Because Jack's employer requires Jack to use his own computer to research the cost and availability of auto parts and other information that he needs for his profession, the computer can be added in with the other tools of his trade.

The exemption allowed by the state of Arizona for tools used in a trade or business is $2,500, so now Jack's tools and the computer have both been protected from inclusion in the bankruptcy estate.

The only downside to this planning is that in order to keep the computer, Jack and Jill will have to continue to pay the store where it was purchased. Since they have already paid more than half of the original cost of the computer, they are willing to do this in order to keep it and all the records stored in its program files.

When the appraised value of their house is compared with the mortgages against it, the remaining equity is well under the *homestead exemption* allowed by the state. Therefore, no action is required to protect the house.

The only jewelry exempted from the bankruptcy estate is the wedding rings. That means the other jewelry that Jack and Jill own may go into the bankruptcy estate. The same is true for the oil paintings because artwork is not an exempt item.

Jack's antique gun collection is even more valuable, and unfortunately, that cannot be exempted either. Faced with losing these assets and seeing them sold by the Trustee to satisfy the claims of their creditors, Jack and Jill are beginning to think about a Chapter 13 filing again. However, their attorney presents another idea to them.

Under the law, Jack and Jill can sell these assets and use the money to make some needed improvements to their house, which is an exempt asset. As long as the funds realized from the sale of the jewelry, artwork, and gun collection are used to improve the house and the improvements are completed before the bankruptcy is filed, the sales cannot be deemed inappropriate or fraudulent by the Trustee.

As part of their prebankruptcy plan, the couple sells the nonexempt assets and uses the proceeds to replace the roof on their house and

Extra Funding

It is possible that financed items can be redeemed by making a settlement with the lien holder that allows the debtor to pay a reduced amount that satisfies the liability and allows retention of the collateral.

Dollar Signs

A **homestead exemption** protects the equity in your home from being absorbed into the bankruptcy estate. The amount of the homestead exemption varies from state to state.

Bank Notes

All property absorbed into the bankruptcy estate will be under the control of the court-appointed Trustee.

repave the driveway. Not only were they able to make these much-needed repairs to their house, they were able to pay for them in full.

It is easy to understand the reasoning behind this decision since the couple benefits from this action in a number of ways. Their home, which is their most important and most valuable asset, has been improved, and the new roof and driveway have actually increased the value of the property and therefore made their equity in the property increase as well.

These repairs would have presented a future liability for Jack and Jill and most likely would have been the source of another debt. Having these improvements done and paid for relieves Jack and Jill of another worry and guarantees their comfort the house for several years to come.

Of course, if the asset you sell is one that holds great sentimental value and emotional attachment, having to sell it to make home improvements could be painful. In that case, you may want to wait until a Trustee is assigned and you can buy the item back from the bankruptcy estate. This is permissible. Depending on the value of the asset, the Trustee could decide that it would not bring enough funds to warrant the time and expense of selling it and let you keep it without paying for it.

NSF Checks

Don't count on the Trustee letting you keep or redeem certain items that are of sentimental or emotional value to you. Although this is possible, the Trustee's viewpoint may differ greatly from your own.

Dollar Signs

A **deficiency judgment** is the amount charged a debtor for the difference between the balance of the lien and the price the creditor gets for the vehicle or other financed property.

You must use common sense and talk these situations over with your attorney. The preplanning period exists to handle all these various scenarios and circumstances.

Get a New Car

Jack and Jill have two vehicles. One of them is the car that Jill drives. It is valued at $6,000 and has no liens against it. This means the equity in this vehicle is $6,000. Their state currently only allows $1,500 per person, per vehicle (or a total of $3,000) that can be exempted in this couple's bankruptcy case.

The other vehicle, Jack's truck, is valued at 18,000, but he still owes $21,000 on it. Obviously, the couple's equity in this vehicle is a negative amount. Unfortunately, the bankruptcy code and exemption statues don't allow you to deduct a negative equity from a positive equity value, so another facet of the prebankruptcy plan is formed.

Jack and Jill's attorney suggests that they look into the possibility of returning the truck to the finance company to satisfy that loan. When a vehicle is returned to a creditor under a Chapter 7 bankruptcy filing, there is no *deficiency judgment* granted.

If the truck had been repossessed by the creditor because the payments were not made, the lien holder could hold Jack and Jill responsible for the difference between what it was sold for and the loan amount. Since repossessed vehicles are often sold to wholesale dealers at auctions, this could be a substantial amount. However, by returning the truck to the creditor through the bankruptcy court, the creditor must settle for whatever the vehicle will bring in the marketplace and write off the balance of the loan.

The next step in this planning strategy is to take the vehicle valued at $6,000 and trade it in on a brand new vehicle. The equity in the newly financed vehicle would be less than $3,000 and therefore exempted from the bankruptcy estate.

This plan works especially well for Jack and Jill because Jack is a mechanic. He is able to sell Jill's car and buy an older, less expensive one that he can fix up and then drive back and forth to work. They use the rest of the money as a down payment on a brand new vehicle. The equity in the old car and the brand new one is less than $3,000, and now both vehicles are under the exemption allowed by their state.

Of course, they must make the payments on the van they purchased, but they have acquired a brand new vehicle that will serve them for a number of years. Also, if they had waited until after the bankruptcy was filed, they would have most likely been denied financing on the new vehicle.

If they had not been able to move forward with this specific plan, Jack and Jill would have lost their second car to the bankruptcy estate and either turned the truck back to the creditor or kept making the payments. Turning the financed vehicle back to the creditor would eliminate this liability and the payments that go along with it. However, they would then have to deal with the problem of finding other transportation.

Bank Notes

The decision regarding vehicles will depend on several factors, including but not limited to the age and condition of the existing vehicles and the loans and payment amounts on them.

Keep in mind, however, that this is a sample strategy that may or may not fit your particular situation. It is presented to show you how various plans can be implemented that make beneficial adjustments to a person's overall lifestyle before a bankruptcy is filed.

The question of vehicles is often the most complex. Automobiles and trucks are expensive assets, but at the same time, they are assets that are greatly depreciated through use. Also, there are so many things in your life that may depend on having a reliable vehicle.

Whatever your particular situation, discuss it thoroughly with your attorney and make sure the action you take is one that won't cause you a hardship after the bankruptcy case is filed and closed. Taking the bus to work everyday could be very inconvenient. Even worse is trying to keep an old car running. If you're not a mechanic like Jack, it can be costly and frustrating.

Intangible Assets

So far, you have been looking at tangible property, assets that can easily be appraised or valued for a specific amount. The next issue that Jack and Jill must discuss in connection with their prebankruptcy planning is an intangible asset.

You may recall that Jack obtained a patent on a tool he designed and constructed. He uses the tool himself to work on automobile engines. The patent cost Jack $5,000 and is good for another 15 years. At the present time, Jack uses this particular tool but has never explored the possibility of manufacturing and marketing the tool to other mechanics or auto repair facilities.

The lawyer explains that a patent is a nonexempt asset and could be absorbed into the bankruptcy estate. The other thing to be considered is the cost of manufacturing and marketing the tool because that could affect the value and salability of the patent.

Jack brings the attorney the diagrams and specifications of the tool that were developed to apply for the patent. On Jack's behalf, the attorney contacts a number of major companies in the automotive business and asks about the feasibility and cost of producing the tool, licensing it, and selling it. Based on the reports and opinions from these professionals in the automotive industry, it is determined that the tool would be rather costly to manufacture and therefore would not make a marketable product in a competitive industry.

This information is used to describe the patent on the list of assets that will become part of the bankruptcy petition. The attorney is confident that the Trustee will realize that the patent does not have any marketable value and will not take it into the bankruptcy estate.

Extra Funding

The value of a patent depends on the marketability of the product the patent covers.

As mentioned earlier, there is also the possibility that a particular asset can be bought back or redeemed by the debtor. Again, this depends on the Trustee's determination of the value of the item and how much time and effort would have to be expended to realize any cash from a sale of the asset.

One of the benefits you receive from your attorney's prior experience is that experienced attorneys generally have a good idea as to what types of assets a Trustee will try to sell. Often the time and expense do not justify the proceeds that can be realized from certain assets, and the Trustee will allow the debtors to retain the items. An attorney who handles bankruptcy cases on a regular basis becomes adept at dealing with the Trustees and becomes familiar with their tendencies and attitudes toward certain assets and situations.

Differences in a Chapter 13 Filing

Other than the obvious difference that Jack and Jill would have to develop a plan of reorganization and pay back their creditors over a three- to five-year period, there are a few other things that should be considered.

Under a Chapter 13 plan, Jack and Jill could retain all of their assets. They could also structure the plan so that some of the creditors would have to reduce the debts to reflect the actual value of the asset that secured it.

The creditors who hold purchase money security interests on appliances and other household goods might make a deal that allows the couple to pay a lesser amount and still keep the merchandise. In most instances, Jack and Jill would lose their credit privileges with that particular company but would settle the debt for a much lower amount.

The same would hold true for the vehicle. The plan would call for the amount of the loan to be reduced to reflect the current value of the vehicle. It is possible that Jack would keep the truck and at the same time lower the loan amount against it, the interest rate, and the payments. This process was mentioned earlier. It is known as the "cramdown" provision. The word as it relates to creditors is well formed to indicate that the creditors are forced by the court order to settle for less than the original amounts they intended to collect from the debtors.

Of course, creditors benefit from Chapter 13 filings because they require that a portion of all the debts be repaid over the timeframe that the plan of reorganization is in effect.

After analyzing how each of the bankruptcy chapters would impact their future financial well being, this fictional couple decided to take their attorney's advice and file under Chapter 7. Under Chapter 7, Jack and Jill will have a number of debts totally discharged and will significantly reduce their overall liability picture. This is because they have a substantial amount of unsecured debt such as medical bills and credit card liabilities.

Bank Notes

Remember that a Trustee is appointed in a Chapter 13 filing. The Trustee collects payments from the debtor, distributes the funds to creditors, and makes sure the debtor honors the terms of the repayment plan.

Planning Your Bankruptcy Strategy

You have seen examples of strategies used in prebankruptcy planning for Jack and Jill. A good deal of the planning is determined by the exemption statues of the state where the bankruptcy is being filed, coupled with the value and types of assets held by the debtors.

The planning for each bankruptcy case must be carefully considered. Many of the aspects of planning are uniform or standard. However, since each bankruptcy case is a little different, the prebankruptcy planning is also unique for each individual debtor. It is prudent to take as much time as you need to form a good plan.

Keep in mind that the plan that takes shape before you file your bankruptcy case may also impact your personal goals for the future. For most people, seeking relief from their debts through the federal bankruptcy courts is a decision that is made only after much soul searching. During this period of reflection and contemplation, it is natural to begin thinking of some of the things that might be possible after the debts are erased.

Perhaps you have short-term plans such as a vacation to clear away the lingering tension from dealing with all those creditors. Perhaps you have long-range plans. Freedom from debts may enable you to use your increased cash flow to improve your current lifestyle.

Hopefully, your plans for the future include more than the acquisition of material possessions. Additional education, for instance, may sharpen skills that will enable you to earn a higher salary or even begin a career in a new field that holds special interest for you.

Information and suggestions in later chapters may help you sort through possibilities that will be open to you after your bankruptcy case is closed. However, the time to begin thinking about your postbankruptcy plan is when you are developing the strategy for the bankruptcy case itself.

If there is something special you want to do after the case is closed, discuss it with your attorney. Your particular goal may require an adjustment in the preplanning strategy. You have probably spent months, even years, thinking about your debts and trying to find a way to handle them. Now is the time to put those thoughts aside and let plans for the future surface.

The Least You Need to Know

➤ Your home is usually your largest asset and is protected by exemptions in all states.

➤ Considering what your financial picture will be after bankruptcy will help you determine the chapter that is most beneficial for you.

➤ Dealing with automobiles and liens against them can be a complex issue of prebankruptcy planning.

➤ Your attorney's experience in dealing with Trustees is a vital part of prebankruptcy planning.

Chapter 12

Redemptions and Reaffirmations

In This Chapter

➤ Redeeming assets

➤ Reaffirming certain debts

➤ Terms and conditions of agreements

➤ Approvals

Before your bankruptcy petition is filed, you will have to decide whether you want to keep any of the property that has a claim against it by a creditor. When your debts are discharged through the court, the creditor can no longer try to collect the liability, but the creditor can take possession of any collateral that secures the debt. If you have a financed vehicle, business equipment, or other merchandise or property, you have the option to make arrangements with the creditor that will allow you to retain the property.

This is done in one of two ways, either by redemption or by reaffirmation. These are legal agreements you enter into with the creditor to settle the debt so that you don't have to forfeit the collateral. Both of these agreements must be approved by the court before they are finalized. The court wants to make sure that the financial terms will not impose a new financial hardship on the debtor.

Redeeming Offers

A redemption is a written offer to a creditor to pay cash in order to redeem an item used to secure the debt. In the sample economic data presented for the fictional couple, Jack and Jill, a number of assets were financed by the retail stores where the merchandise was purchased.

The refrigerator, living room furniture, computer, stereo, and big-screen television are all listed with the names of the companies that hold liens against each one. If Jack and Jill want to keep any or all of these things, they can enter into a redemption agreement with the creditors. For example, the debtors owe $800 on the computer and can offer to pay the resale value of $500 to settle the debt in full and retain the computer.

In Jack and Jill's case, if the creditor agrees to the redemption offer, the couple pays the store $500 and closes out this account. They then get to keep the computer, which is exempt from the bankruptcy estate because it is considered to be tools of the trade.

The retailer or creditor often accepts the redemption agreement to avoid the problems associated with the return and sale of used merchandise. However, the creditor is not required to accept the redemption offer and may insist that the merchandise be returned. The creditor also has the option to request a court hearing to set the redemption value of the item.

NSF Checks

Careful consideration must be given to redeeming property that is nonexempt to make sure it will not be taken into the bankruptcy estate by the Trustee.

One of the essential elements of prebankruptcy planning is discussing each piece of real or personal property that secures a debt with your attorney. An election must be made to keep or forfeit each item of collateral. The bankruptcy code currently requires debtors to file a notice with the court regarding any property that serves as collateral for consumer debts. The notice must indicate the debtors' intention to either retain the property or surrender it. The notice must indicate whether the property is exempt and whether the debtor intends to redeem the property or reaffirm the debt secured by the property.

The code further indicates that the debtor is obligated to carry out the election with 45 days of filing notice of the election. Obviously, the debtor must be able to come up with the funds needed to redeem the property. A cash redemption is generally used only with items of relatively low value.

Funds for the redemption may come from relatives or a postbankruptcy loan; however, it is not prudent to exchange one debt for another. Good judgment and common sense should prevail. Many attorneys advise their bankruptcy clients to restrict redemptions and reaffirmations to property that is essential for their postbankruptcy survival. A refrigerator would be a necessary item; a big screen television would not.

The other thing to remember when considering whether or not to redeem certain items is that you are filing bankruptcy to better your financial situation and cash flow. Carrying over debts that could be discharged will dilute the amount of relief you are granted by the court.

If you reaffirm on a debt, it will not be discharged by the bankruptcy. Later on, if you should default on this debt, the creditor may take action against you. Again, you must give these decisions careful consideration and be open to the advice your attorney provides.

Redemptions and reaffirmations are part of Chapter 7 bankruptcy cases. They are not necessary in a Chapter 13 filing because the plan of reorganization provides for payments or settlements of all debts, secured or unsecured.

Reaffirmation agreements are in a special category. They are not required by law and must be approved by your attorney and the court. The following guidelines apply to reaffirmation agreements:

1. The agreements must be voluntary.
2. The liability reaffirmed must not impose a hardship on the debtor or the debtor's family.
3. The reaffirmation must be in the best interests of the debtor.

Bank Notes

When you reaffirm on a liability, you are telling the court that you want to keep this debt; you do not want it discharged.

Keeping the Homestead

Mortgages are the debts that are most often reaffirmed in a bankruptcy filing. Your equity in the home is exempt from the bankruptcy estate, but to keep that roof over your head, you must make suitable arrangements with the creditor that holds the mortgage on the property.

A reaffirmation agreement on a mortgage is usually drawn up based on the original terms of the loan. The agreement is filed with the court before a discharge of debts is granted. Any debt that has been reaffirmed is then excepted from the discharge.

To give you a better understanding of the terms and conditions, here is a copy of a standard reaffirmation agreement for a mortgage.

REAFFIRMATION AGREEMENT

Case No. 00-0000 (This would be your bankruptcy case number.)

The undersigned debtors, _____, (hereinafter referred to as "you" or "your," whether one or more), agree with the _____ (hereinafter referred to as "Creditor") as follows:

1. On _____, you filed a Petition in the United States Bankruptcy Court for the district of Arizona, seeking relief under Chapter 7 of the United States Bankruptcy Code.

2. In the Schedules of assets and liabilities accompanying your Petition, you listed an obligation to Creditor secured by a lien on the following described real property (hereinafter called the "Collateral"):

   Insert Legal Description of Property

3. You agree and acknowledge that by signing and executing this Agreement, you are reaffirming your obligation to Creditor, according to all of the following terms and conditions:

   a. You agree and acknowledge that all terms and conditions set forth in the Installment Note and Deed of Trust signed and executed by you on or about _____ are reaffirmed by you and shall continue in full force and effect, except as expressly modified in this Agreement. Accurate duplicate copies of the above-described Note and Deed of Trust are attached to this Agreement as Exhibits "1" and "2" and by this reference are made a part of this agreement.

    b. You jointly and severally promise and agree that you will pay to Creditor the sum due on the Promissory Note and Deed of Trust in accordance with the terms thereof (hereinafter called the "Debt") and that as of _____ those sums include:

        Principle Balance $_____

        Attorney Fees and Costs $_____

        Total $_____

        Plus interest at an annual percentage rate of _____ plus monthly impounds for taxes and insurance, together with all late fees incurred after _____.

    c. You and Creditor agree and acknowledge that Creditor will retain its lien on the Collateral until you have paid the full amount of this obligation, plus interest, in full. You also agree and acknowledge that your payment in full of said debt will serve as your redemption of the Collateral.

4. You are aware that the debt which you are reaffirming may be dischargeable in the bankruptcy proceeding that you initiated by filing your Petition, and that if the debt were discharged, you would be under no legal obligation to repay Creditor, although discharge would not affect Creditor's lien on the collateral. You are also aware that you are not required by law or prior agreement to sign the Agreement, and if you fail to honor the terms of this Agreement, the Creditor may resort to legal action to collect the debt and/or to foreclose upon the Collateral under applicable nonbankruptcy law. You may also be liable for Creditor's costs and reasonable attorneys' fees incurred in enforcing this Agreement after default.

5. The Bankruptcy Court will hold a separate hearing, which you must attend, on the discharge of your debts and on your application for approval of this Agreement. This Agreement has been made before you have received such a discharge of your debts from the Bankruptcy Court. Additionally, you understand that within sixty (60) days after the Bankruptcy Court approves this Agreement, you have a right to rescind and cancel it. Notice of rescission shall be in writing and be mailed to the office of Creditor's attorneys _____. The notice shall also acknowledge the Creditor's right to initiate foreclosure proceedings.

6. You also represent that the property is exempt or abandoned property and is not property of the bankruptcy estate, and you hereby agree that all stays against lien enforcement, including the automatic stay provided by 11 U.S.C. S 362, shall be deemed terminated upon the approval of this Agreement by the court.

7. That, as a condition to acceptance of this Reaffirmation Agreement by _____, you promise to pay all such amounts as may be necessary to reinstate, in a current posture, this obligation.

8. You agree that this Agreement has been entered into in good faith by you and Creditor and is in your best interests.

Your attorney is required by the court to review the reaffirmation agreement and sign a declaration stating that the agreement is reasonable and will not pose a hardship on the debtor. A reaffirmation agreement is signed and approved by your attorney and submitted to the court. It can be canceled anytime before the court discharges your debts, or it can be canceled within 60 days after the agreement is filed with the court.

When a debt is reaffirmed, each party has the same rights and liabilities that existed prior to the bankruptcy. The debtor is obligated to pay the loan, and the creditor can sue or foreclose on the property if the payments are not made.

Most mortgage companies have standard forms much like the preceding sample used for reaffirmation agreements and will draw up the papers for your signature. Your attorney will review and approve the documents before you sign them and will add his own declaration of approval to send to the court with the reaffirmation. If you are debtor with a house and a mortgage, this reaffirmation agreement will be an important document in your bankruptcy case.

Pay particular attention to the terms described under numbers 4 and 5 of the sample reaffirmation agreement. You must understand that if you do not reaffirm the mortgage loan or rescind the affirmation, the debt is discharged.

Discharging the debt would only relieve you of the amount of the defaulted payments or the deficiency that might result from a sale, but the mortgage company could still foreclose on the property under the terms of the Deed of Trust you signed when you purchased the house.

Simply put, liens against your property, whether real property or personal property, are still enforceable. Creditors insist on collateral so that they are not left high and dry with no recourse if you default on the loan.

Extra Funding

If a debtor is not represented by an attorney, the court will hold a hearing to decide whether to approve the reaffirmation agreement. The agreement does not take effect until the court approves it.

Autos and Other Assets

Many debtors reaffirm on their auto loans because they have no other means of transportation and must be able to keep their cars. You have already reviewed other options regarding vehicles that can be implemented as part of the prebankruptcy planning. If you are a business owner, you may have to reaffirm on debts secured by equipment or merchandise that enables you to continue your business enterprise. Since people from all walks of life seek relief through bankruptcy, there is no way to categorize all the different types of property that any individual may choose to redeem or retain.

It is possible to reaffirm on any debt, secured or unsecured, but most attorneys will not approve a reaffirmation on an unsecured debt. It defeats the purpose of filing a bankruptcy petition. Your attorney has already reviewed all of your financial data and has a good idea of what your postbankruptcy cash flow will be. Part of his responsibility to you and to the court is to make sure that the bankruptcy action will result in a stable economic future for you and your family.

Keep Your Objectivity

Prebankruptcy planning requires that you maintain your objectivity when it comes to personal property. Decisions based on emotional attachments can be detrimental to your postbankruptcy survival. This is not to say that you should abandon an item of great sentimental value, but you should be selective and reasonable as you consider the importance of these items to you and your lifestyle.

Heed the advice of your attorney and other professionals who are more experienced and knowledgeable about bankruptcy and financial recovery. An attachment to certain material possessions is natural and understandable. However, some of the things that are held most dearly are often things that don't have significant value.

Photographs, a valentine from your sweetheart, a book of poems, or a souvenir that reminds you of your honeymoon or a special vacation are all things that bring you joy but may not hold any monetary value. The Trustee in your bankruptcy case will not be concerned with your personal photographs or mementos. The Trustee will only be looking at the things that can be easily converted to cash to satisfy the claims of your creditors.

Don't stress over the items you may lose in a bankruptcy filing. Instead, focus on all you will gain. This is the primary question you should ask yourself when considering redemptions and reaffirmations: Is this an item I truly have to keep to start over? Remember, the underlying purpose of a bankruptcy filing is the opportunity to begin again. Don't hamper yourself by retaining debts or making new debts in order to keep something you like but don't really need.

The Least You Need to Know

➤ Redemptions and reaffirmations require careful consideration and must be approved by your attorney and the court.

➤ Only low-value items should be redeemed to avoid postbankruptcy problems.

➤ Although equity in your home is exempt up to the amount allowed in your state, you must reaffirm on any mortgages against it.

➤ Bankruptcy does not permanently prevent creditors from confiscating or foreclosing on property used as collateral for loans.

➤ Generally, unsecured debts should not be reaffirmed.

At the sound of the tone, I shall be precisely bankrupt.

Chapter 13

Timing Is Everything

In This Chapter

➤ What to do before Chapter 7 is filed

➤ What to do before Chapter 11 is filed

➤ What to do before Chapter 13 is filed

➤ Timing is everything

Even before the bankruptcy petition is filed, you will begin to breathe easier. Perhaps it is because you are no longer in that terrible state of indecision. You are working to resolve your financial problems, and your involvement in planning a course of action erases much of the stress and emotional turmoil.

You know that it is just a matter of time before the petition is filed and the automatic stay goes into effect. In the meantime, when a bill collector calls, you can say you are in the process of filing bankruptcy and that usually ends the conversation.

Your part of the paperwork has been completed. You should have provided all the information your attorney needs to draw up the actual bankruptcy petition and the schedules that will accompany it.

Chapter 7 Filers

The schedules that will accompany your bankruptcy petition will report all your current income and monthly living expenses. Another schedule will list all your creditors and the amount of the liabilities. This identifies all your debts, including those being reaffirmed.

If any financed items are to be redeemed, the list of debts will include the difference between the cash redemption and the balance of the debt. The remaining balance of a debt settled by redemption will be officially discharged by the court. Notices of redemptions and reaffirmation agreements will be presented to the court along with statements of approval from your attorney.

The filing of your bankruptcy petition should be done on the date that affords the debtor the greatest advantage. The following examples will demonstrate the benefits of good timing.

Tax refunds: If you are expecting a refund of federal or state taxes, delay filing the bankruptcy petition until the tax refund has been received and used for items that the court will not question, such as food or utilities. Otherwise, the tax refund will become a part of the bankruptcy estate and be divided among your creditors.

Tax liabilities: With a few exceptions, a tax liability is not a dischargeable debt. Therefore, it is wise to pay the tax or make payment arrangements with the Internal Revenue Service before filing. The payment schedule can be reported on your list of necessary expenditures.

Many people are not aware that the Internal Revenue Service will work with them on tax liabilities. The worst thing you can do is ignore the notices. The IRS will eventually issue a *tax levy,* which means the government attaches your bank account and anything else you own. Call or write the IRS when you get the first tax bill and set up a payment schedule that you can honor.

Outstanding checks: Make sure the balance in your checking account agrees with the current bank statement that the trustee will request. Delay filing until your account is in order.

Dollar Signs

A **tax levy** is an order issued by the Internal Revenue Service that allows them to collect unpaid taxes by seizing your money or property.

NSF Checks

The Internal Revenue Service will institute collection actions against the personal assets of individuals who are officers, directors, or check signers of companies or corporations with unpaid tax liabilities.

Cash on hand: Any cash in excess of the amount exempted by your state should be spent on normal living expenses. Stock up on groceries and fill the car with gasoline.

Preferential payments: The trustee will go back over your records for the past year, so if you made a payment 10 months ago that could be deemed preferential, delay filing the bankruptcy petition for two months.

Discuss any questions or potential timing problems with your attorney.

Chapter 11 Filers

Your plan of reorganization should be done and ready to submit for court approval. Before you actually file, make sure all the loose ends that could affect your business and your future income have been taken care of.

Since your assets will not go into a bankruptcy estate, you don't have to worry about tax refunds or other income that has not yet been received. These funds will be available to you and will help you make the payments you have outlined in your plan of reorganization.

You do have to worry about tax liabilities and any tax reports that have not been filed. All tax returns should be completed and filed before your plan of reorganization is finalized. If you owe taxes, you can then include them in your repayment plan.

Business owners should be aware that officers, directors, and those with check-signing authority may be personally responsible by law for the unpaid taxes.

If you have co-signers on debts, they are protected from the actions of creditors by your Chapter 11 bankruptcy filing. However, they should be notified and kept informed of the filing and the details of the plan you are implementing.

If you are selling property to help fund the plan of reorganization, you may have to get permission from anyone who has a lien or a secured interest in that property. Leased property belongs to the lessor. Check the lease for any restrictions if you are thinking of assigning the lease to another party.

Check real property and equipment leases, credit cards, and trade accounts for which the contract may be in the name of an individual or for which an individual has guaranteed the debt. This is a common situation with a new business enterprise that does not have an established credit rating. Officers or owners of the business provide their personal guarantee in order to open lines of credit.

A business entity needs competent legal and financial advice before, during, and after filing a Chapter 11. Be sure you have allotted the necessary funds to pay these professionals.

Bank Notes

There is usually no Trustee assigned to a Chapter 11 filing, which allows the business owner to manage the plan of reorganization.

Chapter 13 Filers

Like the Chapter 11 business owner, you must make sure all your financial affairs are in order. Tax issues are of paramount importance and can complicate your bankruptcy petition. Your attorney will advise you regarding any returns that need to be filed either before or after the bankruptcy petition is completed.

Co-signers should be notified in case a creditor calls them or tries to take action against them for a debt included in your plan of reorganization.

NSF Checks

An estimate of attorney fees and court costs should be obtained at the initial consultation with your lawyer so that you can put the necessary funds aside.

All Chapters

Every creditor included in your petition will receive a notice from the court. Make sure that all reaffirmations and redemption offers are in order.

Once again, keep in mind that tax issues should be resolved before a bankruptcy petition is filed. Inadequate tax information may jeopardize your case, so make sure you have revealed all the details of your particular tax situation. For businesses, this includes personal returns, corporate returns, and payroll and unemployment tax reports.

Last but not least, you must have the funds to pay your attorney and the filing fees for your bankruptcy case.

The "Notice To Individual Consumer Debtor(s)" is an information form provided by the United States Bankruptcy Court. You will receive a copy of this notice and will be required to sign and date it to affirm that you have read it.

The following statement is displayed in bold print at the top of the form:

> **The purpose of this notice is to acquaint you with the Four Chapters of the federal bankruptcy code under which you may file a bankruptcy petition. The Bankruptcy Law is complicated and not easily described. Therefore, you should**

seek the advice of an attorney to learn of your rights and responsibilities under the law should you decide to file a petition with the court. Court employees are prohibited from giving you legal advice.

This serves as an official warning to you that bankruptcy is a complex legal action that requires your full understanding and the advice of a competent attorney. The notice goes on to describe the different chapters of bankruptcy and the filing fees for each one. These fees are imposed by the federal court and are remitted to the court when the bankruptcy petition is filed.

These filing fees are standard across the country and are in addition to the legal fees charged by your attorney for handling your case. The filing fees for each chapter are as follows:

Chapter 7: Liquidation, $200 filing fee

Chapter 11: Reorganization, $830 filing fee

Chapter 12: Family farmers, $230 filing fee

Chapter 13: Repayment plan for individuals, $185 filing fee

As you can see, the filing fee for a Chapter 11 reorganization is much higher than for a Chapter 13 repayment plan for an individual consumer. This, in itself, gives you an idea of how complex Chapter 11 is in comparison to the other types of bankruptcy.

Other Timing Issues

Decisions on whether to delay or speed up the filing of a bankruptcy petition can depend on a number of factors. Sometimes there are business and personal considerations that affect the timeframe.

Delay may be necessary to take advantage of a future exemption. A quick filing may prevent creditors from seizing or foreclosing on property.

If the debtor is the midst of a divorce, a bankruptcy petition may stop the divorce settlement actions; you should discuss the effects of delaying or speeding up the bankruptcy filing with your attorney.

If a lawsuit is threatened or in progress, the timing of the filing may determine how and where the disputed matter is decided. For example, an earlier bankruptcy filing could bring the issue into federal court instead of state court. A later filing would leave the matter in the state courts if it is determined that the debtor would receive a better ruling there.

Another very important factor to consider is whether the debtor's economic future is likely to improve. If the debtor is unemployed or is incurring ongoing expensive medical treatments, it may be advantageous to wait until the health problem is resolved or new employment has been obtained. A Chapter 7 bankruptcy can only be filed once every six years, so it should be timed so that the debtor receives the maximum benefit and relief from the filing.

Timing is everything. While you may not be able to predict what the future may hold in the way of additional income or unexpected expenses, you can intelligently assess the current situation and plan your bankruptcy filing accordingly. When the mortgage company is about to foreclose on your home, file quickly and get the benefit of the automatic stay. If you have a substantial tax refund coming, hold off until the check has been cashed and wisely spent so that it won't become a part of the bankruptcy estate and doled out to your creditors.

Bank Notes

Take the extra time needed to sell nonexempt assets and use the funds for home improvements.

Talk openly and honestly with your attorney. Discuss any problem or situation that may affect your current or future finances. Above all, don't view your bankruptcy filing as an end to your problems. Look at it as a new beginning. A fresh start requires good planning, and part of good planning is knowing exactly when to put the plan into motion.

The Least You Need to Know

➤ The filing of a bankruptcy petition should be timed so that it provides the maximum amount of relief to the debtor.

➤ A quick filing is sometimes necessary to save property from being seized or foreclosed on by a creditor.

➤ A later filing may be required if there are ongoing financial problems that will make a fresh start difficult.

➤ Tax issues should be discussed with your attorney so that they do not complicate the bankruptcy case.

Part 4

Your Day in Court

After all the planning and preparation, your attorney files the bankruptcy petition with the federal bankruptcy court. The automatic stay goes into effect. The phone calls from creditors and collection agencies stop. No more late notices are delivered to your door. The mailman is smiling at you again.

The chapters in this part of the book will take you through the legal process that your bankruptcy filing has put into motion.

Chapter 14

Filing a Chapter 7 Bankruptcy Petition

In This Chapter

➤ Your creditors' reactions

➤ What you may keep

➤ State exemptions

➤ What you may lose

You have already learned the basic provisions of a Chapter 7 bankruptcy. When the petition is filed in the federal bankruptcy court, a case number is assigned and the legal process begins. Your petition includes schedules outlining your income and expenses; detailed information about your assets, liabilities, debts, and creditors; and notices of intention regarding redemption and reaffirmation agreements. These agreements must be preapproved by your attorney.

The court will examine the petition and all the documents that are a part of it. The court will be checking to make sure you qualify for relief under Chapter 7 of the federal bankruptcy code. Since you and your attorney have already analyzed your particular situation and know that you do qualify, this initial court review is just a formality.

All the creditors listed in the bankruptcy petition are notified that the automatic stay is in effect. The debtor receives instant relief from the collection actions that were being used by the creditors. Other than the exceptions to the automatic stay presented in an earlier chapter, the creditor still has rights. However, those rights or interests in the property must be presented to the court before the creditor can take any further action.

Creditors Seeking Relief

A creditor who wants to be relieved from the automatic stay must request a court hearing and prove to the bankruptcy judge that there is cause for the automatic stay to be lifted. This is the time when the delineation between a secured debt and an unsecured debt takes on the most importance. It is usually the secured creditor who wants relief from the stay in order to foreclose on real estate or repossess a vehicle.

The creditor must have a lawyer to present the argument against the stay at the court hearing. The lawyer must quickly evaluate the creditor's claim against the debtor and the debtor's property because these hearings generally take place within 10 to 20 days from the time the motion is filed.

There are times when the court grants a creditor relief from the automatic stay. If the debtor's equity in the property is small, the court could rule in favor of the creditor. In some instances, the debtor may be able to make additional payments to increase equity in the property and keep the automatic stay in effect.

A creditor might also appeal to the court for permission to pursue the debtor's insurance coverage to satisfy a claim. For example, the creditor holds a lien against a vehicle that has been destroyed in an accident and wants to collect damages from the company that insures the vehicle for the debtor. The court may grant a relief from the stay to this creditor but limit the collection of the claim to the amount covered by the insurance policy.

NSF Checks

It is in your best interest to keep the payments on secured loans current. This will reduce or eliminate the need to try to increase equity in these assets during the bankruptcy process.

A Chapter 7 bankruptcy case can continue for months before a final discharge is issued and the case is closed. An individual or a small company holding a secured claim may very well be entitled to relief from a stay if the time factor imposes a hardship or jeopardizes the normal operation of the creditor's business enterprise.

In the case of property that is owned by a Chapter 7 debtor and other parties, a creditor can ask the court to lift the stay so that the debtor can be a party to a lawsuit involving the multi-owned property. As long as the automatic stay is in effect, the debtor cannot be named in a lawsuit based on claims to the property. The debtor's interest in the property may even be absorbed into the bankruptcy estate.

The decision of judges on these types of requests is unpredictable. Some judges will rule in favor of the creditor but restrict the creditor's rights against the debtor if the lawsuit results in a judgment. Other judges will deny the creditor's motion and keep the debtor and the debtor's interest in the property out of a lawsuit.

When the court does grant a creditor relief from the stay, it does not remove the related property from the bankruptcy estate or transfer ownership of the property to the lien holder. A creditor who receives relief from the stay is simply allowed to pursue the remedies that would be available to the creditor if the debtor had not filed bankruptcy.

Court decisions on motions for relief of stay can be made at the creditor's initial hearing, or if deemed necessary, an *evidentiary hearing* may be scheduled before a final decision is handed down. A creditor who does not have sufficient grounds for the court to grant relief from the stay can request that the court protect the property held as collateral. A mortgage company, for example, would want to make sure the real estate was insured against damages and the property taxes were paid.

An unsecured creditor can file a motion with the court if there is evidence that the debtor committed fraud, such as falsifying information about employment or income in order to obtain the unsecured loan or credit card.

It is unlikely that the unsecured creditor would receive relief from the stay, but the motion might result in the court's denial of discharge for that particular debt. If the debt is not discharged, the debtor is obligated to pay it as if the bankruptcy petition had not been filed. The creditor is also free to institute collection actions should the debt fall into arrears.

Under a Chapter 7 bankruptcy, an unsecured creditor will generally only receive a small portion of the actual debt. If a debtor has a lot of nonexempt assets that would become a part of the bankruptcy estate and be sold to pay creditors, that debtor would probably not seek relief under a Chapter 7 filing. To preserve the nonexempt assets, such a debtor would file under a Chapter 11 or 13.

Keeping House and Home Intact

Exempt property is excluded from the bankruptcy estate because the purpose behind a bankruptcy filing is to provide relief to the debtor. Stripping debtors of the property they need to start over after bankruptcy would serve no good purpose. Although discharging debts is a primary function of the bankruptcy case, maintaining certain property is just as important to the petitioner.

The federal bankruptcy code provides exemptions for individual debtors only. Businesses such as partnerships and corporations are not entitled to these exemptions.

The main assets covered by the federal exemptions include homesteads, vehicles, household furnishings and goods, and certain personal property. These exemptions are secondary to the exemptions of the state where the bankruptcy is filed.

Lifestyles and economic conditions vary depending on the industries, employment opportunities, and standards of living in each

Dollar Signs

An **evidentiary hearing** is held in court in front of a judge. At the hearing representatives from both sides of an issue present evidence to support their claims.

Bank Notes

Credit card companies often send out preapproval forms that require potential cardholders to list their total annual income. If a person who has recently become unemployed enters an income amount that does not reflect the reduction due to the job loss, he or she *is* falsifying information.

Bank Notes

Exemptions are structured to help individuals keep their home and household from loss. Business property is considered to be "income producing" and therefore may not be exempted.

part of our country. Therefore, the federal bankruptcy courts honor the exemptions of the state where the debtor resides.

In some states, a debtor may choose the federal exemptions if they are more favorable. A debtor cannot pick and choose between state exemptions and federal exemptions. One or the other must be elected for use in the bankruptcy case.

There are specific states that have not authorized the federal exemptions, and debtors who reside in these states must structure their cases based on the exemptions of that state. The property exempted under the state or federal laws is excluded from the bankruptcy estate and cannot be sold by the Trustee to pay the claims of unsecured creditors.

When you file a Chapter 7 bankruptcy petition, you and your attorney will plan your case based on the exemptions allowed in your home state. The preplanning will be similar to the way the fictional couple, Jack and Jill, developed their case in previous chapters. The idea is to get the maximum benefit from the exemptions each state allows.

Now you will look at the exemptions from a number of states and compare the dollar amounts and types of property that their residents are allowed to retain in a bankruptcy filing. This will give you a basic understanding of how the laws across the country determine the way a Chapter 7 bankruptcy case is handled by the courts.

The laws reflect the importance of keeping house and home intact. Citizens need housing, transportation, and tools related to their professions and jobs. Those items are exempted from the bankruptcy estate in most states. However, the extent to which they are protected differs from place to place.

Comparing State Exemptions

You will be reviewing exemptions from the following states: Arizona, Colorado, Illinois, Kentucky, Minnesota, Montana, New York, and Texas. These states, which are located in different areas of the country, provide a fair sampling of the economic and social climates where residents seek relief in the bankruptcy courts.

The type of property and the dollar amount of the exemption allowed in these states is presented for each category that a debtor may need to keep in order to get a fresh start.

Here are the exemptions allowed for a homestead, including condominiums, town homes, cooperative apartments, and mobile homes:

Arizona	$100,000
Colorado	$30,000
Illinois	$7,500 individual; $15,000 couple
Kentucky	$5,000
Minnesota	$200,000; $500,000 if used for agriculture purposes
Montana	$60,000
New York	$10,000

Extra Funding

Some states, such as Minnesota, have a special exemption for those whose homesteads are located on land used for agriculture. This also protects residents of the state who rely on the availability of agricultural products as a source of food.

NSF Checks

The information from these sample states is presented for demonstration purposes only. Since laws are always being revised and updated, you must contact your legal advisor for guidance. Do not rely solely on the information listed here.

Remember that the exemption amount protects only the *equity* in the property.

Texas allows the most liberal exemption because it does not specify a dollar amount, but it does provide the following:

1. For a family, not more than 200 acres, which may be in one or more parcels with the improvements thereon; or

2. For a single, adult person, not otherwise entitled to a homestead, not more than 100 acres, which may be in one or more parcels with the improvements thereon.

One of the provisions of the pending bankruptcy legislation limits the homestead exemption to $125,000 of equity. If this legislation passes, it would affect states such as Texas and Minnesota that have more liberal homestead exemptions. It remains to be seen if this bill will pass and if its passage will then result in court challenges by some of the states.

Many people who file bankruptcy do not own a house but reside in rental property. In most states, any prepaid rent or security deposits required by the landlord are exempt from the bankruptcy estate.

No amount is listed for cash in most states. The general rule is that any cash over and above a reasonable amount to sustain the household will be absorbed into the bankruptcy estate. You have already reviewed the options that a debtor has to dispose of extra funds.

In the cash category, most of the states provide exemptions on life insurance policies and the death benefits paid to a survivor. Funds earmarked for nondischargeable debts such as alimony and child support payments are also exempted. As mentioned earlier, retirement funds are protected from the bankruptcy estate unless it is determined that the additional deposits of these funds were made within 120 days of the bankruptcy filing date.

Exemptions for household furnishings and appliances allowed by the sampling of states is as follows:

Arizona	$4,000
Colorado	$1,500
Illinois	$2,000
Kentucky	$3,000
Minnesota	$4,500
Montana	$4,500
Texas	$30,000 individual; $60,000 family

Texas again seems to allow the most generous exemption amount but broadens this category to take in clothing, jewelry, books, family heirlooms, tools, and motor vehicles. In other words, the exemption covers all the debtor's personal property and therefore is not as ample as it appears.

Dollar Signs

Equity, as it relates to exemptions, is the difference between the value of the property and the liens or mortgages against the property.

Bank Notes

Landlords generally require that you remit extra funds that are held as payment of the last month's rent or to cover cleaning costs and damages to rental property. These types of deposits are usually exempted from the bankruptcy estate.

Extra Funding

The exemption for vehicles is designed to provide the debtor with transportation for work, medical care, and other necessities. It is not for luxury vehicles or fancy sports cars driven for fun and recreation.

Illinois includes wearing apparel, bible, schoolbooks, and family pictures of the debtor as part of the exemption amount. In Kentucky, the $3,000 exemption includes wearing apparel and ornaments (jewelry) along with the household furnishings. The Montana exemption encompasses wearing apparel, jewelry, books, firearms, sporting goods, and musical instruments. However, it specifies that no one item can be valued at more than $600.

New York statutes do not specify an aggregate amount. Instead, the law itemizes the types of items that are exempted. The exemptions include all wearing apparel, household furniture, one refrigerator, all stoves and necessary fuel for 60 days, one radio, one television set, crockery, tableware, and cooking utensils necessary for the debtor and family.

Some of the other states are more specific in identifying the type of property and the exemption amount.

For wearing apparel:

Arizona	$500
Colorado	$750
Minnesota	No limit

For jewelry:

Arizona	Engagement and wedding rings, $1,000; one watch, $100
Colorado	$500
Minnesota	One watch, no limit
New York	A wedding ring, no limit; one watch, $35

In some states, exemptions for miscellaneous items, such as books, pets, sewing machines, and bicycles, are sometimes listed with specific dollar amounts; in other states, these items of personal property are lumped into other categories.

In most states, motor vehicles are classified separately, but again, the exemptions allowed are varied, and each state has certain specifications that it lists.

The states you are reviewing allow the following dollar amounts as exemptions for vehicles:

Arizona	One motor vehicle per individual debtor, $1,500; one motor vehicle for a disabled debtor, $4,000
Colorado	One motor vehicle per individual debtor, $1,000; one motor vehicle used for a disabled or elderly debtor or debtor's dependent, $3,000
Illinois	One motor vehicle, $1,200
Kentucky	One motor vehicle, $2,500
Montana	One motor vehicle, $1,200

New York and Minnesota do not specifically list motor vehicles in their exemption laws. However, both states allow exemptions for machinery used in a trade or profession, and perhaps that category would include necessary transportation.

This brings you to the last category that should be studied, tools used in a trade or profession. The sample states allow exemptions for tools of the trade as follows:

Arizona	$2,500
Colorado	$2,000
Illinois	$750
Kentucky	$3,000
Minnesota	Farming or livestock, $13,000; other trades or professions, $5,000
Montana	$3,000
New York	$600

As you review these exemptions for the sample states, you can see that the amounts allowed vary greatly. This, coupled with the fact that a lot of specific items of personal property are not even addressed, tells you that some of these state laws are old and should be updated.

This only serves to reinforce the need for an experienced attorney to handle your bankruptcy case. Bankruptcy attorneys are familiar with the laws of their state and the interpretations of those laws in the federal bankruptcy courts.

When a Chapter 7 petition is filed, the court will compare the debtor's property with the elected exemptions and decide what property will become a part of the bankruptcy estate.

Nonexempt Property

Under a Chapter 7 bankruptcy filing, any property that is not exempted by federal or state laws may be absorbed into the bankruptcy estate.

Now that you have reviewed the exemptions in a number of different states, you should have a fair idea of what items you would lose in a Chapter 7 bankruptcy case. Some debtors have little or nothing to lose, but if you own a mink coat, jewelry filled with precious stones, a painting by Van Gogh, or a recreational vehicle, you must consider the consequences of losing them.

The laws are meant to protect the everyday things you need to start over again. Luxury items are not exempted, but as demonstrated in the case of Jack and Jill, there are ways to convert nonexempt assets into exempt assets.

Keep in mind that a person with many valuable assets would not put them in jeopardy with a Chapter 7 filing. A Chapter 11 or Chapter 13 filing would probably be more beneficial.

Exemptions do not have any bearing in Chapter 11 or 13 cases because no bankruptcy estate is formed. While a debtor who files a Chapter 7 bankruptcy may lose some nonexempt property, the loss will be offset by the fact that debts will be totally discharged.

Bank Notes

In states where agriculture and livestock are primary industries, special provisions have been built into the exemptions to protect these activities.

Extra Funding

Debtors with a number of valuable assets would be expected to sell them and use the funds to settle their debts.

In recent years, there has been much debate over the bankruptcy exemptions that exist in many states. As you have just seen, certain states have generous exemptions; others do not. The exemption for a debtor's house is the primary area in which the amount of equity that can be exempted from the bankruptcy estate varies widely from state to state.

Many believe that this variance allows debtors to abuse the bankruptcy laws. A debtor with an abundance of cash can protect that cash from falling into the hands of creditors by taking up residence in a state that has no limit on a homestead exemption. Currently, the period in which one must reside in a state before filing a bankruptcy petition is fairly short, less than six months in some states.

This enables this cash-rich debtor with unsecured liabilities to relocate to one of these states, sink all of his or her cash into a house, and then file bankruptcy in that state. The exemptions upheld by the federal bankruptcy court would preserve the cash invested in the debtor's newly acquired homestead. In other words, the creditors would walk away with little or nothing, while the debtor retained his house and all the cash invested in it.

Of course, any secured liabilities would have to be satisfied by turning over the collateral to the creditor, redeeming the property, or reaffirming on the secured loan.

With this in mind, lawmakers have drafted an amendment that has been attached to the pending legislation for bankruptcy reform. This amendment attempts to set a cap on homestead exemptions that would apply to all states. Although the cap being proposed is higher than the current homestead exemption allowed in the majority of states, this provision would directly impact the handful of states that do not have a limit on the amount a debtor can exempt for his or her personal residence.

Obviously, the average debtors who have been struggling to make payments or keep their payments current are not about to pack up and move to Texas or Florida and buy a new house. The average debtors may have all they can handle with trying to keep the kids in shoes or just putting food on the table. Any abuse of the homestead exemption generally comes from people in a much higher income bracket.

If a debtor has the cash needed to buy an expensive house, then that same person has the cash needed to move to another state. The average debtor doesn't have the money to do that. The average debtor is fortunate to be able to pay rent on an apartment or make the payments needed to avoid foreclosure on the house.

Extra Funding

Consider the bankruptcy case of health care and real estate tycoon Abe Gosman, who was able to retain his 64,000-square-foot mansion in West Palm Beach, Florida.

The most interesting and amusing thing about this is that banks and credit card companies have been lobbying for bankruptcy reform for several years. The stockholders of these companies are generally in the same income bracket as the debtors who take advantage of the liberal homestead exemptions in certain states.

If the bill is passed with the homestead exemption amendment attached to it, the supporters of the reform act may find that a loophole in the federal bankruptcy laws has been closed that has previously benefited them or their wealthy friends.

Currently, state exemptions take precedence over the federal exemptions of the bankruptcy code. This brings up another question that concerns this proposed amendment to the bankruptcy bill. If it passes and becomes federal law, will it be challenged by the states that currently have no limit on a homestead exemption? These states are Iowa, Florida, Kansas, South Dakota, and Texas.

Keep in mind that you will find more information on the bankruptcy reform act and the provisions of the bill in the last chapter of this book.

The Least You Need to Know

➤ Creditors can file a motion for relief from the automatic stay.

➤ The court may verify insurance coverage and the payment of property taxes to protect the claim of a secured creditor.

➤ Exemptions vary from state to state.

➤ Luxury items are nonexempt and generally will be taken into the bankruptcy estate in a Chapter 7 filing.

Chapter 15

Filing a Chapter 11 Bankruptcy Petition

In This Chapter

➤ Debtor in possession

➤ Creditors' committee

➤ Disclosure statement

➤ Plan of reorganization

➤ Approval and confirmation

Like Chapter 7 filings, bankruptcy petitions filed under Chapter 11 are assigned case numbers. Creditors are notified, and the automatic stay goes into effect, preventing them from any further collection actions against the debtor or his property. However, the process from that point on is very different.

No bankruptcy estate is formed, and therefore no consideration needs to be given to exemption limits or nonexempt assets. It is this very provision that prompts a business to use this chapter to seek relief from creditors.

Chapter 11 is based on a plan of reorganization that allows the business owner to keep control of the business assets and continue to operate the business enterprise. Sometimes a business, especially a startup operation that has invested a lot of capital and gone into debt purchasing equipment and merchandise, needs more time to get established. It's difficult enough to build a profitable enterprise without the added pressure of creditors' threats and collection actions.

Debtor Stays in Charge

When a Chapter 11 bankruptcy petition is filed, the court does not usually appoint a Trustee. Instead, the petitioner is generally referred to as a "Debtor in Possession." This designation means that the debtor has the rights and powers of a Trustee and is expected to perform the same duties.

Bank Notes

Sometimes the expansion of an existing business can result in financial problems that lead to a Chapter 11 filing.

Extra Funding

Provisions of Chapter 11 may enable a business to get out from under an agreement or lease that has become a drain on profits.

The debtor in possession's responsibilities include the following:

➤ Accounting for property

➤ Examining creditors' claims

➤ Objecting to creditors' claims

➤ Filing monthly operating reports

In addition to competent legal advice, the debtor in a Chapter 11 case may need to consult accountants, appraisers, and other professionals to assist in these matters. The bankruptcy court must approve the employment of any outside party that is going to assist with the administration of the case.

The Chapter 11 bankruptcy filing allows individual business owners, partnerships, and corporations to reorganize their business structure. The debtor is given 120 days from the date the bankruptcy petition is filed to present a plan of reorganization to the court. In developing this plan, the debtor has the opportunity to eliminate contracts, dispose of property, and modify credit agreements and payment terms on leases and other liabilities.

All of this is done while the business continues to operate, so you can understand why many debtors need to hire professionals to help them with the many decisions and details that must be addressed. For a plan of reorganization to be successful, the business must generate the cash needed to fund it and at the same time pay ongoing expenses and wages.

Creditors Are Involved

Shortly after the Chapter 11 petition is filed, the court appoints a committee of creditors. The function of this committee is to represent the interests of unsecured creditors.

These committees are made up according to the classification of debts. For example, the seven creditors who hold the largest claims on goods used in manufacturing the products the debtor sells may be on one committee. At its discretion, the court may appoint other committees for other classifications.

These committees often fail to meet and organize. If the members of the committee do decide to take an active part in the case, they are entitled to consult with the debtor in possession and examine the assets, liabilities, and business operations. They may also take part in the development of the reorganization plan.

Although the creditors are prevented from collection actions by the automatic stay, there are other remedies they can legally use against the debtor.

When a company that supplies merchandise or goods is notified of a Chapter 11 filing or determines by other means that the buyer of the goods or merchandise is insolvent, the company may stop a delivery in progress. Goods in transit may be retrieved before they reach the debtor's place of business.

The bankruptcy code also allows reclamation, wherein the seller of goods may reclaim goods delivered to the debtor immediately before the bankruptcy filing. This requires that the seller present a written notice to the debtor within 10 days of the delivery of goods.

Creditors can also ask for a motion to obtain relief from a stay as outlined in the preceding chapter. Any creditor or committee can request a hearing to ask the court to appoint an examiner or trustee to the bankruptcy case. The creditor would have to present valid evidence to the court for such an appointment, such as fraud, dishonesty, incompetence, or gross mismanagement.

Aside from all of these things, the main purpose of the creditors' committee is to review the plan of reorganization and file acceptances or rejections of it with the court. The committee is entitled to involve their own attorneys, accountants, or appraisers to provide professional advice on their interests. An attorney or accountant employed to represent a creditors' committee may not represent other parties with a vested interest in the bankruptcy case.

Working with the Creditors

It is in the debtor's best interest to communicate with the creditors, individually or as a committee. Attempting to settle liabilities in an organized, legal manner through a Chapter 11 filing is a responsible way to solve the financial problems of the debtor's business.

It is the process of communication and negotiation that enables a debtor to restructure a business and create a plan for the future that will allow the creditors to be paid and the business to continue operating. Unsecured creditors usually receive a greater portion of a debt included in a Chapter 11 reorganization plan than they would under a Chapter 7 filing. Therefore, they should be more receptive and willing to work with the debtor who has filed a Chapter 11.

After the filing of the bankruptcy petition, the debtor cannot seek acceptance or rejection from creditors until certain procedures are followed. Lien holders must receive a written disclosure statement along with the plan or a summary of the plan. The disclosure statement must be presented to the court first and be approved at a hearing. The court will judge whether the disclosure statement contains *adequate information*.

Bank Notes

If you are a debtor preparing to file a Chapter 11 petition, you might want to wait the time necessary to avoid the loss of goods or merchandise needed to continue your business operation.

Dollar Signs

Adequate information is defined as being sufficient in detail to give a hypothetical investor the information necessary to make an informed judgment about the plan and the debtor's company.

The disclosure statement should contain the following information:

➤ The nature and history of the company

➤ The reasons or circumstances behind the bankruptcy filing

➤ The condition of the company's books and records

➤ A description and evaluation of assets

➤ Future prospects for the company

➤ The current financial condition of the debtor

➤ The estimated amount creditors would receive under a Chapter 7 filing

The estimated amount creditors would receive under a Chapter 7 filing is important because this information relates to the amount the creditor will realize under the Chapter 11 reorganization plan. The bankruptcy code stipulates that, under a Chapter 11 plan, the creditor cannot be paid less than the amount that same creditor could expect to receive on the claim if the debtor's property were sold and the proceeds distributed to creditors in a Chapter 7 filing.

Dollar Signs

Accounts receivable are the customer accounts of the company that record sales of merchandise or services that have been delivered to the customer but not yet paid for by the customer.

NSF Checks

Regardless of the size of the business entity, the same careful planning, competent legal advice, and accurate disclosures are vital to the success of the bankruptcy filing and the reorganization plan.

In addition, the disclosure statement should include the sources of information used to prepare it, the accounting methods used by the company, an overview of the company's *accounts receivable*, and details of any litigation that may affect the plan of reorganization.

Although this sounds like a great deal of information to gather, remember that the amount of data depends on the size of the business. A large corporation might have a very lengthy disclosure statement, while a small business enterprise might have only a few pages of information.

The very size and structure of a small business entity puts it into a special category because it generally does not have a large amount of capital or assets. The dollar amount of liabilities is also usually less than the amount carried by a corporation or partnership.

Specific provisions have been built into the bankruptcy code to benefit a small business operation.

A debtor may qualify as a Small Business Debtor if the following criteria are met:

➤ The total amount of debts, secured and unsecured, does not exceed $2 million when the case is filed, and

➤ The debtor is not engaged in owning or managing real property and the activities that result from this type of business.

Generally, the court does not appoint a creditors' committee in the case of a Small Business Debtor, some time periods are shortened, and the procedures for disclosure statements and acceptance of the plan of reorganization are simpler.

As you can see, the filing of a Chapter 11 petition with schedules of assets, liabilities, expenses, and income is only the first step in the process. The disclosure statement and the plan or reorganization must be completed within the next 120 days and be presented to the court and the creditors.

If a debtor fails to comply with the schedule, the creditors can submit their own plan to the court for approval. However, if a debtor's plan cannot be developed and approved by the court and creditors, it is more likely that the debtor's case will be converted to a Chapter 7 liquidation.

The Plan

A debtor's plan of reorganization is meant to take all the liabilities that are threatening to bury the business and modify or reduce them to a manageable state. For a plan to be approved by the creditors and confirmed by the court, it must be proposed in good faith and treat the claims of creditors fairly and equitably. It must also comply with the rules applicable under the federal bankruptcy code.

The bankruptcy code provides for priority claims. Some of these priority claims apply to individual debtors, but as you review the list, you will see that most of them are more applicable to a business entity. Priority claims are unsecured claims in a bankruptcy case. They are paid in the order in which they are listed in the code, and those with a higher listing are paid in full before claims that have a lower ranking receive any cash proceeds.

Priority claims are as follows:

1. Administrative expenses of the bankruptcy
2. Unsecured, postpetition claims (debts incurred after the bankruptcy filing date)
3. Wage claims of employees and independent salespersons up to $4,300 per claim
4. Contributions to employee benefit plans up to $4,300 per employee
5. Claims of farmers and fishermen against debtors operating storage or processing facilities
6. Layaway claims of individuals who didn't get the item for which they placed a deposit
7. Claims for debts to a spouse or children for court-ordered support
8. Recent income, sales, employment, or gross receipts taxes
9. Commitments to maintain the capital of a bank or savings and loan association

Bank Notes

Some businesses have specific needs for certain equipment used to generate income. The loss of this equipment would therefore affect future profits, and the plan of reorganization should explain how the business intends to survive the loss or replace the income with other profitable activities.

If any of these types of claims are owed by the debtor, they must be included in the debtor's plan, and funds are properly designated to them according to their placement on the preceding list.

The federal code also requires that the plan separate or classify the claims. A creditor's claim may be included in a particular class only if it is very much like the other claims or interests in that class. For example, unsecured credit card accounts would be one classification. A class of claims that is altered by the plan of reorganization is considered to be *impaired*.

Dollar Signs

In bankruptcy, **impairment of a claim** or a class of claims means that the debt will not be paid in full.

The plan submitted to the creditors and the court must detail each class of claims and specify whether it is impaired. It is also required that the plan describe how each claim will be dealt with over the course of time the plan is administered.

If a debtor wants to reduce a loan to the fair market value of the collateral and lower the payments on that loan, an explanation of the terms of the adjustment should be included in the plan. Property that is to be returned to a creditor in settlement of a claim must be described along with the specifics of the return and its effect on the debtor's economic future.

Dollar Signs

Stockholders are individuals or other companies that have an interest in a corporation. Stockholders generally vote on any important issues a corporation is considering and would most likely have to approve a Chapter 11 filing and plan.

The Chapter 11 plan should also outline how the plan will be administered. A corporate debtor with *stockholders* has even more provisions that must be included in the plan to ensure that the interests of creditors are protected while the plan is in effect.

Other provisions that may or may not be included in a plan of reorganization are as follows:

➤ Settlements on pending contracts or leases

➤ Information on the collection of claims held by the debtor

➤ Provisions for the liquidation of assets with an outline of how proceeds will be distributed

➤ Information on modifying the rights of creditors

Overall, many of the provisions and details contained in a Chapter 11 will depend on the size and complexity of the business entity filing the bankruptcy petition. Based on the amounts and the number of creditors included in the Chapter 11 petition, the court will have set guidelines for the approval of the plan by the creditors.

Getting the Plan Approved

Before the Chapter 11 plan takes effect, the debtor must send the court-approved disclosure statement and the plan of reorganization to the creditors. This is where the issue of impairment takes on more importance. It is assumed that any class of claims or creditor that is not impaired or altered by the plan accepts it. At the same time, any class of creditors that is impaired to the extent that they receive no payment under the plan is assumed to reject it.

Other creditors with allowed claims or interests under the plan may accept or reject it. The decision must be delivered in writing, signed by the creditor or the creditor's agent.

The bankruptcy code provides that a class of claims accepts the plan if the creditors who hold two thirds of the total dollar amount included in that class and make up more than one half of the number of creditors in that class approve the plan.

The following example demonstrates how this works:

A class of claim contains 12 creditors and a dollar amount of $150,000.

Approval requires 7 creditors who have a combined dollar value of claims of $100,000.

If the plan of reorganization has been approved by creditors in accordance with the guidelines set by the court, it will be confirmed at a hearing.

In the event that some classes of creditors with impaired claims have not approved the plan, the court may still confirm it under the "cramdown" rules.

In simple terms, the "cramdown" provisions are as follows:

1. The plan must be fair and equal to each impaired class and must not be discriminatory to any claim that has not accepted the plan.

2. Secured creditors retain liens on property, or the proceeds of the property, and receive payments that total the value of the collateral as of the effective date of the plan.

3. Secured creditors must receive the equivalent of the value of their claims.

NSF Checks

The "cramdown" rules are not presented here in their entirety or in proper legal terms and must be reviewed and discussed with an attorney in connection with your own Chapter 11 bankruptcy case to avoid problems.

One of the other primary factors that the court will look at before confirming a Chapter 11 plan is whether the plan has a reasonable chance of success. This determination will depend on the current financial condition of the debtor company and its projected future. The confirmation of a plan by the court makes it binding on the debtor and all parties included in the plan. It also gives the debtor control of all the property of the plan, free and clear of claims and interests.

Hopefully, a Chapter 11 debtor who has developed a plan confirmed by the court will be able to honor all the terms over the time period specified. This will give the business a fresh start that will enable it to prosper.

Accommodating Business Matters

If you operate a business, you know that some businesses run a higher risk for failure than others. In the same respect, some businesses are better equipped than others to survive and prosper under a Chapter 11 reorganization plan. A retail company with a substantial amount of inventory, for example, may be able to weather a financial storm because new purchases of merchandise are not immediately needed. On the other hand, a business that must constantly order products or supplies may have more difficulty staying afloat.

Bank Notes

Any business that needs to purchase products or supplies on an ongoing basis should make sure the plan of reorganization does not alienate vendors whose products are vital to the continued operation of the business.

Restaurants must purchase food items on a daily basis to keep the business operating properly. In addition, many of the necessary purchases have a very short shelf life. Produce and some dairy products must be used within a specified amount of time to preserve their quality and appeal.

Once a Chapter 11 plan is implemented, a food business may find that vendors who are forced to accept payments under the plan will no longer extend credit to the business owner. This places an additional burden on the owner. The cash flow will be reduced by the need to pay for purchases upfront.

It is always possible to establish relationships with new vendors, but that may depend on the size of the city where the business is located. Even in a very large city, news of a business owner's financial problems can spread within a particular industry and strain the relationships between buyers and sellers.

All of this underscores the necessity for competent legal and financial assistance before, during, and after the development of a plan of reorganization in a Chapter 11 bankruptcy filing.

The Least You Need to Know

➤ A Chapter 11 bankruptcy filing gives the debtor 120 days to prepare a plan of reorganization.

➤ Creditors may stop delivery of goods in transit when notified of the bankruptcy filing.

➤ The bankruptcy code has specific rules and requirements that apply to the plan of reorganization and its structure.

➤ Creditors must receive a copy of the reorganization plan and a disclosure statement from the debtor.

➤ Creditors must approve the plan of reorganization before it is confirmed by the court.

Chapter 16

Filing a Chapter 13 Bankruptcy Petition

In This Chapter

➤ Creditors and proofs of claims

➤ Co-debtors and the automatic stay

➤ Repayment plan

➤ Approval and confirmation

➤ Discharge

If you are a regular wage earner whose income exceeds your monthly living expenses you can seek relief from creditors under a Chapter 13 bankruptcy filing. One of the advantages of Chapter 13 is that you will remain in control of your property. No consideration has to be given as to whether assets are exempt or nonexempt.

This is not to say that assets will not be lost in the bankruptcy filing. Some items of collateral may have to be turned over to secured creditors to satisfy claims. Other items could be sold or liquidated to stabilize finances and keep the repayment plan on track.

A Trustee is appointed in a Chapter 13 filing. The Trustee will review the documents, deal with creditors, and oversee the repayment plan approved by the court.

Creditors Speak Up

In Chapter 13, the debtor does not deal directly with creditors. Instead, creditors are notified by the court that a Chapter 13 has been filed and that the automatic stay is in effect. All collection actions must cease, including foreclosures and wage garnishments.

An unsecured creditor with an interest in the bankruptcy filing is required to file a proof of claim with the court. Failure to file the proof of claim properly and in the time period set by the court may result in the creditor losing the right to be paid under the debtor's plan.

Once your attorney has filed the Chapter 13 bankruptcy petition, he or she will keep you informed of all the deadlines set for the creditors by the court.

In some jurisdictions, the court may supply the proof of claim form, which requires the following information from the creditor:

1. The name of the debtor
2. The number assigned to the bankruptcy case by the court (your case number)
3. The name and address of the creditor
4. The amount and nature of the claim

The creditor may also have to provide a copy of any legal judgment, contract, or agreement pertaining to the claim.

A secured creditor, especially a bank, mortgage company, or finance company, may also file a proof of claim with the supporting documentation for the lien. However, the secured creditor's interest in the property or collateral used for the loan is usually not affected by a failure to file the proof of claim.

Extra Funding

The majority of unsecured creditors, such as credit card companies, have legal departments that handle proof of claim filings.

Remember Your Co-Signers

Some debtors have a friend or relative who has helped them get loans or other types of credit accounts. This person often becomes liable for the claim if the debtor defaults on it. This co-debtor may be a co-signer on the loan or a personal guarantor for the debt.

A co-signer is someone who agrees to share your responsibility on a debt. Financial institutions often require co-signers when the person applying for the loan does not meet their income or credit requirements. A person who is applying for credit for the first time has no credit history and will most likely need a co-signer in order to obtain the financing.

A son, for example, may need a parent to co-sign on his first auto loan. If the son defaults on the loan, the finance company will look to the parent to repay the debt. A guarantor also shares in the responsibility of a debt by offering the lender a personal guarantee that the liability will be paid in full.

If the debt is a consumer loan (a loan taken out for personal or household purposes), the automatic stay covers the co-debtor even though the co-debtor is not a party to the bankruptcy filing.

Initially, the guarantor or co-signer is protected on other types of debts by the automatic stay, but as you learned in a previous chapter, the creditor can file a motion to have the stay lifted. In a Chapter 13 filing, the creditor is generally allowed to pursue the other party or the co-signer for payment of the debt if any of the following circumstances apply:

➤ If the co-debtor received proceeds from the loan

➤ If the creditor's interest would be destroyed or damaged without relief from the automatic stay

➤ If the debtor has chosen not to pay the debt under the Chapter 13 plan

In the last instance, the automatic stay may terminate within days of the creditor's request for relief. These rules may apply to both secured and unsecured debts. If you have people in your life who were kind enough to help you obtain credit, you need to be aware of how your bankruptcy filing might affect them. You will need your attorney's advice and expertise to handle this situation appropriately.

Bank Notes

Many financial institutions require that an owner personally guarantee loans taken out for a business. This is because a new business does not have an established credit history that can be verified.

Presenting a Plan to the Court

If a repayment plan is not filed with the bankruptcy petition, the debtor has 15 days to present it to the court. The time for preparing and filing this plan is short because the debtor will not be negotiating with creditors or seeking their approval of the plan, like the Chapter 11 filer does. Also, in a Chapter 13 bankruptcy filing, only the debtor can present a plan to the court.

If you are filing a Chapter 13 petition, it is prudent to develop the repayment plan during the prebankruptcy period when you and your attorney are discussing all the aspects of your case and the options open to you. Creditors receive a copy of the plan but do not have the option of approving it. The approval and confirmation are up to the court.

Dollar Signs

Good faith indicates the debtor's assurance that he or she can live up to the terms and payments proposed in the plan.

Dollar Signs

Disposable income is the amount remaining after the payment of normal, reasonable living expenses.

When the court reviews the repayment plan, it will determine whether certain requirements have been met. The requirements are as follows:

1. The plan must be proposed in *good faith*.

2. The plan must allow the unsecured creditors an amount equal to what they would have received under a Chapter 7 bankruptcy filing. This is called the "best interest of creditors test."

3. The plan must outline the payment of all *disposable income* into the plan for at least three years. This provision is known as the "best efforts test."

In addition to the "best interest" and "best efforts" tests, the debtor's plan must provide for full payment of priority claims, such as spousal maintenance or child support payments. With respect to secured claims, the lien holder must receive a minimum amount equal to the value of the collateral. Although the objections of creditors are limited in a Chapter 13 case to the "interest" tests previously outlined, a secured creditor can take issue with the value placed on the collateral that is the basis for the claim. Objections of this type generally require negotiations between the debtor's attorney and the creditor. If the parties cannot reach an agreement or a compromise, the court will rule on the issue.

Repayment plans have primary clauses and sections that are used to implement them. Some are presented in the sample plan that follows:

UNITED STATES BANKRUPTCY COURT
Eastern District of Ohio

John and Susan Brown, Case No. 00-12345

Chapter 13 Plan

1. The future earnings of the debtors are submitted to the Trustee, and the debtor shall pay to the Trustee the sum of $650 for 36 months or until all claims are paid.

2. From the payments received, the Trustee shall make disbursements as follows:

    (a) To the expenses of administration: $25

    (b) To the secured creditors whose claims are as follows:

        (1) ABC Finance Co. $300

        Collateral: 1999 Nissan valued at $10,800

        (2) Arizona Land Co. $55

        Loan #12367

        Collateral: One acre of land in Big Bear, AZ valued at $2,000 (see legal description attached)

    (c) To priority creditors in the order prescribed by 11 USC 507:

        (1) None listed

(d) To unsecured creditors whose claims are allowed. Unsecured creditors shall be paid approximately 40 cents on the dollar.

   (1) Visa $28

   (2) MasterCard $56

   (3) Sears $31

   (4) J.C. Penney $31

   (5) Discover Card $31

   (6) City Bank $31

   (7) Telco Finance $31

   (8) Mechanics Credit Union $31

   (See mailing addresses and documentation attached)

3. The following contracts of the debtor are rejected, and the debtor shall return possession of the collateral. No claim for damages resulting from rejection is allowed.

   (a) Click Leasing Company 1999 Mercury Cougar

4. The debtors shall pay directly the monthly amounts to the following fully secured creditor:

   (a) Big Bear Mortgage Co. $552

5. The date this case was filed shall be the effective date of this plan as well as the date when interest ceases to accrue on unsecured claims.

6. The court may, after a hearing designated by the court, may increase or reduce the amount or the time for payments where it appears that circumstances so warrant.

7. Option provisions pursuant to 11 USC 1322: None

Dated: 12-10-01

_____   _____

John Brown   Susan Brown

_____

This sample Chapter 13 plan is fairly simple and easy to understand. Depending on the financial situation of the debtor filing the bankruptcy, the plan can be longer, shorter, or more involved. Using this plan, you will now examine how it was developed for this fictional couple's fictional bankruptcy case.

In the preceding chapter, you reviewed the list of priority claims as set forth in the federal bankruptcy code. Only one of them applies to this fictional case, the administrative expenses of the bankruptcy. This is the first item identified in the disbursement portion of the plan.

The Browns were able to reduce their liability on the auto loan to the value of the 1999 Nissan. The original balance was several thousand dollars higher with a high interest rate. The land was valued at approximately the same value as the balance of the liability, so that loan was not altered. There were no other priority claim debts, so that brings us to the unsecured creditors. The plan designates that each of the unsecured creditors will receive approximately 40 cents on the dollar for their claims.

Using your math skills, you can see that Visa will receive 36 payments of $28 each, or a total of $1,008. If the balance Visa is receiving is 40 cents on the dollar (or 40 percent of the original balance due), the Browns have reduced this liability by approximately $2,500. The same holds true for the other unsecured creditors. Each of them is reducing the liability and accepting less than half of what was owed to them.

Actually, the Brown's Chapter 13 payment plan is a good one for the unsecured creditors because some plans might allow unsecured creditors as little as 10 cents on the dollar amount of the claim. The sample plan also calls for the return of a leased vehicle that was costing the Browns $400 per month. No claim for damages to the leasing company for the early termination of the lease is provided in the plan.

Bank Notes

Administration costs generally depend on the size and complexity of the bankruptcy case.

Extra Funding

A Chapter 13 case that is converted to a Chapter 7 bankruptcy is often referred to as a Chapter 20.

The plan the Browns have submitted to the court for approval has relieved them of several thousands dollars of debts. The Browns and their lawyer developed the plan based on their disposable income, and they feel they will be able to handle the terms and payments outlined in the plan.

The Seal of Approval

Once the court and the Trustee have reviewed all the information from the debtors and creditors and have determined that the plan meets the "best interests" and "best efforts" tests, the plan is approved. When a Chapter 13 plan is approved and confirmed by the court, it is binding for the debtors and the creditors. The debtor remits the amount specified in the plan to the Trustee each month, and the Trustee makes the payments as outlined in the plan.

If the Browns' circumstances were to change, the plan provides for modifications with court approval. For example, the term of the plan could be extended, or the amount paid into the plan each month by the debtors could be reduced. The Browns also have the right to convert their Chapter 13 case to a Chapter 7 case.

In some instances, if a debtor fails to perform according to the Chapter 13 plan, the Trustee can set the plan aside and convert the bankruptcy case to a Chapter 7. The nonexempt property of the debtor would then go into the bankruptcy estate and be sold. The creditors would then receive only a portion of the amount generated by the sale of the nonexempt property.

Final Page of Chapter 13

The last thing to occur in a Chapter 13 is the discharge of debts. The difference between the original balances on the debts and the amount paid under the plan will be discharged once the plan has been completed. Certain circumstances may allow the debts to be discharged even if the debtor did not complete the payments under the plan. This is sometimes called a hardship discharge, and it may be granted when situations arise that the debtor has no control over, such as illness or job loss.

Some debts remain with the debtor unless they have been paid in full through the payment plan. Liabilities for student loans, child support, and some taxes are not dischargeable under any of the bankruptcy chapters. It is possible to make payments on some of these debts and pay them off over the three-year period during which the plan is in effect. A tax liability or a student loan, for example, could be paid off during the term of the plan. Child support payments probably could not be eliminated by the plan because they usually continue until the child reaches adulthood.

The legislation pending in Congress may increase the number of Chapter 13 filings across the country. Many attorneys and politicians think it will. However, bankruptcy filings are not strictly determined by the choice of the citizens who use this means to start over.

Bankruptcy filings are linked to other factors such as the unemployment rate, interest rates, and the availability of medical insurance benefits. Many people seek relief in the bankruptcy courts for circumstances beyond their control. That's why the hardship discharge exists in Chapter 13 and will most likely continue to be used.

The Least You Need to Know

➤ Chapter 13 repayment plans must be presented to the court within 15 days of the bankruptcy filing.

➤ A Trustee is appointed to administer the plan.

➤ A plan can be modified if the circumstances of the debtor change during the term of the plan.

➤ A Chapter 13 filing can be converted to a Chapter 7 by the debtor or, in some cases, the Trustee.

➤ Debts under Chapter 13 are not discharged until the repayment plan has been fulfilled.

Chapter 17

The Actual Court Appearance

In This Chapter

➤ The meeting of creditors

➤ Chapter 7 meetings

➤ Chapter 11 meetings

➤ Chapter 13 meetings

Within 10 days after filing a bankruptcy petition, you will receive a notice from the United States Bankruptcy Court telling you when and where you must appear. This procedure is referred to as a Section 341 Meeting of Creditors because it comes under Section 341 of the federal bankruptcy code. It is also called the "first meeting of creditors."

In many states, this meeting is not convened in a courtroom and is not presided over by a judge. Instead, the meeting is generally held in a conference room or office and is presided over by an interim Trustee assigned to the bankruptcy case. In Chapter 7 and Chapter 13 cases, the interim Trustee usually becomes the permanent Trustee for that particular case.

This formal meeting is held between 20 and 50 days from the date that the bankruptcy petition is filed. All of the creditors named in the bankruptcy petition will receive a similar notice. While the meeting is mandatory for the debtor, the creditors are not required to attend. The creditors who do show up at the meeting are usually the ones who have large or secured claims.

If the bankruptcy petition is a joint filing, all debtors seeking relief under the bankruptcy petition must attend the meeting of creditors with their respective attorneys. This means both husband and wife or all business partners must attend the meeting of creditors.

Generally, the date of this meeting is written in stone. In other words, it cannot be rescheduled unless there is proof of a genuine emergency. In rare cases, a debtor's presence at the meeting could be waived by a judge if evidence of good cause for the absence was presented to the court. Otherwise, failure of debtors to appear at the meeting of creditors may prompt the presiding Trustee to recommend to the court that the bankruptcy case be dismissed.

Bank Notes

Since the interim Trustee who presides over the meeting of creditors has expended the time and effort to study the petition and schedules, it is more efficient for the court to keep that person on the case.

NSF Checks

If you do not have the required ID, discuss alternatives with your attorney. For example, someone who does not have a driver's license would have to provide some other form of identification.

Bank Notes

The Trustee will also confirm that the debtors have read and signed the information sheet provided by their attorneys or the United States Trustees' office. The content of this federal form was presented in a previous chapter.

The Trustee may oversee and administer a case, but any motions, complaints, or other legal complications are turned over to the federal bankruptcy court, where a judge will rule on the issues. Upon arrival at the meeting, debtors are required to provide identification and verification of their social security numbers. A driver's license or other photo ID, along with a copy of your social security card or W-2 form, will be requested by the Trustee at the start of the meeting.

Once the Trustee has verified that the debtors are indeed the same ones who filed the bankruptcy petition, the meeting can begin.

Chapter 7 Meets With or Without Creditors

As the meeting begins, the Trustee will administer an oath to the debtors in which they swear to tell the truth, the whole truth, and nothing but the truth. It's very similar to, if not exactly the same as, the oath you've heard in courtrooms and on all the legal shows on television. The administration of the oath and everything else that takes place at the meeting is recorded on audiotape or taken down by a court reporter for the official record.

In many Chapter 7 cases, no creditors are present. If there is a creditor or a representative of a creditor at the meeting, the person may want to question the debtor. Your lawyer will be at your side to help you answer any queries a creditor may present. Sometimes the creditor is there to try to convince the debtor to reaffirm on the claim.

It is possible that a finance company with a lien on a vehicle will show up at the meeting and offer to cut a deal with the debtor. For example, if you are three months behind in the payments, the finance company could offer to forget about the arrearages and forgive all the late fees if you will reaffirm on the debt and start making payments again.

Creditors, especially finance companies that do not ordinarily buy and sell vehicles or other properties, don't want the hassle of trying to recover their loss by repossessing and selling the property. Because the property is being returned through a bankruptcy, they may only receive partial reimbursement for their claim and will not be able to get a deficiency judgment for the difference.

The creditor would much rather talk you into keeping the property and resuming your payments on the loan. However, you and your attorney should already have decided what property you are redeeming and what loans you are reaffirming. You should not be swayed by a creditor's last-ditch efforts to seduce you back into the claim.

Regardless of whether creditors are in attendance, one of the duties of the Trustee is to make sure that the debtor understands everything that is covered at the meeting and the bankruptcy process itself.

The Trustee will want to know if the debtor is aware of the following points connected with a bankruptcy filing:

➤ The consequences of a bankruptcy filing and the effect it may have on the debtor's credit history

➤ The choice to convert the filing to another bankruptcy chapter

➤ The effects of receiving a discharge of debts under the chapter filed

➤ The consequences of reaffirming a debt

In addition, the Trustee or the debtor's attorney will question the debtor regarding the bankruptcy petition and its related schedules. Some standard questions you might be asked are as follows:

1. Did you examine the schedules that are a part of your petition before signing them?

2. Did you include all of your assets?

3. Did you include all of your debts?

4. Do you wish to make any corrections or additions to the schedules that are part of your petition?

The Trustee may also question the debtor about various aspects of the schedules, such as how the value of certain assets was determined. Again, your attorney will be there to help you answer the questions and to provide any supplementary information the Trustee requests. Although this may sound like a long, drawn-out session, in reality, it will probably last less than 30 minutes. The purpose of this initial meeting is to verify and, if necessary, clarify information.

Extra Funding

Chapter 7 filers who do not have any saleable assets will generally not meet with the Trustee again after the meeting of creditors.

Chapter 11 Filers May Not Get Off So Easy

The complexity of a Chapter 11 reorganization may result in a longer, more involved meeting of creditors. First of all, the individuals serving on the committee of creditors are more likely to be there to question the debtor. The meeting is still presided over by a United States Trustee, who will ask the debtor some of the same questions outlined previously for a Chapter 7 filer.

Creditors who attend the meeting will have their own agendas and their own questions to ask. Since these creditors have a vested interest in the debtor's business, they may want to know about the business operation and its current and future operations. Generally, the creditors are looking for reassurance that the business will generate enough income to fund the plan of reorganization. The type of questions asked of a Chapter 11 debtor will depend greatly on the nature and scope of the business enterprise as well as the amount of the claims, both secured and unsecured, that will become part of the repayment plan.

It is possible that no creditors will attend the meeting for a Chapter 11 filer with a small, simple business operation. Although it is in their best interest to appear and communicate with the debtor, some may leave everything in the hands of the court. Under the federal code, rule 2004, an examination can be requested by any party with an interest in the bankruptcy filing.

The examination of the debtor under this rule results from a motion filed with the court. Although a motion can be filed for an examination in any bankruptcy case, it is more common in Chapter 11 filings. Again, this is because these cases are primarily filed by businesses, and businesses tend to incur greater liabilities and larger claims than individual debtors.

Bank Notes

A 2004 examination generally occurs only when a creditor provides the court with a valid reason for an in-depth inspection of the debtor or the debtor's business operation.

The examination may pertain to the acts, conduct, or property of the debtor as well as the debtor's financial condition. In a Chapter 11, the examination extends to the operation of the business, its future potential for income, and the funding of the plan of reorganization.

Since creditors will have an opportunity to vote on the actual plan of reorganization, it follows that some of them will want to obtain as much information as possible about the debtor and the debtor's business enterprise. The creditors may also want to determine whether the debtor is capable of administering the plan of reorganization or whether a Trustee would better serve their interests. They also need to know if they need accountants or other professionals to protect their claims. Like Chapter 7, if no creditors are present, the meeting is short and fairly routine.

Chapter 13 Filers and Unsecured Creditors

Creditors may or may not show up at the meeting of creditors for a Chapter 13 bankruptcy case. However, unsecured creditors have 90 days after the date set for the meeting to file a proof of claim with the court.

As previously explained, failure to file the proof of claim in a timely manner may eliminate the unsecured creditor from receiving payments under the debtor's plan. As with the other chapters, the Trustee will administer the oath and verify the accuracy of the petition and its schedules. The Trustee will also ascertain that the debtor understands the bankruptcy laws and their consequences.

A Creditor's Right to Confront the Debtor

A bankruptcy case is like any other legal action in that there are two sides to be considered. The debtor is on one side of the case; the creditors are on the other side. The law provides that both sides have an opportunity to present their story.

That is the purpose of the meeting of creditors. It gives the opposing sides a chance to speak out or try to make a deal. However, if creditors have an objection to the bankruptcy case, it is not presented at the 341 meeting. It must be presented to the court, where it will be ruled on by a judge.

The debtor, who instigated the legal action by filing a bankruptcy petition seeking relief through the courts, is required to appear at the meeting to verify information and answer questions. The creditor isn't required to attend and, in many Chapter 7 and Chapter 13 cases, foregoes the opportunity to meet with the debtor.

Even when the creditor does appear, the Trustee and the debtor's attorney ensure that the proceedings are conducted fairly and properly. The meeting of creditors is a routine procedure and should not be anticipated with fear or apprehension. The federal bankruptcy laws are there to afford protection and relief, and all who come before the United States Trustee must abide by the rules and protocol established by the courts and the laws. If a creditor has evidence of fraud or any other type of misconduct in connection with a bankruptcy case or a debtor, it must be presented through the proper legal channels. A motion has to be filed and heard by the court.

Extra Funding

There is generally no sure way to determine in advance what creditors, if any, will show up at a 341 meeting.

A creditor will not jump up in the middle of a meeting of creditors and hurl accusations at the debtor. Granted, this takes most of the drama out of the meeting of creditors, but if you've been traveling the rocky road of financial distress, you don't need any more drama in your life. You need peace of mind and the chance to make a fresh start. The meeting of creditors is a smooth, well-paved road. Your lawyer has navigated it many times and will be there to guide you as you travel toward economic stability.

It is probably the name, "meeting of creditors," that causes the most trepidation for the bankruptcy filer. For a debtor who has suffered through months of phone calls from creditors and collection agencies and has received stacks of late notices, the possibility of meeting a creditor face to face may bring on a case of hives.

Don't rush out and buy an anti-itch ointment. Remember that your previous encounters with creditors, before the automatic stay went into effect, were entirely different than they will be under the jurisdiction of the bankruptcy court.

For one thing, before you sought legal advice and filed a bankruptcy petition, it was you versus all those creditors. Needless to say, you were probably outnumbered. You may have also been uninformed about your rights and the rules that the creditors and their agents were bound to follow in dealing with you.

Filing a bankruptcy petition and receiving the automatic stay is like getting that final out in a close ballgame. Before you filed, you were out on the pitcher's mound facing the top of the lineup. It was the bottom of the ninth, and your team was only hanging on by one run. The bases were loaded, and you knew that one wrong pitch would have runners thundering across home plate. Your fastball was sinking like lead, and your curveball was hanging over the plate, inviting the batters to swing for the fence. You wanted to throw a spitball, but your mouth felt like cotton.

With the game on the line, you found an attorney and filed a bankruptcy petition. Your attorney is an experienced, skilled player who relieves you on the mound and retires the opposing side in order, saving the game for you.

The bankruptcy Trustee oversees the proceedings. Like a Major League umpire, the Trustee is an impartial person who makes sure the game is played honestly and correctly. In your case, the opposing hitters may not even show up at the plate, but even if they do, you can relax and depend on your attorney to keep them from scoring against you.

This analogy is not intended to make light of the bankruptcy process or the claims of your creditors. The comparison is simply a way to help you remember that the bankruptcy process and the meeting of creditors should not cause you to lose sleep at night. Once your bankruptcy petition is filed, put yourself in the hands of your attorney and the Trustee. They are professionals who will answer your questions and protect your interests.

The Least You Need to Know

➤ The meeting of creditors is mandatory for the debtor, but creditors do not always attend.

➤ Debtors must provide photo identification and proof of their Social Security number to the presiding Trustee.

➤ An interim Trustee conducts the meeting of creditors and is usually permanently assigned to Chapter 7 and Chapter 13 cases.

➤ Under rule 2004, creditors can request an examination of the debtor, the debtor's property, or the business entity.

Chapter 18

Duties of the Bankruptcy Trustee

In This Chapter

➤ The United States Trustee program

➤ The Trustee in Chapter 7

➤ The Trustee in Chapter 11

➤ The Trustee in Chapter 13

If you file a bankruptcy petition, the Trustee assigned to your case will become an important part of the legal process. Your relationship with the Trustee may be of short duration or may last for years. The Trustee is the liaison between you and your creditors. Understanding the function and responsibilities of this person will help you establish a relationship that will serve your best interests.

Your first contact with the Trustee is at the meeting of creditors. Keep in mind that this meeting and any subsequent meetings with the Trustee will be conducted in a business-like manner. The Trustee may seem sympathetic to you and the financial problems that brought you together. However, he or she is sworn to administer your case according to the rules and regulations of the federal bankruptcy code.

Who Is the Trustee?

The Executive Office for the United States Trustee is in Washington, D.C. From this office, the United States Trustee program is administered and managed. This program was established by the Bankruptcy Reform Act of 1978. It is funded in part by fees paid by individuals and businesses that file bankruptcy petitions with the federal courts. The United States Trustees and assistant United States Trustees are appointed by the Attorney General in 21 regions across the United States.

The following chart shows each region and the states included in that region's jurisdiction:

U.S. TRUSTEE PROGRAM

Judicial Districts Covered by USTP Regions

U.S. Trustee Regions and Corresponding Judicial Districts

Region 1:
Maine
Massachusetts
New Hampshire
Rhode Island

Region 2:
Connecticut
New York (Eastern, Northern, Southern, and Western Districts)
Vermont

Region 3:
Delaware
New Jersey
Pennsylvania (Eastern, Middle, and Western Districts)

Region 4:
Maryland
South Carolina
Virginia (Eastern and Western Districts)
West Virginia (Northern and Southern Districts)
District of Columbia

Region 5:
Louisiana (Eastern, Middle, and Western Districts)
Mississippi (Northern and Southern Districts)

Region 6:
Texas (Eastern and Northern Districts)

Region 7:
Texas (Southern and Western Districts)

Region 8:
Kentucky (Eastern and Western Districts)
Tennessee (Eastern, Middle, and Western Districts)

Region 9:
Ohio (Northern and Southern Districts)
Michigan (Eastern and Western Districts)

Region 10:
Illinois (Central and Southern Districts)
Indiana (Northern and Southern Districts)

Region 11:
Illinois (Northern District)
Wisconsin (Eastern and Western Districts)

Region 12:
Iowa (Northern and Southern Districts)
Minnesota
North Dakota
South Dakota

Region 13:
Arkansas (Eastern and Western Districts)
Nebraska
Missouri (Eastern and Western Districts)

Region 14:
Arizona

Region 15:
California (Southern District)
Hawaii
Guam
Northern Mariana Islands

Region 16:
California (Central District)

Region 17:
California (Eastern & Northern Districts)
Nevada

Region 18:
Alaska
Idaho (exclusive of Yellowstone National Park)
Montana (exclusive of Yellowstone National Park)
Oregon
Washington (Eastern and Western Districts)

Region 19:
Colorado
Utah
Wyoming (including those portions of Yellowstone National Park in Montana and Idaho)

Region 20:
Kansas
New Mexico
Oklahoma (Eastern, Northern, and Western Districts)

Region 21:
Georgia (Middle, Northern, and Southern Districts)
Florida (Middle, Northern, and Southern Districts)
Puerto Rico
U.S. Virgin Islands

Only two states, Alabama and North Carolina, do not take part in the United States Trustee program. In these two states, each court district has a Bankruptcy Administrator who appoints a panel of Trustees. Members of this panel are then assigned to the cases filed in that circuit court district.

The best way to describe the United States Trustee program is through its mission statement: "The United States Trustee program acts in the public interest to promote the efficiency and to protect and preserve the integrity of the bankruptcy system. It works to secure the just, speedy, and economical resolution of bankruptcy cases; monitors the conduct of parties and takes action to ensure compliance with applicable laws and procedures; identifies and investigates bankruptcy fraud and abuse; and oversees administrative functions in bankruptcy cases."

Bank Notes

Random rotations and assignments are a way to ensure that debtors cannot time the filing of their bankruptcy cases in the hopes of having a particular Trustee handle it.

The United States Trustee in each district appoints individuals to serve as Trustees for the bankruptcy cases filed in that jurisdiction. Trustees may have legal backgrounds but do not have to be lawyers. The selected Trustees are included on a panel of Trustees that will receive random appointments to bankruptcy cases in their geographical area.

The Executive Office in Washington, D.C., provides administrative and management support to the regional offices as well as general policy and legal guidance. However, there are a number of specific responsibilities that the United States Trustee of each region must oversee and direct. They are as follows:

➤ The appointment and supervision of individual Trustees who are assigned to bankruptcy cases

➤ Necessary legal action to enforce the requirements of the bankruptcy code and to prevent fraud and abuse

➤ Referring matters for investigation and criminal prosecution when appropriate

➤ Ensuring that bankruptcy estates are administered promptly and efficiently and that professional fees are reasonable

➤ Appointing and convening creditors' committees in Chapter 11 business reorganization cases

➤ Reviewing disclosure statements and requests and applications for professionals in Chapter 11 cases

➤ Sponsoring matters relating to the bankruptcy code and rules of procedure in court

The individual Trustee assigned to a bankruptcy case reports to the United States Trustee in the region where the bankruptcy is filed. Private or individual Trustees have their own set of requirements and responsibilities in connection with each case assigned to them. Their responsibilities extend to the debtors, the creditors, and any other parties connected to the bankruptcy filing.

The Trustee's Role in Chapter 7

The first duty of the Trustee is to examine the bankruptcy petition and all the documents that are part of it. This includes notices of reaffirmation and redemption and any other pertinent paperwork.

The questions the Trustee asks are based on the scrutiny of all the information pertaining to the bankruptcy case. In a Chapter 7, the Trustee then takes charge of the nonexempt property that has become part of the bankruptcy estate. In some cases, the Trustee will determine that the filing is a "no-asset" case. That means it is a bankruptcy case in which there are no nonexempt assets with enough value to generate funds for distribution to the unsecured creditors.

If the Trustee determines that there are assets that can be sold for significant amounts, the debtor will be instructed to turn those assets over to the Trustee. The normal time for the disposing of assets and discharge of debts that ends the bankruptcy case is approximately 60 days.

Although it is sometimes possible to redeem certain property from the bankruptcy estate, this would not be necessary in a no-asset case because all the property would remain with the debtor. In an asset case, the Trustee looks at the property in the bankruptcy estate with an eye toward extracting enough income from it to make the sale process worthwhile. Subsequent meetings with the Trustee may allow a debtor to redeem any property that is deemed more trouble to sell than it is worth.

Just as the United States Trustees have certain responsibilities, the individual Trustees assigned to Chapter 7 cases have obligations that must be addressed and carried out. The federal code regulating Trustees specifies that the Trustee in a Chapter 7 case must do the following:

1. Collect and liquidate property of the bankruptcy estate.
2. Account for all property received under the bankruptcy estate.
3. Examine the financial affairs of the debtor.
4. Review any proofs of claim filed in the case and eliminate any claim that is improper.
5. Answer creditors' questions.
6. Administer the bankruptcy estate and close it as quickly and efficiently as circumstances allow.
7. Oppose the debtor's discharge if there are valid reasons to do so.
8. Prepare and file a report and an accounting of the bankruptcy estate with the court and the United States Trustee.

In a case that is determined to be a no-asset case, there would be no need for some of these duties to be performed. Where there are assets (other than real estate) to be sold, the Trustee can dispose of them by holding an auction at a designated location or through one of the Internet companies that specializes in auctions.

If there is real estate to be sold, the Trustee will generally hire a realtor to list the property and accept contracts from qualified buyers.

Bank Notes

The United States Department of Justice describes the bankruptcy Trustee as a "watch dog" over the bankruptcy process.

Extra Funding

Even when there are assets in the bankruptcy estate that can be sold, the creditors generally only receive a small percentage of the original liability.

The actual sale of the property will have to be approved by the court before it is finalized. Any proceeds from the liquidation of the property in the bankruptcy estate will be placed in an interest-bearing account.

Payments to creditors are usually not made until the court approves the Trustee's final report on the assets and their disposition. The Trustee is allowed to draw on these funds if expenses are incurred in maintaining or securing the property. Administrative costs of the court and the bankruptcy estate are paid first, before the claims of creditors. Distribution of the other funds is done according to the priority rules outlined in a prior chapter.

In connection with the examination of all the debtors' documents and financial affairs, the Trustee is responsible for reporting any discrepancies or suspicions of fraud to the United States Trustee in an efficient and timely manner. Sometimes creditors and other interested parties contact the Trustee with allegations regarding a debtor and a bankruptcy filing.

It is up to the Trustees to investigate these charges and report their findings to the court. Any suspicion of fraud or unscrupulous actions in relation to a bankruptcy case would give the Trustee a valid reason to object to the discharge of debts for the Chapter 7 filer.

This would most likely prompt the United States Trustee to request an investigation of the debtor and his or her attorney. While all of this sounds like a large load for the Trustee to carry, remember that most Chapter 7 cases are honest filings, by honest citizens, that move along smoothly and routinely.

When a Trustee Is Assigned to Chapter 11

In a Chapter 11 reorganization, the debtor or business owner assumes the role of the Trustee and is bound by the same rules that a court-appointed Trustee must follow. A lot of information has already been offered in previous chapters about Chapter 11 reorganization, and you know that in addition to keeping the business operation running, the debtor would be responsible for administering the plan and making payments to creditors. In most instances, the debtor would turn some of these duties over to professional accountants or legal advisors.

NSF Checks

If a committee of creditors prevailed upon the court to assign a Trustee in a Chapter 11 filing, the debtor would lose control of his business operation and administration of the plan or reorganization.

The assignment of a Trustee to a Chapter 11 case could be construed by the debtor as a reason to abandon the plan and convert the bankruptcy to a Chapter 7 liquidation.

The Trustee's Role in a Chapter 13 Filing

A Trustee assigned to a Chapter 13 bankruptcy case has the same duties and responsibilities as the Chapter 7 Trustee, with a few additions. In a Chapter 13 case, the Trustee must attend and testify at any hearing that concerns the following:

➤ The value of property subject to a lien

➤ Confirmation of a repayment plan

➤ Modification of the plan after confirmation

When a Trustee administers a Chapter 13 plan, it means the Trustee monitors incoming funds from the debtor and makes sure they are remitted in a timely manner, distributes the funds in accordance with the plan, and advises (other than on legal matters) and assists the debtor in performing under the plan.

That's All, Folks ...

The information you have just reviewed should have dispelled any thoughts you may have had about the Trustee having a cushy job. The Trustee walks the middle of the road and must honor his or her obligations to all the parties involved in the bankruptcy.

Excellent administrative skills are required along with the ability to examine financial records and make intelligent decisions. A certain amount of tact and diplomacy may also be needed to deal with distraught debtors and the claims of creditors. And then there are the lawyers, accountants, and other professionals that may be involved in any given case.

The United States Department of Justice has a Web site that will provide more information on the United States Trustee program or federal bankruptcy courts in your region. You can access the site at www.USTWeb@usdoj.gov. You can also contact your regional United States Trustees office; those listings can also be found on the Web site.

Bank Notes

The Trustee assigned to a Chapter 13 plan will be working with the debtors and the creditors for a three- to five-year period.

The Least You Need to Know

➤ The United States Attorney General appoints the United States Trustees.

➤ The United States Trustees program covers all federal court jurisdictions with the exception of Alabama and North Carolina.

➤ The United States Trustee appoints a panel of individual Trustees who are assigned to the bankruptcy cases in that region.

➤ The Trustee assigned to your bankruptcy case is an important part of the legal process and the resolution of your case.

➤ More information on the United States Trustee program can be obtained from the United States Department of Justice.

Chapters Should Have Happy Endings

In This Chapter

➤ Public records

➤ The final steps

➤ Discharge of debts

➤ Tax consequences

➤ Maximum relief

Filing bankruptcy is not a pleasant experience. However, from the information you have gathered so far, you should be convinced that it is not an altogether terrible ordeal either. Although filing bankruptcy can be a complicated process for debtors with businesses or tons of assets, with a competent legal advisor, it can be handled with a minimum of pain and suffering. Chapter 11 and Chapter 13 filers will be involved in the process for an extended period of time, but Chapter 7 filers will be done with the meetings and paperwork and be out of debt in a fairly short amount of time.

All debtors who seek relief through bankruptcy should look at the process as a business transaction. Some transactions are more complex and take longer than others, but you enter into a business deal to get something you want. As long as that is accomplished, the amount of time and effort that went into the deal is worthwhile.

People go into bankruptcy because they want to eliminate debts and take control of their finances. If there were not a legitimate need for a legal process to accomplish these things in this country, the laws would not exist. The federal bankruptcy code is a maze of rules and regulations, but it is a system that works. There are consequences and side effects to bankruptcy, but the end result is what counts.

You Could Be in the Newspaper

The official filing of any legal action is recorded in the public record. Bankruptcy is a legal action, and therefore the filings are often published in the newspaper. You've seen the public records column in your daily paper: births, deaths, divorces, and bankruptcies. When you think about it, they do go together. Births are new beginnings, deaths and divorces are endings, and bankruptcy is the end of financial problems and the beginning of a fresh start.

Not all newspapers publish public records on a daily basis. It's one of those things that editors may throw in the paper to fill an empty space on a page. If the paper sells lots of ads for the day you filed or there are a lot of newsworthy stories, your bankruptcy may not be published at all.

If you live in a large city, your name could get lost among all the others published that day. If you live in a very small town, your bankruptcy filing could stick out like a neon light flashing in the desert at night.

NSF Checks

Bankruptcy is not something that can be kept secret, and trying to keep it under wraps will just make your life more difficult.

The best thing you can do is be open and honest with family, friends, co-workers, employers, and anyone else who is near and dear to you. As discussed in earlier chapters, they are probably aware of your financial problems anyway. This doesn't mean you should tell everyone you meet that you just filed bankruptcy; just be aware that people will know about it and may ask you about it.

You should also be aware of another important fact. The majority of people really aren't too concerned about your problems. They are too busy worrying about their own problems.

The only parties who will actually be affected by your bankruptcy are you and your creditors. By the time you file bankruptcy, you've already dealt with your emotions and the effect this will have on your life and your future. As for the creditors, leave their reactions for your attorney, the court, and the Trustee to handle.

The Last Few Steps for Chapter 7

If you're a Chapter 7 filer, you will have to turn any nonexempt assets over to the Trustee to be sold. You will also have to negotiate a settlement on any property you wish to redeem from the Trustee. Your attorney can help you with this process if it is necessary.

When you redeem an item from the Trustee, the amount you pay to redeem it becomes part of the funds generated by the bankruptcy estate. Remember, the Trustee will not allow you to redeem property for a small dollar amount that might be sold to another buyer for a higher price. The Trustee has an obligation to get as much income as possible out of the bankruptcy estate to distribute to the creditors.

You will also have to make the payments on any debts you re-affirmed in the bankruptcy process. It is important to keep them current because the terms of the reaffirmation agreement allow the lien holder to take action if you default. Any debts that are non-dischargeable, such as support payments, certain taxes, and student loans, should be kept current as well. These debts will continue to be your responsibility until they are paid in full.

Reaching the End of Chapter 13

The last steps for Chapter 13 filers include having their repayment plan confirmed by the court and putting it into operation. Without all the monthly payments that were strangling you before the filing, you should be able to come up with the monthly amount prescribed by your plan and still have the cash you need to pay everyday expenses. The obligations and restrictions of a Chapter 13 plan on a debtor are few. Obviously, honoring the payments for your plan is your first and foremost duty when you file Chapter 13.

Another important restriction is the provision that you will not incur any significant new debt without the court's approval. The court naturally wants to ensure that you will maintain the payments for the plan and will not do anything to jeopardize your ability to do so. You are also obliged to keep insurance premiums current on any asset that is collateral for a debt.

Chapter 13 debtors are allowed to move or change jobs as long as it does not disrupt the regular payments required by the plan. Court approval for things like a new car loan or the purchase of a new residence is possible but may take up to 45 days to process. Remember that the repayment plan can be modified, but this is not recommended unless there is a good reason or necessity to do so.

Extra Funding

Child support payments generally continue until the dependent reaches age 18. This liability is one that will not be eliminated by a bankruptcy filing.

Bank Notes

A dire circumstance such as job loss or unexpected health problems would be more likely to necessitate a conversion to a Chapter 7 filing rather than a modification of the Chapter 13 plan.

Drawing Chapter 11 to a Close

Chapter 11 business filers have longer to develop a plan of reorganization, but the quicker it is presented and approved the better. Putting it into operation as soon as possible is in everyone's best interests and may avoid additional expenses and fees.

Your creditors are going to be disgruntled by the bankruptcy filing. Receiving payments sooner rather than later under the plan of reorganization will go a long way toward improving their attitude and their willingness to work with you again. This is especially important if you have creditors who supply goods or merchandise for your business.

Since the Chapter 11 debtor acts in the same capacity as a court-appointed Trustee, it is prudent to use the same objectivity and caution that the bankruptcy court would exercise. Treat everyone as fairly and efficiently as possible.

The Official Discharge of Debt

The timetable for the final discharge will vary according to the type of bankruptcy petition filed and the size and complexity of your bankruptcy case. Chapter 7 cases can go on for several months before the final discharge of debts takes place. Chapter 11 and 13 cases are not discharged until the plans have been fulfilled. Regardless of how long it takes to reach the final discharge, it is the time when you are freed from the demands of creditors.

When a discharge of debts is issued by the bankruptcy court, the order provides that all debts, except for those that are reaffirmed or nondischargeable, included on the petition are permanently erased from the debtor's life. The order does not prevent a debtor from paying a debt that was discharged. If a debtor chooses to make payments on a liability that was discharged through the bankruptcy filing and then decides not to pay it after all, the creditor may not take any action against the debtor.

Remember that Chapter 11 and 13 filers can convert to a Chapter 7 bankruptcy filing if new circumstances make the plan to pay creditors impossible to honor. Contact your legal advisor to guide you through the conversion.

NSF Checks

If any of your creditors attempt to collect a debt that has been discharged, contact your attorney immediately.

Once a Chapter 11 or 13 filer completes the payment plan, the debts that remain are discharged by the court. The amount of these dischargeable debts will be the difference between the original liability and the total of the payments made under the plan. For example, if a creditor's original claim was $4,000 and the creditor received payments totaling $2,500 during the course of the repayment plan, then the difference of $1,500 would be discharged by the court when the plan was completed.

If the plan included nondischargeable debts that were not fully satisfied during the time the plan was in effect, the debtor would be obligated to continue making the payments on that debt until it was paid in full. This would apply to student loans, certain taxes, and support payments.

The IRS and the Discharge of Debts

The Internal Revenue Service may look at the cancellation of a debt outside of bankruptcy as taxable income, especially for a partnership or corporate business. However, for the individual debtor, the discharge of debts has no tax consequences. The Internal Revenue code excludes the gain realized by the cancellation of a debt in a bankruptcy filing as income.

In some instances, a debtor's tax credits (such as losses) carry forward, or the exclusion of gain on the sale of a personal residence may be absorbed into the bankruptcy estate and used by the Trustee in the administration of the estate. Again, all tax matters should be investigated and discussed with your attorney or tax adviser before the bankruptcy petition is filed.

Relief Is Like a Security Blanket

Since each bankruptcy case is different and each debtor has his or her own agenda, goals, and plans for the future, the measure of relief that results from a bankruptcy filing varies.

No one comes out of a bankruptcy totally unchanged. Some things will be lost; however, with proper planning and good legal advice, the things that are lost should be minor compared to what is gained. To demonstrate how a bankruptcy may affect your financial condition and lifestyle, let's turn to our fictional couple, Jack and Jill, once again. Their Chapter 7 bankruptcy changed their financial picture and also enabled them to make some positive personal changes in their lifestyle.

You may recall that Jack and Jill converted some of their nonexempt personal property into exempt property before the bankruptcy filing. Jack's gun collection, a few items of jewelry, and two oil paintings were sold, and the proceeds from these sales were used to make home improvements. Also before filing, the couple traded Jill's car valued at $6,000 in on a new van and purchased an older vehicle that needed repairs and had a low value as their second car. Jack's mechanical abilities made it possible for him to repair the older vehicle so that it was suitable for their needs.

When the bankruptcy was filed, Jack's truck that was worth less than the outstanding loan balance was turned back to the creditor. Since this was done through the bankruptcy court, the creditor was not able to pursue a deficiency judgment on the vehicle.

Jack and Jill had other personal property that was financed. Through the bankruptcy proceedings and with the help of their attorney, the couple redeemed the computer Jack needs for work. The two mortgages on their house were reaffirmed with the lien holders, as were the loans on their refrigerator and living room furniture.

The personal property that was turned back to the creditors was the big screen television set and the stereo. Both of these were considered luxury items that they could live without. All of you who watch sports events on big screen televisions are probably taking exception to the previous statement, but that's the way this fictional bankruptcy shaped up.

The only item that might have gone into the bankruptcy estate was Jack's patent on the tool he designed. However, based on the information gathered and filed with the bankruptcy petition, the Trustee decided that the patent didn't have enough marketability or value to generate funds. In the end, Jack and Jill's case was determined to be a no-asset case. That is, there were no nonexempt assets that could be sold through the bankruptcy estate to provide cash to pay the unsecured creditors.

Extra Funding

In general, a bankruptcy filing should provide the maximum amount of relief allowed by law.

NSF Checks

Remember that these sample vehicle strategies will not work for everyone. Each situation is unique, and many debtors cannot qualify for a loan on a new vehicle because their credit rating is poor or their income is too low.

Before the bankruptcy, Jack and Jill's liabilities were as follows:

Creditor	Balance Due	Payment
Mid-Atlantic Mtg. (1st Mtg.)	$81,500	$580
First Mechanics Bank (2nd Mtg.)	$30,000	$250
First Mechanics Bank (Truck)	$21,000	$467
Atlantic Medical Center	$24,000	$500
Dr. Richard Brown	$600	$50
ABC Appliance Store	$350	$25
Designer Furniture Store	$2,400	$60
Big Screen City	$1,000	$40
Stereo City	$550	$25
Computer City	$800	$40
Visa	$7,800	$234
MasterCard	$9,100	$273
Discover	$4,200	$135
Citibank	$2,700	$81
USA Bank-student loan	$8,600	$200
Totals	**$194,601**	**$2,960**

Here's how their schedule of liabilities was revised through the Chapter 7 bankruptcy filing:

Creditor	Balance Due	Payment
Mid-Atlantic Mtg.(1st Mtg.)	$81,500	$580
First Mechanics Bank (2nd Mtg.)	$30,000	$250
Union Auto Loans	$31,000	$530
ABC Appliance Store	$350	$25
Designer Furniture Store	$2,400	$60
USA Bank-student loan	$8,600	$200
Totals	**$153,850**	**$1,645**

Extra Funding

A student loan can be refinanced to adjust the payments in accordance with the lender's guidelines.

Even though the couple increased their liability on the vehicle loan by $9,000 by returning the truck and buying the new van, they reduced their overall debt by $40,751. This is a substantial difference. The payments on their current liabilities are $1,315 less than they were prior to the bankruptcy filing. Among the remaining debts is a student loan that cannot be discharged through a bankruptcy filing. All the other nonsecured debts were discharged.

For Jack and Jill, the bankruptcy filing made another important change possible. Jill was able to quit her job, and although that eliminated her salary, it also eliminated the $688 per month she was paying for childcare. This was a huge consideration for this fictional couple because Jill felt guilty about the time her job took away from her children. In addition, more than half of her salary was eaten up by childcare expenses and the cost of convenience foods that many working parents rely on to feed their families.

Also, even though the court discharged the debt they owed to Dr. Richard Brown, the couple opted to continue to pay him anyway, as he continued to provide medical care for the twins. Finally, you can see how the bankruptcy affected Jack and Jill's monthly income versus the amount paid out each month.

	Before Chapter 7	After Chapter 7
Monthly income:	Jack $3,947	$3,947
	Jill $1,312	$0
Total income:	**$5,259**	**$3,947**
Monthly debt payments:	($2,960)	($1,645)
Dr. Brown's bill:		($50)
Monthly cash expenditures:	($2,223)	($1,535)
Total payouts:	**($5,183)**	**($3,230)**
Net cash over/short:	$76 over	$717 over

With more than $600 left over for incidental expenses each month, Jack and Jill are back on top of the hill again.

Your Own Happy Ending

A bankruptcy filing can change your financial picture and improve your lifestyle. However, it is not an instant, sure-fire solution to all your problems. Unemployment, health problems, and a host of other things that happen to you and yours can continue after a bankruptcy filing and may prevent you from getting as financially solvent as you would like to be.

The purpose of bankruptcy is to give you a certain measure of relief and allow you to concentrate on the future instead of worrying about liabilities incurred in the past. Once the automatic stay goes into effect, most of the tension and stress associated with a multitude of unpaid bills is relieved.

The final discharge of debts and the close of the bankruptcy case generally do not elicit as great a feeling of liberation. However, it is a significant event. All debts discharged are now permanently eliminated. These creditors are gone from your life. There may be a few twinges of guilt associated with their total banishment. That is a natural reaction and one that should be recognized and then quickly dismissed.

NSF Checks

Don't expect a bankruptcy filing to make such a dramatic difference in your own life. The case of Jack and Jill is fictional and is presented for demonstration purposes only. How a Chapter 7 filing affects the average person depends on many factors that need to be discussed with your legal advisor.

Preparing to Start Over

It is too late to go back and change things. Your time and energy should now be focused on ensuring your future rather than trying to make up for the past. Most likely, the debts discharged were for liabilities held by large banks and credit card companies. As you learned in the beginning of this book, you are just an account number to these companies.

All of these companies usually have a special account set up in their accounting systems called Allocation for Bad Debts. When their accountants prepare a budget each year, a certain amount is posted to that account, estimating the amount of money that the company expects to lose on loans that are canceled for one reason or another.

At the end of the year, the Allocation for Bad Debts account is analyzed and adjusted. The actual amount the company lost on the credit they extended to individuals and companies that failed to satisfy their debts is written off the books and deducted on their tax return.

Extra Funding

Financial companies do not expect to collect 100 percent of what is owed to them. The very nature of the business is that a certain percentage of loans will become uncollectable and have to be written off their books.

Lending money to others can be a lucrative operation, but the risk factor is always there, too. However, you don't read about too many credit card companies going broke. Our country's economy is measured in part by how much money is being spent by consumers, and credit card companies are always trying to talk Americans into spending more by offering them higher credit limits and incentives.

How many times have you made a purchase at a department store and had the clerk offer to deduct 10 percent from the sale amount if you would apply for a store credit card? That is just one indication of the store's belief that once you have the credit card you will spend more.

Fortunately, you've already learned the dangers attached to those offers and should now be better prepared to revise your own economic strategy. The final chapters of this book offer advice and suggestions to help you rebuild your credit and stay solvent.

The Least You Need to Know

➤ Bankruptcy filings are a matter of public record and may be published in your hometown newspaper.

➤ Before your Chapter 7 debts are discharged, nonexempt assets will be sold and the funds distributed to the unsecured creditors.

➤ Chapter 13 filers cannot incur significant new debt without approval from the bankruptcy court.

➤ For the average individual, a discharge of debts does not trigger any tax consequences.

Part 5

Life After Bankruptcy

You are now looking back on the bankruptcy filing and thinking it was not as bad as you had anticipated. Any legal process has complications and a certain amount of red tape. It's the way the system works, and believe it or not, most of the procedures were put in place to protect you.

Regardless of how much your creditors received or are scheduled to receive in the coming months, it is time to put their claims behind you and concentrate on your future. You filed bankruptcy to get a fresh start for yourself and, if applicable, your family or your business. This part of the book offers advice and suggestions on moving forward financially and coping with some of the problems that a bankruptcy filing may present.

Chapter 20

You and Your Credit Report

In This Chapter

➤ Are all your debts wiped off?

➤ Credit report data

➤ New leases on life and property

➤ Starting over

Depending on the circumstances that drove you into bankruptcy, you may still have issues that were not settled by the filing. For example, if the bankruptcy was prompted by a divorce, there may be many emotional hurdles that are difficult to think about much less jump over. Health problems are another reason that people seek relief from creditors through the bankruptcy system, and unemployment is still a primary cause of financial disaster.

Bankruptcy is often a side effect that results from situations that are far more serious than financial problems. However, it is beneficial because clearing away debts that are unrelated to everyday essentials may free up funds that can be used for more vital expenses. It also provides the peace of mind that comes from knowing the bill collectors will not be able to carry off property required for the basic needs of life.

The point is that although bankruptcy may provide financial relief, if you have other, ongoing issues, you need to explore other options to help you stabilize your future.

For those who are fortunate enough to truly get a fresh start through a bankruptcy filing, you may also need assistance to ensure that wiping out your old debts does not lure you into temptations that will create new liabilities. It will take some time for things to settle down after a bankruptcy. You don't want to take any action for 60 to 90 days. Consider this a cooling off period in which you can establish a normal routine.

If you have reaffirmed on any of your debts, you will be making those payments in addition to taking care of your normal household expenses. If you are working with a repayment plan, you will be making the payments prescribed by the plan as well as maintaining your other expenses.

The main thing is that you should try to avoid making any substantial financial changes in your lifestyle, such as moving to a new residence or trying to make any major purchases. You should have the property needed to sustain yourself and your family for the first few months, so you can relax and think about your long range plans for the future.

The fictional couple, Jack and Jill, took the opportunity that bankruptcy afforded to have Jill quit her job. However, this was not a major financial decision because the additional expenses that went along with Jill's employment, such as child care and no-fuss meals, minimized the effects of her salary.

In other words, as long as the change is a positive one for the family and doesn't jeopardize the newly created financial status, it is fine. For all other situations, you may want to take the time suggested to make sure the change is necessary and beneficial. You may be surprised to find that, with time, some ideas and goals lose importance, while others become more attractive.

NSF Checks

Chapter 13 filers need to be especially careful not to take on new obligations with payments that may make the plan more difficult to honor. Court approval is necessary for large purchases that are financed, but a number of small obligations can also add up to trouble.

Your Credit History Is Still Riddled with Holes

Adverse credit information can remain on your credit report for seven years. A bankruptcy filing can remain on your credit report for 10 years. Of course, you were already told that before you filed your bankruptcy petition. Given your other problems, this fact didn't matter too much. What was foremost in your mind was getting the automatic stay that would get those creditors and collectors out of your life.

There is nothing wrong with that, especially since your credit report was already a mess. Given the problems that made you decide to file bankruptcy, there was nothing you could do about the late fees and collection actions that were being posted to your report. At that time, your credit history was the least of your worries. Stopping the tow truck from carting off your only means of transportation was much more urgent.

The bankruptcy has discharged your debts and restored some order to your economic condition. Once enough time has passed to allow you to contemplate things in a calm atmosphere without the pressure of creditors, you may be ready to look at your credit report and see if you can do anything to improve it.

The first step in solving any problem is to gather all the information so it can be analyzed and studied. Unfortunately, a bankruptcy does not clear all the bills from your credit history. They are still there, along with all the gory details and derogatory reports that your creditors provided to the credit bureaus. The record of your bankruptcy filing will also be on the report.

If you are faint of heart, you may not want to look at your credit report. It could be a painful reminder of the days when a ringing telephone made you cringe. However, if you want to develop a plan for the future, it is a problem that should be addressed.

There are three major credit bureaus in the United States. They are:

1. Equifax Credit Bureau
2. Experian (formerly TRW Credit Bureau)
3. Trans Union Corporation Consumer Disclosure Center

To get complete information on your credit history, you will need to request your credit report from all three of these bureaus. Detailed contact information for each can be found in Appendix A of this book. Credit reports can be ordered by mail, by telephone, or through the Internet. The reason you request all three reports is because of the reporting procedures of creditors. Creditors may report to all three of these bureaus, or they may report to one or the other of them.

Information on one bureau's report may not be found on another. Companies that access these reports generally work with one bureau and make their decisions to approve or deny credit based on the information that bureau has in your file. When you apply for credit, you don't know which bureau the report will come from, so if you are going to clean up anything on your credit history, you have to make sure it is cleaned up with every reporting bureau.

There may be a charge for each report requested. It is a nominal fee, and you are better off just paying it and getting the information sent directly to you.

Bank Notes

Remember that there are no quick fixes. Credit repair agencies that charge for services cannot remove adverse information on your credit report if the information is true.

Extra Funding

Some companies offer you a free credit report, but there usually is some type of service connected to the retrieval of the report on your behalf.

What's on Your Report?

If you've never looked at a credit report before, the following lists show what you can expect to find on one.

It will contain personal information including:

➤ Your name
➤ Current and previous addresses
➤ Social Security number

➤ Telephone number

➤ Date of birth

➤ Current and previous employers

If you are married and have joint credit accounts, similar information about your spouse may also appear on the report.

Your credit history includes reports about your accounts with the following:

➤ Retail stores

➤ Banks

➤ Finance companies

➤ Mortgage companies

It also includes matters of public record such as:

➤ Tax liens

➤ Court judgments

➤ Bankruptcy filings

Bank Notes

Any information that might influence a potential creditor's decision on your credit worthiness is recorded and kept in your credit history.

At the end of the report is a list of inquiries. This is a listing of all the people who have received copies of your credit report.

You may be wondering how the credit bureaus obtain the personal information that appears on your report. The information mainly comes from creditors, but it can also be obtained from public records. Sometimes the personal information comes directly from the consumer who contacts the credit bureau.

As mentioned earlier, when a creditor reports a delinquency on an open account, the information stays on your report for a full seven years from the date of the delinquency. Bankruptcies are reported for 7 to 10 years, depending on the chapter that was filed. If an account has been paid in full without any adverse information attached to it, the bureau may report it as closed for 10 years.

The majority of companies can access your credit history very quickly because they subscribe to one or all of the bureaus and have direct links to the information via fax or computer. Although it seems like your whole life may be displayed on a credit report, there is certain information that cannot be revealed by a credit bureau.

The following data is either not available to the credit reporting bureau or is not allowed to be listed on your report:

➤ Bank account information

➤ Medical histories

➤ Cash purchases

➤ Business accounts for which you are not personally liable

➤ Race, gender, religion, or national origin

Cleaning Up Your Credit Report

If you get copies of your credit reports from all three major credit bureaus and there are no errors on any of them, it may qualify you for the world record book. Granted, people who have very few credit accounts and have kept the same address and the same employer for a number of years may have reports that are free of errors. However, people who have experienced financial problems have pages of data, numerous accounts, lots of delinquencies, and lists of inquiries. All of this adds up to the likelihood of errors.

As someone who has just come out of a bankruptcy, should you be concerned about errors on your credit history? Yes. Should you spend the time and effort required to correct the errors? Maybe. Obviously, it depends on the magnitude of the errors. It also depends on what kind of bankruptcy you filed and what you are considering in the future.

Go over the reports carefully and mark all the accounts that were discharged by the bankruptcy court. If you're a Chapter 11 or 13 filer, note which accounts are being paid and the adjusted balances of each. Pay particular attention to debts you have reaffirmed. Make sure the payments and balances are accurate.

If there are serious errors on your credit reports, you can file a dispute with the credit bureau. The Federal Fair Credit Reporting Act requires that your dispute be investigated within 30 days. If the credit bureau cannot verify the disputed information, a correction must be made to your credit history, and you will be notified of this action.

Your credit report may not do you any good at this moment in time, but by making sure the information is accurate and noting any discrepancies, you are giving yourself an advantage that you can draw on for the future. The advantage is this: By knowing exactly what is on your credit reports and by keeping copies of them and of any corrections you noted yourself or officially disputed, you will not be caught off-guard by potential employers, landlords, creditors, or any other parties that may access your credit report.

You may have heard the saying, "The best defense is a good offense." Armed with the proper information, you can discuss your credit history and explain any item of significance. You won't be apologizing but will be open and honest about it, and that in itself will show that you are a person of integrity. If your bankruptcy was due to medical reasons or an unexpected job loss, try to document the circumstances that put you in financial distress.

Knowing exactly what is on your credit report will prepare you to answer questions or provide explanations.

Bank Notes

You may want to check your credit report every three months. This allows time for new information to be posted and old information to be removed.

Bank Notes

Documents such as letters from doctors verifying health issues or paperwork that relates to employment losses should be requested and kept as part of your personal records.

Try to Stay Still

Credit reports are routinely run for a number of reasons, and many of them have nothing to do with obtaining credit. Employers, for example, may request credit reports on people they are considering for certain positions. Most landlords and property management companies request them before entering into a lease agreement with a potential tenant.

If you are an apartment dweller, try to stay put for at least a year after you file bankruptcy. During that year, pay your rent on time each month. A good reference from a former land-lord will generally allow you to obtain a lease on a new apartment because it will offset the information on your credit report.

Just as you faced up to your financial problems and opted to file bankruptcy, you will be much better off if you own up to the fact that your credit rating will probably be a hin-drance to you. Accept that probability and you will find ways to work around it.

Exceptions

Life is full of surprises, and new opportunities sometimes pop up when you least expect them. Although it is suggested that you take several months to let things settle down after a bankruptcy, you never know what fate may have in store for you. Don't get so complacent that you let a good thing pass you by. Even if you are in the midst of a Chapter 13 repay-ment plan, you can make changes that are beneficial to you and your family.

Just consider all changes objectively. Move forward whenever possible but don't make hasty decisions. Explore all your options and make sensible decisions that will actually improve your life and your current economic situation. A new job with a higher salary and better benefits would be a good choice. A new sports car with tinted windows and a sunroof may not be so good.

Extra Funding

Chapter 13 plans can be modi-fied to accommodate changes in employment or residency. Any modification must be approved by the court.

Remember the financial problems you left behind and keep things in perspective. Keep your credit report in a spot where it can be reviewed. If you are tempted to go out on a limb again, look at the credit report to remind yourself of how shaky and unstable those limbs can become.

Your bankruptcy allowed you to start over. You've got a new lease on life, so make the most of it. Starting over financially is simply an exten-sion of the plan and the strategies you began to devise when you made the decision to file bankruptcy.

In some ways, a new beginning is an awesome challenge. This is espe-cially true when old habits still lie close to the surface, waiting for a chance to spring up and take you in the wrong direction again. No one is perfect, and you may find yourself making the same old mistakes again. However, the difference is that after all you've experienced, you should be able to recognize the pitfalls and find a way around them.

Finding and maintaining good financial balance is like learning to ride a bicycle again. You may be a little shaky at first. You may even tumble off the bike a few times. Don't get discouraged. False starts and a few falls are to be expected. Once you're up and rolling again, keep your speed under control and keep your eyes on the road ahead.

The Least You Need to Know

➤ Allow yourself some time to settle down and establish a new routine after a bankruptcy filing.

➤ You should request a credit report from the following three companies: Equifax Credit Bureau, Experian, and Trans Union Corporation Consumer Disclosure Center.

➤ Dispute any major errors on the reports.

➤ Potential employers and landlords often request a copy of your credit report.

➤ Know what's on your credit report so you can discuss it openly and honestly.

➤ Document any information that is needed to explain your bankruptcy filing.

Chapter 21

New Credit Accounts

In This Chapter

➤ Credit cards

➤ Auto loans

➤ Mortgages

➤ Other loans and leases

Although the bankruptcy and other derogatory information stays on your credit report for 7 to 10 years, all hopes of new credit accounts are not lost. Chapter 11 and Chapter 13 filers are working to settle their debts through their payment plans, and that in itself will start to improve their credit rating.

A credit rating is something you won't see on your credit reports when and if you request them. However, a rating is included with the reports requested by banks, mortgage companies, and any other commercial organization that accesses your credit file. The rating is based on how fast or slow you have paid your bills. Slow or late payers get a low rating; those who pay their bills on time get a higher rating.

If you have already thrown your hands in the air in a sign of surrender, figuring that after all the financial turmoil you've been through your rating is probably a double minus zero, take them down again. A bankruptcy plus a poor credit rating may stop you from getting some types of credit, but there will still be some doors that will swing open for you.

In this chapter, you will learn about some of those doors and how to avoid having them hit you in the backside as you walk through them.

Credit Card Offers

While you won't be receiving scads of preapproved credit card invitations, chances are you will receive a few. That's right, even after a Chapter 7 bankruptcy filing, some credit card companies will still solicit your business.

Bank Notes

Retaining an existing account may be easier than applying for a new one. This is especially true if you are still suffering the effects of a job loss or illness.

Of course, the companies with balances that were discharged through the Chapter 7 may never send you another invitation, but there are always others. Companies that know you filed bankruptcy—it's a matter of public record and is boldly reported on your credit history—will still want you to become one of their cardholders.

Why is that? It's simple arithmetic. A Chapter 7 bankruptcy can only be filed once in a six-year period. These companies figure that they have all that time to extract interest from you.

Unfortunately, a credit card is a necessary evil. If you doubt that, try to rent a car or book a hotel room without one. Being acutely aware of this fact, some bankruptcy filers do not include one or more of their credit cards in the bankruptcy petition. Generally, it's an account with a small balance or no balance at all. This keeps the account open and usable; if this is possible, it is probably the best way to go.

If you have learned the lessons that bankruptcy teaches, you know that one credit card is enough. It's all you need to rent a car or book a hotel room. If you have learned the lessons well, you will use the card sparingly and will pay off the balance in full each month when the bill arrives.

All consumers, whether they have filed bankruptcy or not, should live by this rule. After all, it's a way to get free credit. Use the credit, pay it back before any interest accrues, and you won't find yourself in that vicious circle of revolving credit ever again.

If all your credit card accounts were included in the bankruptcy, accept a card from a new company. One card from one company. Then lock it away somewhere. Don't carry it around in your purse or wallet where you'll be tempted to use it for that sparkling pair of earrings or that silk designer shirt.

How About a New Car?

Surprisingly, you may also be able to get an auto loan within a few months of your bankruptcy discharge. Again, it's because an auto loan is a short-term loan. The loan company may take the position that your loan will be paid in full before six years pass and you can file a Chapter 7 bankruptcy again.

In addition, the loan is secured by a vehicle that can be repossessed if you default on the loan. Old tow trucks never die; they just get new paint jobs. Since a reliable vehicle may be a necessity for getting to work every day, you may have no choice but to buy one fairly soon after your debts are discharged. A new car may be easier to finance than a used one, and a used car can turn into more trouble than it's worth. Shop around and get the best vehicle you can afford.

Again, banks or finance companies that had their claims eliminated by a Chapter 7 discharge will not be anxious to do business with you now. However, like the credit card companies, there are other financial institutions that may be willing to take a chance on you. These generally will be companies who charge higher interest rates, so check out all the terms of the contract before making a commitment.

Remember, it's fine to move forward and improve your lifestyle, but consider all deals and contracts carefully. Make sure you're not going to jeopardize your newfound financial stability with unwise and unnecessary purchases. Tailor the payments on a vehicle to fit your current budget. Sometimes it is better to finance a vehicle for a longer time to get lower payments.

Also, if you are a Chapter 13 filer in the midst of a payment plan, keep in mind that any major purchase, such as a new car, must be approved by the court and your Trustee. If you are a Chapter 11 filer, transportation needs should have been figured into your long-range plan of reorganization and should not be an issue after the plan is approved by the court.

Extra Funding

Loans for new vehicles are easier to obtain because the value of the collateral (the new vehicle) is higher and will not depreciate as quickly as the value of a used car.

Can You Buy a House?

You may be able to buy a house and get a mortgage within a short period of time after your debts are discharged by a Chapter 7 filing. There are what are known as sublenders who are willing to underwrite a mortgage loan for someone who has filed bankruptcy; however, the interest rate is going to be substantially higher than a first-class lender's rates. You will also have to come up with a down payment of at least 15 percent of the purchase price of the house.

The potential problems in dealing with a sublender were discussed in a previous chapter that presented advice on obtaining home-equity loans to be used for debt consolidation. These cautionary statements are even more important when you are applying for a first mortgage on a house.

A first mortgage will most likely be for a much larger amount than a second mortgage loan. The greater the liability, the more care should be exercised before the obligation is finalized. Again, if buying a house in the first two years after a bankruptcy has been filed is a necessity, do it with caution and care.

It is possible to get a mortgage from a sublender, pay on it for a few years, and then refinance the house with a better interest rate. The danger in trying to do this is that you never know how the interest rates are going to fluctuate. Sometimes the rate goes up and doesn't come down for a long time. In that case, you may be stuck with the higher rate, which translates into larger payments and little or nothing gained in equity.

NSF Checks

Second-class lenders, or sublenders, generally charge interest rates that are 2 to 6 percent higher than a first-class lender's rates.

A regular, conventional loan on a house with a first-class lender is generally not obtainable for four years after a bankruptcy filing. The four-year waiting period begins on the date of your final discharge. Once this amount of time has passed and you have begun to rebuild your credit rating, a variety of mortgage plans will be open to you.

Some of these loan programs offer good interest rates and reasonable down-payment requirements. As with vehicles, it is generally easier to get financing on a new house than on an older home. This is because contractors enter into agreements with banks and other financial institutions in which the contractor promises to steer buyers their way in exchange for attractive loan programs.

VA and FHA Loans

The Veterans Administration has loan programs for people who have served in the armed forces. The Veterans Administration requires a bankruptcy filer to wait two to four years from the date of discharge. The main benefit of getting a loan through a VA program is that a veteran can buy a house for no money down.

FHA loans, mortgage loans guaranteed by the government or the Federal Housing Administration, may be obtained two years after the date of your final bankruptcy discharge. The Federal Housing Administration also offers a number of programs with good interest rates and low down payments. However, since this is a government agency, there will be a lot more paperwork, and it will generally take longer to get a loan approved.

Bank Notes

If you served in any branch of the armed forces, contact the Veterans Administration to apply for an eligibility certificate that will enable you to participate in a VA loan program. Your lender can provide contact information.

All banks and mortgage companies can process conventional loans, FHA loans, and VA loans. The loan officers will help you complete the paperwork and will explain the advantages of one loan program over another. In addition to the time periods mentioned, most lenders, whether they are doing conventional, FHA, or VA loans, require that the borrower have at least 12 months of good payment and credit history to qualify for a mortgage.

Prequalifying for Your Home Loan

In today's real estate market, sellers and agents generally want a buyer to be prequalified for a mortgage loan before a contract for sale is drawn up. With a bankruptcy on your credit history, it will probably take additional time to get prequalified. Detailed explanations for your bankruptcy filing and the adverse information on your credit report will be required by most lenders.

If there is a real estate foreclosure on your credit history, it makes it all the more difficult to obtain financing on new property. It may take several years for you to establish a credit history positive enough to offset the negativity of a foreclosure. Of course, there are exceptions to every rule. You may find a lender who is willing to work with you. Some lenders judge each applicant on an individual basis and will explore all the possibilities for you.

Mortgage lenders generally obtain credit reports from all three credit bureaus to make sure they have complete information on a borrower. This is another reason why you should also request reports from all the bureaus, so that your information includes everything a lender will be able to access.

Although a mortgage is secured by the house you buy, lenders do not want to be in the real estate business. They can confiscate the property if you default on the mortgage payments, but then they have to go to the trouble and expense of reselling the property to recover their loan amount.

A mortgage is a long-term loan. You are expected to pay on it for 15 to 30 years. Since you can file another Chapter 7 bankruptcy after six years have lapsed, some mortgage companies routinely refuse credit to a borrower who has previously filed a Chapter 7.

Besides your credit history, lenders look at your current employment situation, the probability of your continued employment, and your income-to-debt ratio. Any of these things can work against you. Any of these things can prevent you from obtaining a mortgage loan at a reasonable interest rate.

There is no way to know what a lender's reaction is going to be to your present situation and your past credit history. All you can do is try and see what happens. Even if you are turned down by the lender, you will learn how the process works and be able to use that knowledge to deal with another lender who may be more sympathetic and willing to work with you. If you are working with a reputable real estate company, ask the agent to recommend a loan officer who has been in the business for a reasonable amount of time. An experienced loan officer knows all the ins and outs of working with people with less-than-perfect credit histories.

Don't Let Turn-Downs Get You Down

In the first few years after you've filed bankruptcy, you may find it difficult to obtain credit of any kind. How difficult it is and how long it takes to get back in the good graces of creditors depends on the type of bankruptcy you filed and the number and amount of debts that were discharged. For the most part, you will probably not be able to get any type of unsecured loan from a bank. Even credit card companies may require that you deposit funds into an account that will be held to guarantee the credit limit on the card.

Don't get discouraged and don't be tempted to seek loans from disreputable lenders or those that charge ridiculous interest rates. Avoid any long-term contracts or leases. Although the deal may sound great, you must study the long-range totals of payments, interest, and equity to be gained through the agreement.

Potential creditors will be checking on you. You should be checking on them as well. Make sure that anyone who offers you credit is reputable. Remember the old saying, "A deal that sounds too good to be true usually is."

Second-class lenders and creditors are very adept at selling, and most do not have your best interests in mind. You are the one who must keep your best interests in mind. If someone tells you to sign today because the great deal won't be available tomorrow, drop your pen and run. Your greatest ally is time. Time will enable you check out the creditor and the contract. Time will enable you to rebuild your credit and stay solvent.

Bank Notes

The probability of continued employment is an important factor in qualifying for a loan. Your employer will be asked to provide information on this.

Extra Funding

Remember that by law, you can rescind a loan agreement within three business days of acceptance.

Making a Fresh Start

The importance of your credit status is actually determined by you. The bankruptcy will stay on your report for 7 to 10 years. There is nothing you can do to change that. It is out of your control.

Although you cannot go back and alter the past and erase the damaging information that your credit history contains, you can control what appears on your credit history in the future. That is why it is prudent to check out lenders who are willing to extend credit to you immediately after a bankruptcy. While some of them take advantage of people who have histories of financial trouble, not all of them are disreputable.

As mentioned earlier, some lenders will work with you after a bankruptcy because they know the law and know that you will be unable to file another Chapter 7 bankruptcy for at least six years. That gives them plenty of time to collect payments and interest from you.

Reputable lenders will not use high-pressure tactics to get you to sign a contract. On the other hand, second-class lenders school their representatives in the powers of persuasion. Don't be taken in by their smooth talk and deadline ultimatums.

The type of credit obligations you incur after a bankruptcy should not be undertaken simply to try and show the world that you can control your finances and pay your bills. Don't make unnecessary purchases just because you can. Many people get into financial trouble because they do not take the time to consider all the consequences of a major purchase. Driving that shiny new car may be fun, making the payments on it may offset all the pleasure.

Financial problems often begin because consumers are not willing to wait for things. The loss of a little virtue called patience is what the credit card industry is built on. Somewhere along the way, consumers became impatient, and the concept of "buy now and pay later" was born. This child of the modern generation has grown into a gigantic industry that can swallow you whole if you let it. Take all the time you need to consider your purchases and make sure they will not cause you more problems than they are worth.

Remember that filing bankruptcy is intended to give you a fresh start. You should have been able to retain the things you need for your current lifestyle. As time goes on, you will undoubtedly need to add or replace some of those material items, but each addition or replacement should be carefully considered and researched.

Immediately after a bankruptcy case is closed, the motto to live by may be "Good things come to those who wait." Unless you have an urgent, immediate need, refrain from major purchases. Before your bankruptcy filing, time was an enemy. Creditors were demanding quick results and fast payments that you couldn't deliver.

Now that those demands have been eliminated, time can be your best friend. Move forward leisurely, setting a pace that will enable you to establish the routine that works for you and your new lifestyle.

The Least You Need to Know

➤ Credit cards and short-term loans may be available to you despite your bankruptcy filing.

➤ It will take two to four years from the date your debts were discharged in a bankruptcy case to become eligible for a home mortgage through a first-class lender.

➤ Avoid sublenders with high interest rates and too-good-to-be-true deals.

➤ Many lenders look for 12 months of good payment history before extending credit.

Chapter 22

Rebuilding Your Credit Rating

In This Chapter

➤ Reestablish credit

➤ Avoid impulse buying

➤ Accumulate an emergency fund

➤ Learn from past mistakes

Just as it took many months, maybe even years, for your financial problems to develop, it may take some time for them to totally disappear. Bankruptcy affords a fresh start, but it is not a 100-yard dash to stability and tranquility. It is more like a long-distance marathon, in which the runner needs a certain amount of stamina and determination to finish the race.

Although your debts are gone and your cash flow is greatly improved, you probably will not be able to obtain credit as easily or quickly as you did before the downward spiral into economic disaster began. Many creditors may want to see a steady improvement in your credit report before they finance any new purchases for you.

Slow and Steady Wins the Race

You begin to rebuild your credit from the date your debts are discharged or your payment plan begins. It is a slow process. It requires that you make all payments on time and in full. These payments include every liability and every expense you are expected to pay.

Two of your primary, ongoing expenses are rent or mortgage payment and utility bills. Even though the electric, gas, and water companies do not generally report to the credit bureaus, they are an excellent source of credit references. People who do not have any other kind of established credit are often able to get letters from the utility companies verifying that they have paid their bills in full and on time.

If you have reaffirmed on any debts, make sure those payments are kept current. If you obtain a credit card, use it for essentials only and pay off the balance in full when the bill comes. Don't let the balance accumulate. There is no short cut to establishing a good payment history. It must be done month by month, year by year, at a slow but steady pace.

As time passes, the old delinquent accounts will begin to fade further and further into the past and be replaced by your new, consistent, and reliable payment schedules. Check your credit report from time to time to make sure it contains the correct information and reflects your efforts to improve it. If there are errors on your report that need to be corrected, write to the credit bureau and request that they verify the information and update their records.

If you are having difficulty obtaining any type of credit after your bankruptcy, the following suggestions may help:

➤ Apply for a small loan through the bank or credit union where you have a checking or savings account. If necessary, deposit sufficient funds into a savings account to guarantee the loan amount. Then make every loan payment on time. This will establish a good payment history with the bank and will be reported to the credit bureau.

➤ Apply for a credit card and, if necessary, guarantee the amount of the credit limit by depositing funds into the bank that manages the card. Use the card for an essential expense every month, such as gasoline or groceries. Pay it in full and on time.

➤ Make a substantial down payment on a purchase and arrange for a payment schedule to satisfy the balance. Even paying the balance off in a short period of time, such as 90 days, will help you establish a good payment record. However, don't buy something you really don't need just to do this. That's how you got in trouble the first time around.

Bank Notes

Lenders want to know if a bankruptcy filing was a one-time problem or a sign that the consumer cannot handle credit obligations.

No one can repair your credit but you. You do it slowly and steadily with smart shopping and discipline. The ultimate goal is to demonstrate that you have the ability and the means to pay your bills on time.

No Wild Shopping Sprees

"Shop till you drop" is a slogan that should have new meaning for you now. Shopping too much causes you to drop into debt—deep, dark, unrelenting debt.

If you filed bankruptcy because of circumstances beyond your control, such as job loss or illness, you can skip this section. However, if your financial problems were caused in part by all those shoes, dresses, or suits with designer labels in your closet, you'd better read this section twice.

If your financial problems were caused by too many vacations, fancy sports cars, or a compulsion to own things you don't need just for the fun of it, you may need to read this section every day for the rest of your life.

Impulse buying is not smart. It is not healthy, and therefore it should not be categorized as fun. If bankruptcy didn't curb your desire to clean out the shopping mall, you may need counseling. Get the help you need before you put yourself and your family into economic jeopardy again.

Here are a list of questions you should ask yourself when you're considering a nonessential purchase. A nonessential purchase is anything that you don't really need but that you want anyway.

1. Will buying this item save the rain forests?
2. Will buying this item guarantee world peace?
3. Will buying this item make all politicians honest?

If you can truly answer "yes" to any of these questions, go ahead and complete the purchase. Whatever the price, it will be worth it. Otherwise, walk away and use the money you would have spent for something you or your family needs or put it in the bank for that rainy day when the roof springs a leak. You may not have enough to repair the roof, but a new bucket may come in handy.

Extra Funding

Debtors Anonymous has chapters across the country to help impulse shoppers stay in control. Look in your local telephone directory to locate a chapter near you.

Establish an Emergency Fund

Even if you're not a compulsive shopper, having extra cash in your pocket may be a temptation. After your bankruptcy case has been closed, you will most likely have some extra bucks to spend. That's great. That's one of the reasons you filed bankruptcy, and now is the time to use those dollars to ensure your future.

The best thing you can do with that extra cash is put it into a savings account. If you're not disciplined enough to take it to the bank yourself, arrange for a payroll deduction that is deposited directly into the savings account. That way, the cash is in there before you get a chance to get your hot little hands on it.

Use all the creativity you have stored up inside of you to find new and innovative ways to save money. A big factor in bankruptcy is that most people don't have an emergency fund to fall back on. When trouble lands on their doorstep, it usually has a price tag attached to it. Having the extra funds to handle the problem will keep you from falling behind on your regular payments.

Even if all you can save is the loose change in your pocket each day, do it. Find a cute piggy bank, a tin can, a cup, or whatever works and dump that change in there every night. At the end of each month or week, cart the change to the bank and deposit it.

One word of warning: Bank tellers hate it when people show up with loose change. Before you take yours to the bank, count the coins and roll them in coin wrappers.

Building a savings account is like re-establishing a good credit rating. It takes effort and discipline to develop the habit. You've probably cultivated your share of bad habits during your lifetime. Make the effort to cultivate a good habit, one that will benefit you and yours. If you borrow money, you are expected to repay it. Wouldn't it be nice to own the bank and give yourself a loan whenever the need arose? That's the idea behind a savings account.

The other benefit of having a savings account is that it shows that you are disciplined and in control of your money. Credit applications always ask if you have a checking or savings account. Some even ask for the approximate balance in those accounts. A savings account demonstrates that you are working toward a stable, secure financial future.

A savings account is just one more way to offset the negative information on your credit report. It doesn't have to contain a staggering amount of money; it just has to be open and receiving regular deposits.

Your Brighter Future

A bankruptcy case is often a turning point in a debtor's life. Granted, there may be some people who file bankruptcy petitions every six years. However, for most people, it is a once-in-a-lifetime experience, and once in a lifetime is quite enough for them.

NSF Checks

Some banks charge a fee for the time it takes to count and process loose change.

Regardless of the type of bankruptcy you filed, the process may very well have caused you to reevaluate your priorities and spending habits. Hopefully, a person whose bankruptcy was caused by undisciplined spending may be able to gain control and identify the factors that trigger this behavior. You may have learned how to budget, restrict your spending, and save some money.

For those who were forced into bankruptcy by circumstances they could not foresee or control, there may still be things they can change in their life to make another trip to bankruptcy court improbable.

The establishment of the emergency fund discussed earlier should be a part of everyone's plan for the future. If you can manage to put some funds aside, it will help you maintain expenses when unexpected situations arise that cause financial havoc.

Some of the agencies and solutions that were offered in the opening chapters of this book may be even more helpful after a bankruptcy. Without the stress of collection actions and creditors calling, you can concentrate on making the changes that will enable you to avoid economic pitfalls in the future. Being willing to make changes and explore options is just as important after bankruptcy as it was before the decision was made to file a petition.

For a business owner operating under a Chapter 11 reorganization, pulling all the pieces together and making them fit into your financial plan should have taught you a great deal. Your experience may have made you a better businessperson and possibly a top notch negotiator. Of all the bankruptcy filers, the business operator has the largest task. He or she must be able to make the business a more profitable operation and honor the payment schedule set up for creditors. Many business owners depend on a salary or a percentage of the profits to support themselves and their families. This means the business owners must monitor expenses at home and at the office.

If you are a small business owner, there are a number of organizations that you can turn to for information and advice. One such group is SCORE, which stands for Service Corps of Retired Executives. SCORE has 389 chapters across the United States and a total of 11,000 volunteers who provide a variety of services for the small business. SCORE volunteers come from a diverse background, and chances are the chapter in your area will have an executive who has successfully run a business similar to yours. These retired executives have a wealth of information and experience to share, and there is no charge for the one-on-one counseling sessions.

Bank Notes

If you haven't learned about budgets and good financial planning, you may benefit from educational courses on those subjects.

Through the SCORE Web site, business owners can e-mail questions and concerns and receive a quick response. Visit the Web site at www.score.org. Other contact information for SCORE can be found in Appendix A of this book. Whether you are business owner or an individual, the relief you have obtained through bankruptcy is only the first step in building a secure economic base.

The reasons you filed bankruptcy may have disappeared when the court discharged your debts. However, as you work toward a brighter tomorrow and true financial security, don't forget what those reasons were and how they affected your life. By remembering, you arm yourself with the resolve and determination you need to help you avoid or minimize financial setbacks in the future. If nothing else, you should have learned how to organize your financial affairs; that alone will help you achieve your goals.

Extra Funding

The SCORE organization also sponsors a variety of workshops on subjects such as Smart Staffing, Marketing with Diversity, and Understanding Payroll Taxes.

With an understanding of the legal process, the proper attitude, and a competent attorney, it is possible to survive bankruptcy. Furthermore, it is possible to survive and prosper.

The Least You Need to Know

➤ Repairing your credit requires time and the diligence to make payments consistently and timely.

➤ If impulse shopping is even partially responsible for your bankruptcy filing, seek counseling to avoid repeating your mistakes.

➤ Establishing an emergency fund will help you handle financial setbacks in the future.

➤ The bankruptcy process should have taught you how to organize your financial affairs.

Chapter 23

The Bankruptcy Reform Act of 2001

In This Chapter

➤ Means testing

➤ Homestead exemptions

➤ Miscellaneous proposals

➤ Chapter 12

➤ Abusive creditor practices

The federal Bankruptcy Reform Act has been under construction for a number of years. Banks and credit card companies continue to lobby for changes in the bankruptcy system. The reason is obvious. The credit card companies hold claims that are unsecured, so they are the ones who generally get nothing in a Chapter 7 filing.

Legislators have been trying to get a bill enacted into law since 1998. One version of the reform act was actually approved by both the House of Representatives and the Senate and was sent to the president to be signed into law. President Clinton vetoed it, saying that the provisions were unfair to low-income Americans. With a new party in the White House, the bankruptcy bill has been resurrected and is again making its way through the House of Representatives and the Senate.

This time, there are a few new provisions, and as of this writing, the two legislative groups have not been able to agree on the bill because of the amendments that are being tacked onto the reform act. The House of Representatives approved one version of the new bankruptcy laws, and the Senate approved a different version. The bill must now go to a committee made up of legislators from both groups to hash out a single version everyone can agree on.

If and when the committee is formed and is able to compromise on the issues, the bill will be revised and sent to the president, whoever he or she may be at the time, to be signed into law. The law will take effect six months after the bill is signed. However, there is always the possibility it will be vetoed again.

In this chapter, you will review general information about the pending legislation. If you are reading this book, you are probably contemplating bankruptcy, and therefore you should be aware of the proposed changes that may affect your filing.

Who Will Be Eligible for Chapter 7?

Earlier chapters in this book presented information on means testing and how the pending legislation would force some debtors to file a Chapter 13 rather than a Chapter 7. Means testing exists in the current bankruptcy code. However, the new proposal provides specific guidelines for determining whether a debtor has the ability to repay unsecured debts such as credit card balances.

There are three elements to the pending changes for means testing under the federal bankruptcy code. They are as follows:

1. The definition of current monthly income

2. A list of allowed deductions

3. Defined "trigger points" for determining the ability to repay unsecured debts

"Current monthly income" is described in the bill as a monthly average of all the income received by the debtor during the six months preceding the *date of determination*.

The current monthly income of the debtor includes regular contributions to household expenses made by other parties. In other words, if your mother-in-law lives with you and gives you grocery money, she would be contributing to the household, and that contribution would be included in your total income for the month. Social security benefits are excluded from the current monthly income amount.

The allowed monthly deductions vary a little depending on which version of the pending legislation you are reviewing, but the primary deductions allowed are the same. They are as follows:

➤ Set allowances for food, clothing, personal care, transportation, housing, and entertainment, as established by the Internal Revenue Service for negotiating the payment of delinquent taxes

➤ Actual expenses of the debtor in categories recognized by the Internal Revenue Service but not assigned a maximum limit

Dollar Signs

The **date of determination** for the means testing is defined as the last day of the calendar month that precedes the bankruptcy filing.

➤ $\frac{1}{60}$ of all secured debt due in the five years following the bankruptcy filing and of all past-due debt secured by property necessary for support

➤ $\frac{1}{60}$ of all priority debt

➤ Charitable contributions of up to 15 percent of gross income

As you can see, if this bill passes as outlined above, lawyers may have to take some accounting courses just to determine the current monthly income of their clients. Once the current monthly income is figured, the lawyer can move on to the next issue covered by the pending legislation, the *trigger points*.

The bottom line, or "trigger points" as our legislators call them, determine whether a debtor is eligible to file a Chapter 7 petition. If a debtor has $166.67 left over after the allowed deductions have been subtracted from the average monthly income, he or she does not qualify for a Chapter 7 filing regardless of the amount of general unsecured debts the debtor may have. Or if the debtor has at least $100 of income left over, and the income is sufficient to pay at least 25 percent of the debtor's unsecured debt over a five-year period, he or she will be required to file a Chapter 13 repayment plan.

The debtor will be required to file a statement showing how his or her means test was calculated, and that statement is supposed to be distributed to the creditors named in the petition.

The bill does have a provision for "special circumstances" in which a debtor may document situations or problems that would necessitate expenses not covered by the allowed deductions. In these cases, the amount of leftover income might be adjusted to fall below the trigger points.

The purpose of the bankruptcy reform bill is to close up loopholes in the law and prevent people from abusing it. However, the fact remains that most people who file bankruptcy have generally been struggling for years to make their payments. If they could pay their debts, they would. They can't, so they seek relief in bankruptcy court.

Dollar Signs

Trigger points are the specified limits that will determine whether a debtor is eligible to file a Chapter 7 or will be required to file a Chapter 13 repayment plan.

NSF Checks

A debtor who is determined by the "trigger points" test to have abused the bankruptcy system will have his or her Chapter 7 case dismissed or converted to a Chapter 13, and his or her attorney may be assessed a fine.

A Proposed Ceiling on Homestead Exemptions

The U.S. Senate attached an amendment to its version of the bankruptcy reform bill. Some of the senators explain this addition to the legislation by relating stories about wealthy citizens who have filed bankruptcy. These rich folks had millions of dollars in debts discharged but, at the same time, were able to retain luxurious homes valued in the millions. The point is that these people took their cash and invested it in million-dollar homes in states that have no limit on homestead exemptions. This, of course, sheltered the cash from the creditors and left the debtors sitting pretty after the bankruptcy filing.

You may recall that the homestead exemptions in the state of Texas, for example, allow a single debtor to retain 100 acres of property and the dwelling or improvements thereon. A debtor with a family may retain 200 acres and the dwelling or improvements thereon.

There is no limit on the value of the acreage or the house built on the acreage. Unlimited homestead exemptions such as this also exist in Iowa, Florida, Kansas, and South Dakota.

The tacked-on amendment calls for a limit of $125,000 on all homestead exemptions. Of course, the senators and congressman from Iowa, Florida, Kansas, South Dakota, and Texas oppose the limiting of the homestead exemption. The voters from their states expect these legislators to prevent this measure from being approved.

At first glance, you may think that this amendment to the bankruptcy reform bill has no real bearing on the average person, who is living in a small house with a big mortgage and is struggling to pay bills, feed the kids, and keep the old car running. In fact, the exemption limit of $125,000 is actually higher than the homestead exemptions allowed in most states. However, property values are increasing all over the country. A simple two-bedroom house in the state of California costs more than $200,000. This is not a luxury home; it's a standard home with basic features.

Extra Funding

The actor Burt Reynolds filed bankruptcy in the state of Florida. It is reported that his discharged debts totaled about $10 million, but he was allowed to keep a house worth $2.5 million in that state.

One congressman complained that his constituents purchased homes for $50,000 that were now valued at $200,000. Those people would be forced to liquidate their homes under the provisions of the proposed amendment. As you might imagine, this amendment is causing a good deal of debate and may possibly lead to the failure of the bill itself.

Still another provision connected to this amendment requires that a person reside in a state for 730 days (two years) before claiming the exemptions of that state. It is believed that some debtors relocate to states where the exemptions are more favorable, reside there for a short time, and then file bankruptcy. Again, this is not something the average person could do; it's a ploy of the wealthy to save their assets from creditors and the bankruptcy estate in a Chapter 7 filing.

Extra Funding

Some politicians believe that limiting the homestead exemption in all states will threaten a 130-year-old right of the states and may result in individual states challenging the provision if the bill becomes law.

Still another section of the new bill tacks on a provision that excludes the value of improvements made to the homestead intended to hinder or delay creditors during the seven years prior to the bankruptcy filing. You may recall that in the fictional case presented in previous chapters, Jack and Jill sold assets that would have gone into the bankruptcy estate and used the cash to make home improvements. This provision would prohibit such action prior to a bankruptcy filing.

Other Proposed Amendments and Provisions

A change to the redemption process is also included in the Bankruptcy Reform Act that would pretty much eliminate redemption as an option for most debtors. The provision states that a redemption would require full payment of the amount of the claim, and the creditor's claim would be based on the retail replacement value of the collateral. To make it even more difficult, the bill goes on to say that if a debtor does not redeem or reaffirm on a secured claim, the automatic stay is lifted.

Although tax liens are not dischargeable under the current bankruptcy code, they are lower on the priority payment list than family support obligations. The pending legislation would move the tax liens up in priority status. Therefore, if property with a tax lien were sold by the Trustee in a Chapter 7 case, the proceeds from the sale would go to satisfy the tax lien before support was paid.

The replacement value issue appears in another section of the bill dealing with motor vehicles. It would create a change in the "cramdown" provision for vehicles that were purchased within three to five years (the Senate version says three years, the House version says five years). The value of the vehicle could not be reduced to less than the amount of the remaining claim. The value of the vehicle would be determined by retail replacement value. Under the current laws, the claim on motor vehicles can be reduced in accordance with the current market value of the vehicle.

There are also some proposed changes in the filing of income tax returns. Debtors would have to provide copies of their most recent tax returns to the Trustee seven days prior to the first meeting of creditors. The information may then be made available to any party with an interest in the bankruptcy. This is going to be a muddy area because it involves privacy issues. The bill provides that privacy regulations be adopted and defined by the federal court administration.

> **Bank Notes**
>
> Under the "cramdown" provision of the current rules, a creditor can be forced to reduce a claim to the amount of the market value of the collateral.

Another provision requires that Chapter 13 debtors file any tax returns past due for the four years preceding bankruptcy within specified time periods that begin with the first meeting of creditors.

When it comes to federal income tax, the best thing you can do for yourself is to file all tax returns in a timely manner and make payment arrangements with the Internal Revenue Service for any unpaid tax liabilities. Don't wait until you get into bankruptcy court to attend to tax matters.

Also related to Chapter 13 cases, the bill provides that confirmation hearings may not take place until at least 20 days after the 341 meeting. Under current law, the confirmation could be done sooner. The existing bankruptcy code allows debtors to file a Chapter 7 bankruptcy every six years. The reform act extends the time period between bankruptcy filings to eight years.

Both versions of the reform act contain provisions that require audits conducted by certified or licensed public accountants of all information filed by the debtor in at least 0.4 percent of consumer cases. Chances of your case being subjected to an audit sound pretty slim, but it will probably depend on the size and number of cases filed in your geographical area.

In addition, both bills require that debtors receive some type of debt counseling within 180 days prior to filing a bankruptcy petition. Exceptions to this provision would be made based on hardship circumstances, in which case the debtor would receive the counseling within 30 days after the filing date of the bankruptcy case.

Extra Funding

If this legislation becomes law, your attorney would be able to advise you concerning the counseling and educational programs.

Pilot educational programs for debtor financial management would be tested in six judicial districts over an 18-month period and then be evaluated for effectiveness and cost. Debtors might be denied a discharge until they complete the program, but telephone and Internet courses would be permissible.

One last provision of the proposed bill puts family support payments before the administration costs of the bankruptcy case in the list of priority payments. This would place the support payments in first place on the list.

As you can see, the proposed Bankruptcy Reform Act targets specific areas of the bankruptcy code. These are areas that are considered to have loopholes that allow abuse of the bankruptcy system.

Chapter 12

Chapter 12, which is similar to Chapter 13, is for family farmers. It is for debtors whose primary source of income is the operation of a family farm. The new bill proposes making Chapter 12 a permanent part of the bankruptcy code, instead of a provision that expires every few years and has to be renewed.

New Rules for Creditors

Although specific provisions for creditors are not outlined in the Bankruptcy Reform Act, part of the reform process is supposed to impose stricter rules on creditors. Like the consumer provisions of the bankruptcy bill, these restrictions may never be enacted into law. However, some of the concerns voiced by consumer groups and legislators are worth repeating here. If nothing else, it will help you use caution when dealing with the credit card companies.

Offers arrive in mailboxes across the country on a daily basis. Consumers are bombarded with preapproved credit cards, credit cards with low rates, and high credit limits. Many consumers accept these cards without realizing that the tiny printing on the back of the form is actually a contract.

When you accept the offer and sign the form, you are agreeing to all those terms and conditions. The terms for a low-interest card generally state that after a specified time period, the interest will rise to the regular rate, which can be in excess of 20 percent. The fine print that most people don't bother to read also states that if you miss a payment or are late with a payment, the low rate is rescinded and the higher rate takes effect.

Some legislators want to require that the credit card companies disclose this "fine print" information in big print, advising consumers of the consequences of missing a payment or being late more than once. Some believe that the credit card statement itself should have an added feature that advises the customer of how long it will take to pay off the credit card balance if he or she makes only the minimum payment each month. Many people do not realize that it will take them years to pay off a balance that is compounded with interest charges each day.

Our country has truth-in-lending laws for other types of credit transactions. If you purchase a home or a car, you receive a statement that tells you exactly how many payments will have to be made, the amount of the payments, and how much you will actually be paying in interest and principle over the life of the loan. The credit card industry is basically giving out loans, so they should be held to the same standards of truth in lending. Will this ever happen? Perhaps. Or maybe like the bankruptcy reform bill, it will take years before such measures are enacted into law.

In the meantime, until the Bankruptcy Reform Act is enacted into law, all bankruptcy filings will be handled in accordance with the federal bankruptcy code and the exemptions of your home state that are currently in effect.

Remember that the bill does not prevent a truly insolvent debtor from obtaining relief under a Chapter 7 bankruptcy filing. The main purpose of the reform act is to require debtors who have the means to pay a portion of their liabilities to do so. While the passage of new bankruptcy regulations would benefit the banks and credit card companies, it will also focus attention on some of the problems these financial institutions may have brought upon themselves.

Some believe that the credit card companies have lobbied for changes to cut the losses they have experienced because of their own business practices, such as extending credit to high-risk borrowers. Although making credit card companies adhere to the same rules that govern other types of loan transactions is probably not in the near future, there are some steps that legislators are considering that would address some of the problems.

The following solutions are being considered:

➤ Studies are being considered that would determine whether credit card companies are offering credit to consumers without verifying their employment status or their ability to make payments.

There are many claims that credit cards have been issued in the names of people who are deceased or underage. In today's world, 10 year olds with credit cards in their names could successfully make purchases over the telephone or the Internet.

Recently, merchants have begun to ask customers to produce a photo ID along with the credit card when charging a purchase. This is a good practice. It protects the merchant as well as the credit card holders.

➤ Require credit card companies to disclose payment and interest terms in a better, clearer manner.

➤ Prohibit credit card companies from closing accounts that are paid off each month instead of letting the balance revolve and grow.

Not many companies cancel accounts that are paid in full each month. The goal of the credit card companies is to keep customers on the books for as long as possible, bombarding them with all sorts of enticing offers. The companies know that most people eventually will fall into the ever-spinning cycle of revolving credit.

Bank Notes

One of the ways consumers get into trouble is through the deceptive practices credit card companies use to attract new cardholders.

As Congress and consumer advocates try to sort out all the problems of the credit industry, it continues to grow. As the credit industry grows, so does the number of consumers who find themselves in trouble. The American Bankruptcy Institute reports that bankruptcies in the United States have risen steadily over the last 20 years. It also estimates that more than 97 percent of bankruptcies are filed by individuals rather than businesses.

The connection between the ease with which credit can be obtained these days and the escalating bankruptcy rate is obvious. Therefore, the blame must be shared by both the credit card companies and the consumers.

The goal of this book is to detail the bankruptcy laws in a clear and concise fashion, allowing the average person to understand how the system works and how it can be used to obtain relief from debt. It is also intended to help people survive bankruptcy and establish a secure financial future. Solutions to long-term, sizeable problems usually come about through education and increased awareness. Hopefully, this book has provided the reader with both.

The Least You Need to Know

➤ The pending laws will not go into effect until six months after the president signs the bill.

➤ An amendment to the bill attempts to put a cap on the homestead exemptions.

➤ Redemptions allowed under the new law would require the debtor to pay the creditor the replacement retail value instead of the resale value of the property.

➤ Bankruptcies filed before this bill becomes law are subject to the federal bankruptcy code and exemptions that are in effect at the time of filing.

Resource Directory

Attorney Referral Services

American Bar Association
541 N. Fairbanks Ct.
Chicago, IL 60611
312-988-5000
www.abanet.org

Attorney Finder
P.O. Box 5530
Mesa, AZ 85211
602-253-7344
www.attorneyfinder.com

LawInfo.com
1782 La Costa Meadows Dr., Suite 100
San Marco, CA 92069
1-800-397-3743
www.lawinfo.com

Credit and Debt Counseling Services and Organizations

National Foundation for Credit Counseling
801 Roeder Rd., Suite 900
Silver Springs, MD 20910
1-800-388-2227
questions@nfcc.org

American Consumer Credit Counseling
24 Crescent St.
Waltham, MA 02453
1-800-769-3571
help@consumercredit.com

Association of Independent Consumer Credit Counseling Agencies (AICCCA)
11350 Random Hills Rd., Suite 800
Fairfax, VA 22030-6044
703-934-6118

Debtors Anonymous
P.O. Box 920888
Needham, MA 02492-0009
781-453-2743
new@debtorsanonymous.org

Federal Job Training/Retraining Programs

The Employment and Trade Administration
www.doleta.gov

One Stop Career Center

ETA-sponsored job placement and training programs in 10 regions across the country. The following list gives contact numbers for each region and state covered:

> Region 1: CT, ME, MA, NH, RI, VT (617-565-3630)
>
> Region 2: NJ, NY, PR, VI (212-337-2139)
>
> Region 3: DE, DC, MD, PA, VA, WV (215-596-6336)
>
> Region 4: AL, FL, GA, KY, MS, NC, SC, TN (404-562-2092)
>
> Region 5: IL, IN, MI, MN, OH, WI (312-353-0313)
>
> Region 6: AR, LA, NM, OK, TX (214-767-8263)
>
> Region 7: IA, KS, MO, NE (816-426-3796)
>
> Region 8: CO, MT, ND, SD, UT, WY (303-844-1650)
>
> Region 9: AZ, CA, HI, NV, GU (415-975-4610)
>
> Region 10: AK, ID, OR, WA (206-553-7700)

Education and Student Loan Information

U.S. Department of Education
400 Maryland Ave. SW
Washington, DC 20202
1-800-USA-LEARN
www.ed.gov

Sallie Mae Servicing Corporation
P.O. Box 9500
Wilkes Barre, PA 18773-9500
1-888-272-5543

Health Organizations

American Cancer Society
1-800-ACS-2345
www.2.cancer.org

American Heart Association
National Center
77272 Greenville Ave.
Dallas, TX 75231
1-800-AHA-USA1
www.americanheart.org

American Diabetes Association
1701 N. Beauregard St.
Alexandria, VA 22311
1-800-342-2383
www.diabetes.org

Easter Seals
230 W. Monroe St., Suite 1800
Chicago, IL 60606
1-800-221-6827
www.easter-seals.org

Barter and Trade Organization

National Association of Trade Exchanges
24600 Center Ridge Rd., Suite 480
Westlake, OH 44145
440-835-3654
www.nate.org

Credit Bureaus

Equifax Credit Bureau
P.O. Box 740241
Atlanta, GA 30374-0241
1-800-548-4548 (residents of GA, VT, MA)
1-800-233-7654 (residents of MD)
1-800-685-1111 (all other states)
www.equifax.com

Experian (formerly TRW Credit Bureau)
P.O. Box 949
Allen, TX 75013-0949
1-888-397-3742
www.experian.com

Trans Union Corporation
Consumer Disclosure Center
P.O. Box 390
Springfield, PA 19064-0390
1-800-916-8800
1-800-682-7654
www.tuc.com

Resources for Small Business Owners

Service Corps of Retired Executives (SCORE)
1-800-634-0245
www.score.org

Glossary

These terms are related to bankruptcy and the federal bankruptcy code:

341 meeting   The first meeting of creditors in a bankruptcy case that is required under section 341 of the federal bankruptcy code.

adversary proceeding   A lawsuit filed through the bankruptcy court that is related to the debtor's case.

administrative claims   The costs of administrating a bankruptcy case.

automatic stay   A court order that prohibits creditors and collectors from taking collection actions against a debtor who has filed a bankruptcy petition.

bankruptcy code   Title 11 of the United States code that sets forth the rules and regulations that govern the bankruptcy system.

bankruptcy estate   The property and interests of a debtor that are placed under the jurisdiction of the court and Trustee and held for the purpose of generating funds to be distributed to creditors.

bar date   The last date for filing a proof of claim.

breach of peace   Committing an unlawful act to repossess property of a debtor.

Chapter 7   A bankruptcy action that calls for the liquidation of a debtor's nonexempt assets to pay creditors and then relieves the debtor of the obligation of dischargeable debts.

Chapter 11   A bankruptcy action primarily used by businesses, in which a plan of reorganization is developed that allows the debtor to keep control of assets and operate the business while making payments to creditors.

Chapter 12   A bankruptcy action for family farmers that allows them to pay their debts over a prescribed time period from future earnings.

Chapter 13   A bankruptcy action for regular wage earners that allows them to develop a repayment plan under which creditors are paid all or part of the claims over a three- to five-year period.

Chapter 20   The term used when a Chapter 13 bankruptcy petition is converted to a Chapter 7.

collateral   Property that secures a loan.

confirmation   The court order that approvals the plans developed in a Chapter 11 or Chapter 13 bankruptcy case.

conversion   The process by which one chapter of bankruptcy is changed to another chapter of bankruptcy.

cramdown   The process by which a creditor's claim is reduced by order of the bankruptcy court.

creditor   A person or company that holds a claim or debt against a debtor.

debtor   A person or company that owes a debt to the creditor.

debtor in possession   The debtor in a Chapter 11 bankruptcy case who remains in control of assets and assumes the role of Trustee.

default   The failure to pay a debt in a timely manner.

denial of discharge   The termination of a bankruptcy case due to fraud or misrepresentation wherein the court refuses to order relief from claims for the debtor.

discharge   The legal elimination of debts and claims through the bankruptcy process.

dischargeable debts   Debts that may be discharged through a bankruptcy filing.

disclosure statement   A detailed account of the debtor's financial condition that must accompany any plan of reorganization and be approved by the court.

dismissal   The termination of a bankruptcy case without a denial or discharge of debts.

disposable earnings   The income remaining after all expenses allowed by law have been deducted.

examiner   An officer of the court appointed to investigate any allegations of mismanagement or misconduct by a debtor in a bankruptcy case.

exempt   Property that is excluded from the bankruptcy estate by federal or state laws and therefore is not available to satisfy the claims of creditors.

exemptions   Lists of the types and values of properties protected from the claims of creditors by federal and state laws.

fiduciary   A person or organization with the responsibility of acting on behalf of another. The fiduciary is required to act with good faith, diligence, and loyalty toward the represented entity.

fraudulent conveyance   The transfer of property to another person without reasonable compensation in order to keep the property from the claims of creditors or the bankruptcy estate.

garnishment   A legal procedure by which a creditor claims a portion of a debtor's salary in payment of a debt.

holdouts   Holders of claims who refuse to accept a plan of reorganization in a Chapter 11 bankruptcy case.

homestead   The house in which you reside.

impairment class   A class of claims that will not be paid in full under a Chapter 11 plan of reorganization.

judgment   The formal order of a court to pay a claim after a lawsuit.

lien   An interest in property that secures a debt or judgment.

liquidated debt   A debt that has a value that can be precisely calculated.

no-asset case   A bankruptcy case in which the debtor has no nonexempt assets that can be transferred to the bankruptcy estate.

nondischargeable   A debt that cannot be eliminated through a bankruptcy action.

objective futility   The inability of a debtor to successfully reorganize under Chapter 11.

oversecured claim   A debt that is secured by collateral with a value that exceeds the amount of the claim.

personal property   Property that is not real estate or permanently affixed to real estate.

petition   The document that is filed with the court to begin a bankruptcy case.

preference   A transfer or a payment to a creditor for a claim that is made within a certain timeframe before the filing of a bankruptcy petition.

prepetition   Claims or actions that take place before the filing of a bankruptcy petition.

priority   A provision of the bankruptcy code that establishes the order in which claims are to be paid.

promissory note   The document signed by a debtor that promises to pay the claim described therein.

proof of claim   A form filed with the court by a creditor to establish a claim against a debtor.

reaffirmation   A legal agreement between a creditor and a debtor to retain the terms and conditions of a debt, such as a mortgage or car loan.

redemption   The process by which a debtor pays a creditor all or part of a claim in order to retain collateral.

relief from stay   A court order that lifts the automatic stay and allows a creditor to pursue collection activities or remedies against a debtor or property in bankruptcy.

repossess   The action that a creditor takes to retrieve collateral for a claim that is in default.

schedules   Required lists of assets, liabilities, income, and expenses that are part of a bankruptcy petition.

secured debts   Claims or loans that are guaranteed by the value of collateral or property

security agreement   An additional document signed when a debt is secured that specifically identifies the collateral.

Trustee   A court-appointed official who monitors and presides over a bankruptcy case and administers the bankruptcy estate.

undersecured claim   A claim that is secured by collateral valued at less than the amount of the debt.

unsecured debts   Debts that are not guaranteed by collateral or property.

Official Bankruptcy Forms

The bankruptcy forms and worksheets reproduced in this appendix are here for your use. These forms were made available by the Federal Judiciary Administrative Office of the U.S. Courts. You may want to double-check to make sure you have the most current version of these forms by visiting http://www.uscourts.gov/bankform/, as they are subject to change.

List of Forms (in Order of Appearance)

1. Voluntary Petition
2. Voluntary Petition—Page 2
3. Exhibit "A"
4. Declaration under Penalty of Perjury on Behalf of a Corporation or Partnership
5. Application and Order to Pay Filing Fee in Installments
6. List of Creditors Holding 20 Largest Unsecured Claims
7. Involuntary Petition
8. Schedules
9. Summary of Schedules
10. Schedule A—Real Property
11. Schedule B—Personal Property
12. Schedule B—Continuation Sheet 1
13. Schedule B—Continuation Sheet 2
14. Schedule C—Property Claimed As Exempt
15. Schedule D—Creditors Holding Secured Claims
16. Schedule D—Continuation Sheet
17. Schedule E—Creditors Holding Unsecured Priority Claims
18. Schedule E—Continuation Sheet
19. Schedule F—Creditors Holding Unsecured Nonpriority Claims
20. Schedule F—Continuation Sheet
21. Schedule G—Executory Contracts and Unexpired Leases
22. Schedule H—Codebtors
23. Schedule I—Current Income of Individual Debtor(s)
24. Schedule J—Current Expenditures of Individual Debtor(s)

25. Declaration Concerning Debtor's Schedules

26. Statement of Financial Affairs

27. Individual Debtor's Statement of Intention

28. Notice of Commencement of Case Under the Bankruptcy Code, Meeting of Creditors, and Deadlines

29. Form B9A Chapter 7 Individual or Joint Debtor No Asset Case

30. Form B9B Chapter 7 Corporation/Partnership No Asset Case

31. Form B9C Chapter 7 Individual or Joint Debtor Asset Case

32. Form B9D Chapter 7 Corporation/Partnership Asset Case

33. Form B9E Chapter 11 Indidual or Joint Debtor Case

34. Form B9E (ALT.) Chapter 11 Individual or Joint Debtor Case

35. Form B9F Chapter 11 Corporation/Partnership Asset Case

36. Form B9F (ALT.) Chapter 11 Corporation/Partnership Asset Case

37. Form B9G Chapter 12 Individual or Joint Debtor Family Farmer

38. Form B9H Chapter 12 Corporation/Partnership Family Farmer

39. Form B9I Chapter 13 Case

40. Proof of Claim

41. General Power of Attorney

42. Special Power of Attorney

43. Order and Notice for Hearing on Disclosure Statement

44. Order Approving Disclosure Statement and Fixing Time for Filing Acceptances or Rejections of Plan, Combined with Notice Thereof

45. Ballot for Accepting or Rejecting a Plan

46. Order Confirming Plan

47. Caption (Full)

48. Caption (Short Title)

49. Caption of Complaint in Adversary Proceeding Filed by a Debtor

50. Caption for Use in Adversary Proceeding Other than for a Complaint Filed by a Debtor

51. Notice of Appeal under 28 U.S.C. § 158(a) or (b) from a Judgment, Order, or Decree of a Bankruptcy Judge

52. Discharge of Debtor

53. Certification and Signature of Non-Attorney Bankruptcy Petition Preparer (See 11 U.S.C. § 110)

54. Notice of Motion or Objection

55. Notice of Objection to Claim

(Official Form 1) (9/97)

FORM B1	**United States Bankruptcy Court** _____District of_____	**Voluntary Petition**

Name of Debtor (if individual, enter Last, First, Middle):	Name of Joint Debtor (Spouse) (Last, First, Middle):
All Other Names used by the Debtor in the last 6 years (include married, maiden, and trade names):	All Other Names used by the Joint Debtor in the last 6 years (include married, maiden, and trade names):
Soc. Sec./Tax I.D. No. (if more than one, state all):	Soc. Sec./Tax I.D. No. (if more than one, state all):
Street Address of Debtor (No. & Street, City, State & Zip Code):	Street Address of Joint Debtor (No. & Street, City, State & Zip Code):
County of Residence or of the Principal Place of Business:	County of Residence or of the Principal Place of Business:
Mailing Address of Debtor (if different from street address):	Mailing Address of Joint Debtor (if different from street address):

Location of Principal Assets of Business Debtor
(if different from street address above):

Information Regarding the Debtor (Check the Applicable Boxes)

Venue (Check any applicable box)
- ☐ Debtor has been domiciled or has had a residence, principal place of business, or principal assets in this District for 180 days immediately preceding the date of this petition or for a longer part of such 180 days than in any other District.
- ☐ There is a bankruptcy case concerning debtor's affiliate, general partner, or partnership pending in this District.

Type of Debtor (Check all boxes that apply)
- ☐ Individual(s)
- ☐ Corporation
- ☐ Partnership
- ☐ Other_____
- ☐ Railroad
- ☐ Stockbroker
- ☐ Commodity Broker

Nature of Debts (Check one box)
- ☐ Consumer/Non-Business
- ☐ Business

Chapter 11 Small Business (Check all boxes that apply)
- ☐ Debtor is a small business as defined in 11 U.S.C. § 101
- ☐ Debtor is and elects to be considered a small business under 11 U.S.C. § 1121(e) (Optional)

Chapter or Section of Bankruptcy Code Under Which the Petition is Filed (Check one box)
- ☐ Chapter 7
- ☐ Chapter 9
- ☐ Chapter 11
- ☐ Chapter 12
- ☐ Chapter 13
- ☐ Sec. 304 - Case ancillary to foreign proceeding

Filing Fee (Check one box)
- ☐ Full Filing Fee attached
- ☐ Filing Fee to be paid in installments (Applicable to individuals only) Must attach signed application for the court's consideration certifying that the debtor is unable to pay fee except in installments. Rule 1006(b). See Official Form No. 3.

Statistical/Administrative Information (Estimates only)
- ☐ Debtor estimates that funds will be available for distribution to unsecured creditors.
- ☐ Debtor estimates that, after any exempt property is excluded and administrative expenses paid, there will be no funds available for distribution to unsecured creditors.

THIS SPACE IS FOR COURT USE ONLY

Estimated Number of Creditors	1-15	16-49	50-99	100-199	200-999	1000-over
	☐	☐	☐	☐	☐	☐

Estimated Assets	$0 to $50,000	$50,001 to $100,000	$100,001 to $500,000	$500,001 to $1 million	$1,000,001 to $10 million	$10,000,001 to $50 million	$50,000,001 to $100 million	More than $100 million
	☐	☐	☐	☐	☐	☐	☐	☐

Estimated Debts	$0 to $50,000	$50,001 to $100,000	$100,001 to $500,000	$500,001 to $1 million	$1,000,001 to $10 million	$10,000,001 to $50 million	$50,000,001 to $100 million	More than $100 million
	☐	☐	☐	☐	☐	☐	☐	☐

(Official Form 1) (9/97)

Voluntary Petition *(This page must be completed and filed in every case)*	Name of Debtor(s):	**FORM B1**, Page 2

Prior Bankruptcy Case Filed Within Last 6 Years (If more than one, attach additional sheet)		
Location Where Filed:	Case Number:	Date Filed:

Pending Bankruptcy Case Filed by any Spouse, Partner or Affiliate of this Debtor (If more than one, attach additional sheet)		
Name of Debtor:	Case Number:	Date Filed:
District:	Relationship:	Judge:

Signatures

Signature(s) of Debtor(s) (Individual/Joint)

I declare under penalty of perjury that the information provided in this petition is true and correct.

[If petitioner is an individual whose debts are primarily consumer debts and has chosen to file under chapter 7] I am aware that I may proceed under chapter 7, 11, 12 or 13 of title 11, United States Code, understand the relief available under each such chapter, and choose to proceed under chapter 7.

I request relief in accordance with the chapter of title 11, United States Code, specified in this petition.

X _____
Signature of Debtor

X _____
Signature of Joint Debtor

_____
Telephone Number (If not represented by attorney)

_____
Date

Signature of Debtor (Corporation/Partnership)

I declare under penalty of perjury that the information provided in this petition is true and correct, and that I have been authorized to file this petition on behalf of the debtor.

The debtor requests relief in accordance with the chapter of title 11, United States Code, specified in this petition.

X _____
Signature of Authorized Individual

_____
Printed Name of Authorized Individual

_____
Title of Authorized Individual

_____
Date

Signature of Attorney

X _____
Signature of Attorney for Debtor(s)

_____
Printed Name of Attorney for Debtor(s)

_____
Firm Name

_____
Address

_____

_____
Telephone Number

_____
Date

Signature of Non-Attorney Petition Preparer

I certify that I am a bankruptcy petition preparer as defined in 11 U.S.C. § 110, that I prepared this document for compensation, and that I have provided the debtor with a copy of this document.

_____
Printed Name of Bankruptcy Petition Preparer

_____
Social Security Number

_____
Address

_____

Names and Social Security numbers of all other individuals who prepared or assisted in preparing this document:

If more than one person prepared this document, attach additional sheets conforming to the appropriate official form for each person.

X _____
Signature of Bankruptcy Petition Preparer

_____
Date

A bankruptcy petition preparer's failure to comply with the provisions of title 11 and the Federal Rules of Bankruptcy Procedure may result in fines or imprisonment or both 11 U.S.C. §110; 18 U.S.C. §156.

Exhibit A

(To be completed if debtor is required to file periodic reports (e.g., forms 10K and 10Q) with the Securities and Exchange Commission pursuant to Section 13 or 15(d) of the Securities Exchange Act of 1934 and is requesting relief under chapter 11)

☐ Exhibit A is attached and made a part of this petition.

Exhibit B

(To be completed if debtor is an individual whose debts are primarily consumer debts)

I, the attorney for the petitioner named in the foregoing petition, declare that I have informed the petitioner that [he or she] may proceed under chapter 7, 11, 12, or 13 of title 11, United States Code, and have explained the relief available under each such chapter.

X _____
Signature of Attorney for Debtor(s)   Date

Form B1, Exh.A (9/97)

Exhibit "A"

[If debtor is required to file periodic reports (*e.g.*, forms 10K and 10Q) with the Securities and Exchange Commission pursuant to Section 13 or 15(d) of the Securities Exchange Act of 1934 and is requesting relief under chapter 11 of the Bankruptcy Code, this Exhibit "A" shall be completed and attached to the petition.]

[Caption as in Form 16B]

Exhibit "A" to Voluntary Petition

1.　　If any of the debtor's securities are registered under Section 12 of the Securities Exchange Act of 1934, the SEC file number is _____.

2.　　The following financial data is the latest available information and refers to the debtor's condition on _____.

a.　　Total assets　　　　　　　　　　　　　　　　$ _____

b.　　Total debts (including debts listed in 2.c., below)　　$ _____

　　　　　　　　　　　　　　　　　　　　　　　　　　　　Approximate
　　　　　　　　　　　　　　　　　　　　　　　　　　　　number of
　　　　　　　　　　　　　　　　　　　　　　　　　　　　holders

c.　　Debt securities held by more than 500 holders.

　　　secured / /　　　unsecured / /　　subordinated / /　　$ _____　　_____

　　　secured / /　　　unsecured / /　　subordinated / /　　$_____　　_____

　　　secured / /　　　unsecured / /　　subordinated / /　　$ _____　　_____

　　　secured / /　　　unsecured / /　　subordinated / /　　$_____　　_____

　　　secured / /　　　unsecured / /　　subordinated / /　　$_____　　_____

d.　　Number of shares of preferred stock　　　_____　　_____

e.　　Number of shares common stock　　　　_____　　_____

　　　Comments, if any: _____
　　　_____
　　　_____

3.　　Brief description of debtor's business: _____
　　　_____
　　　_____

4.　　List the names of any person who directly or indirectly owns, controls, or holds, with power to vote, 5% or more of the voting securities of debtor:
　　　_____
　　　_____
　　　_____

203

Form B2
6/90

Form 2. DECLARATION UNDER PENALTY OF PERJURY
ON BEHALF OF A CORPORATION OR PARTNERSHIP

I, [the president *or* other officer *or* an authorized agent of the corporation] [*or* a member *or* an authorized agent of the partnership] named as the debtor in this case, declare under penalty of perjury that I have read the foregoing [list *or* schedule *or* amendment *or* other document (describe)] and that it is true and correct to the best of my information and belief.

Date _____

Signature _____

_____
(Print Name and Title)

Form B3 (Official Form 3)
(9/97)

Form 3. APPLICATION AND ORDER TO PAY FILING FEE IN INSTALLMENTS

[Caption as in Form 16B.]

APPLICATION TO PAY FILING FEE IN INSTALLMENTS

1.   In accordance with Fed. R. Bankr. P. 1006, I apply for permission to pay the Filing Fee amounting to $_____ in installments.

2.   I certify that I am unable to pay the Filing Fee except in installments.

3.   I further certify that I have not paid any money or transferred any property to an attorney for services in connection with this case and that I will neither make any payment nor transfer any property for services in connection with this case until the filing fee is paid in full.

4.   I propose the following terms for the payment of the Filing Fee.*

   $ _____   Check one ☐   With the filing of the petition, or
                                 ☐   On or before _____
   $ _____ on or before _____

   $ _____ on or before _____

   $ _____ on or before _____

*   The number of installments proposed shall not exceed four (4), and the final installment shall be payable not later than 120 days after filing the petition. For cause shown, the court may extend the time of any installment, provided the last installment is paid not later than 180 days after filing the petition. Fed. R. Bankr. P. 1006(b)(2).

5.   I understand that if I fail to pay any installment when due my bankruptcy case may be dismissed and I may not receive a discharge of my debts.

_____   _____
Signature of Attorney   Date   Signature of Debtor   Date
                                          (In a joint case, both spouses must sign.)

_____   _____
Name of Attorney   Signature of Joint Debtor (if any)   Date

CERTIFICATION AND SIGNATURE OF NON-ATTORNEY BANKRUPTCY PETITION (See 11 U.S.C. § 110)

   I certify that I am a bankruptcy petition preparer as defined in 11 U.S.C. § 110, that I prepared this document for compensation, and that I have provided the debtor with a copy of this document. I also certify that I will not accept money or any other property from the debtor before the filing fee is paid in full.

_____   _____
Printed or Typed Name of Bankruptcy Petition Preparer   Social Security No.

_____
Address

Names and Social Security numbers of all other individuals who prepared or assisted in preparing this document:

If more than one person prepared this document, attach additional signed sheets conforming to the appropriate Official Form for each person.

x_____   _____
Signature of Bankruptcy Petition Preparer   Date

A bankruptcy petition preparer's failure to comply with the provisions of title 11 and the Federal Rules of Bankruptcy Procedure may result in fines or imprisonment or both. 11 U.S.C. § 110; 18 U.S.C. § 156.

205

Form B3 continued
(9/97)

UNITED STATES BANKRUPTCY COURT
_____ DISTRICT OF _____

In re _____,   Case No. _____
                    Debtor

                                                                    Chapter _____

ORDER APPROVING PAYMENT OF FILING FEE IN INSTALLMENTS

                    IT IS ORDERED that the debtor(s) may pay the filing fee in installments on the terms proposed in the foregoing application.

                    IT IS FURTHER ORDERED that until the filing fee is paid in full the debtor shall not pay any money for services in connection with this case, and the debtor shall not relinquish any property as payment for services in connection with this case.

                                        BY THE COURT

Date: _____   _____
                                            United States Bankruptcy Judge

Form B4
11/92

Form 4. LIST OF CREDITORS HOLDING 20 LARGEST UNSECURED CLAIMS

[Caption as in Form 16B]

LIST OF CREDITORS HOLDING 20 LARGEST UNSECURED CLAIMS

Following is the list of the debtor's creditors holding the 20 largest unsecured claims. The list is prepared in accordance with Fed. R. Bankr. P. 1007(d) for filing in this chapter 11 [*or* chapter 9] case. The list does not include (1) persons who come within the definition of "insider" set forth in 11 U.S.C. § 101, or (2) secured creditors unless the value of the collateral is such that the unsecured deficiency places the creditor among the holders of the 20 largest unsecured claims.

(1)	(2)	(3)	(4)	(5)	
Name of creditor and complete mailing address including zip code	*Name, telephone number and complete mailing address, including zip code, of employee, agent, or department of creditor familiar with claim who may be contacted*		*Nature of claim (trade debt, bank loan, government contract, etc.)*	*Indicate if claim is contingent, unliquidated, disputed or subject to setoff*	*Amount of claim [if secured also state value of security]*

Date: _____

_____
Debtor

[Declaration as in Form 2]

207

FORM B5.
(6/90)

FORM 5.   INVOLUNTARY PETITION

United States Bankruptcy Court _____District of_____	INVOLUNTARY PETITION

IN RE (Name of Debtor - If Individual: Last, First, Middle)	ALL OTHER NAMES used by debtor in the last 6 years (Include married, maiden, and trade names.)
SOC. SEC./TAX I.D. NO. (If more than one, state all.)	
STREET ADDRESS OF DEBTOR (No. and street, city, state, and zip code) COUNTY OF RESIDENCE OR PRINCIPAL PLACE OF BUSINESS	MAILING ADDRESS OF DEBTOR (If different from street address)

LOCATION OF PRINCIPAL ASSETS OF BUSINESS DEBTOR (If different from previously listed addresses)

CHAPTER OF BANKRUPTCY CODE UNDER WHICH PETITION IS FILED

☐ Chapter 7   ☐ Chapter 11

INFORMATION REGARDING DEBTOR (Check applicable boxes)

Petitioners believe:
☐ Debts are primarily consumer debts
☐ Debts are primarily business debts (complete sections A and B)

TYPE OF DEBTOR
☐ Individual   ☐ Corporation Publicly Held
☐ Partnership   ☐ Corporation Not Publicly Held
☐ Other: _____

A. TYPE OF BUSINESS (Check one)
☐ Professional   ☐ Transportation   ☐ Commodity Broker
☐ Retail/Wholesale ☐ Manufacturing/   ☐ Construction
☐ Railroad   ☐ Mining   ☐ Real Estate
                            ☐ Stockbroker   ☐ Other

B. BRIEFLY DESCRIBE NATURE OF BUSINESS

VENUE

☐ Debtor has been domiciled or has had a residence, principal place of business, or principal assets in the District for 180 days immediately preceding the date of this petition or for a longer part of such 180 days than in any other District.

☐ A bankruptcy case concerning debtor's affiliate, general partner or partnership is pending in this District.

PENDING BANKRUPTCY CASE FILED BY OR AGAINST ANY PARTNER
OR AFFILIATE OF THIS DEBTOR (Report information for any additional cases on attached sheets.)

Name of Debtor	Case Number	Date
Relationship	District	Judge

ALLEGATIONS
(Check applicable boxes)

1.   ☐ Petitioner(s) are eligible to file this petition pursuant to 11 U.S.C. § 303(b).
2.   ☐ The debtor is a person against whom an order for relief may be entered under title 11 of the United States Code.
3.a. ☐ The debtor is generally not paying such debtor's debts as they become due, unless such debts are the subject of a bona fide dispute;
                                     or
  b. ☐ Within 120 days preceding the filing of this petition, a custodian, other than a trustee, receiver, or agent appointed or authorized to take charge of less than substantially all of the property of the debtor for the purpose of enforcing a lien against such property, was appointed or took possession.

COURT USE ONLY

FORM 5 Involuntary Petition
(6/92)

Name of Debtor _____

Case No. _____
(court use only)

TRANSFER OF CLAIM

☐ Check this box if there has been a transfer of any claim against the debtor by or to any petitioner. Attach all documents evidencing the transfer and any statements that are required under Bankruptcy Rule 1003(a).

REQUEST FOR RELIEF

Petitioner(s) request that an order for relief be entered against the debtor under the chapter of title 11, United States Code, specified in this petition.

Petitioner(s) declare under penalty of perjury that the foregoing is true and correct according to the best of their knowledge, information, and belief.

X_____
Signature of Petitioner or Representative (State title)

Name of Petitioner   Date Signed

Name & Mailing
Address of Individual   _____
Signing in Representative
Capacity   _____

X_____
Signature of Attorney   Date

Name of Attorney Firm (If any)

Address

Telephone No.

X_____
Signature of Petitioner or Representative (State title)

Name of Petitioner   Date Signed

Name & Mailing
Address of Individual   _____
Signing in Representative
Capacity   _____

X_____
Signature of Attorney   Date

Name of Attorney Firm (If any)

Address

Telephone No.

X_____
Signature of Petitioner or Representative (State title)

Name of Petitioner   Date Signed

Name & Mailing
Address of Individual   _____
Signing in Representative
Capacity   _____

X_____
Signature of Attorney   Date

Name of Attorney Firm (If any)

Address

Telephone No.

PETITIONING CREDITORS		
Name and Address of Petitioner	Nature of Claim	Amount of Claim
Name and Address of Petitioner	Nature of Claim	Amount of Claim
Name and Address of Petitioner	Nature of Claim	Amount of Claim
Note: If there are more than three petitioners, attach additional sheets with the statement under penalty of perjury, each petitioner's signature under the statement and the name of attorney and petitioning creditor information in the format above.	Total Amount of Petitioners' Claims	

_____continuation sheets attached

209

Form B6
(6/90)

FORMS 6. SCHEDULES

Summary of Schedules

Schedule A - Real Property
Schedule B - Personal Property
Schedule C - Property Claimed as Exempt
Schedule D - Creditors Holding Secured Claims
Schedule E - Creditors Holding Unsecured Priority Claims
Schedule F - Creditors Holding Unsecured Nonpriority Claims
Schedule G - Executory Contracts and Unexpired Leases
Schedule H - Codebtors
Schedule I - Current Income of Individual Debtor(s)
Schedule J - Current Expenditures of Individual Debtor(s)

Unsworn Declaration under Penalty of Perjury

GENERAL INSTRUCTIONS: The first page of the debtor's schedules and the first page of any amendments thereto must contain a caption as in Form 16B. Subsequent pages should be identified with the debtor's name and case number. If the schedules are filed with the petition, the case number should be left blank.

Schedules D, E, and F have been designed for the listing of each claim only once. Even when a claim is secured only in part or entitled to priority only in part, it still should be listed only once. A claim which is secured in whole or in part should be listed on Schedule D only, and a claim which is entitled to priority in whole or in part should be listed on Schedule E only. Do not list the same claim twice. If a creditor has more than one claim, such as claims arising from separate transactions, each claim should be scheduled separately.

Review the specific instructions for each schedule before completing the schedule.

FORM B6-Cont.
(6/90)

UNITED STATES BANKRUPTCY COURT
_____District of _____

In re _____,   Case No. _____
        Debtor   **(If known)**

SUMMARY OF SCHEDULES

Indicate as to each schedule whether that schedule is attached and state the number of pages in each. Report the totals from Schedules A, B, D, E, F, I, and J in the boxes provided. Add the amounts from Schedules A and B to determine the total amount of the debtor's assets. Add the amounts from Schedules D, E, and F to determine the total amount of the debtor's liabilities.

AMOUNTS SCHEDULED

NAME OF SCHEDULE	ATTACHED (YES/NO)	NO. OF SHEETS	ASSETS	LIABILITIES	OTHER
A - Real Property			$		
B - Personal Property			$		
C - Property Claimed as Exempt					
D - Creditors Holding Secured Claims				$	
E - Creditors Holding Unsecured Priority Claims				$	
F - Creditors Holding Unsecured Nonpriority Claims				$	
G - Executory Contracts and Unexpired Leases					
H - Codebtors					
I - Current Income of Individual Debtor(s)					$
J - Current Expenditures of Individual Debtor(s)					$

Total Number of Sheets of ALL Schedules ➤

Total Assets ➤ $

Total Liabilities ➤ $

FORM B6A
(6/90)

In re _____,   Case No. _____
                    Debtor   **(If known)**

SCHEDULE A - REAL PROPERTY

Except as directed below, list all real property in which the debtor has any legal, equitable, or future interest, including all property owned as a co-tenant , community property, or in which the debtor has a life estate. Include any property in which the debtor holds rights and powers exercisable for the debtor's own benefit. If the debtor is married, state whether husband, wife, or both own the property by placing an "H," "W," "J," or "C" in the column labeled "Husband, Wife, Joint, or Community." If the debtor holds no interest in real property, write "None" under "Description and Location of Property."

Do not include interests in executory contracts and unexpired leases on this schedule. List them in Schedule G - Executory Contracts and Unexpired Leases.

If an entity claims to have a lien or hold a secured interest in any property, state the amount of the secured claim. See Schedule D. If no entity claims to hold a secured interest in the property, write "None" in the column labeled "Amount of Secured Claim."

If the debtor is an individual or if a joint petition is filed, state the amount of any exemption claimed in the property only in Schedule C - Property Claimed as Exempt.

DESCRIPTION AND LOCATION OF PROPERTY	NATURE OF DEBTOR'S INTEREST IN PROPERTY	HUSBAND, WIFE, JOINT, OR COMMUNITY	CURRENT MARKET VALUE OF DEBTOR'S INTEREST IN PROPERTY, WITHOUT DEDUCTING ANY SECURED CLAIM OR EXEMPTION	AMOUNT OF SECURED CLAIM

Total▶

(Report also on Summary of Schedules.)

FORM B6B
(10/89)

In re _____,   Case No. _____
           Debtor   **(If known)**

SCHEDULE B - PERSONAL PROPERTY

Except as directed below, list all personal property of the debtor of whatever kind. If the debtor has no property in one or more of the categories, place an "x" in the appropriate position in the column labeled "None." If additional space is needed in any category, attach a separate sheet properly identified with the case name, case number, and the number of the category. If the debtor is married, state whether husband, wife, or both own the property by placing an "H," "W," "J," or "C" in the column labeled "Husband, Wife, Joint, or Community." If the debtor is an individual or a joint petition is filed, state the amount of any exemptions claimed only in Schedule C - Property Claimed as Exempt.

Do not list interests in executory contracts and unexpired leases on this schedule. List them in Schedule G - Executory Contracts and Unexpired Leases.

If the property is being held for the debtor by someone else, state that person's name and address under "Description and Location of Property."

TYPE OF PROPERTY	N O N E	DESCRIPTION AND LOCATION OF PROPERTY	HUSBAND, WIFE, JOINT, OR COMMUNITY	CURRENT MARKET VALUE OF DEBTOR'S INTEREST IN PROPERTY, WITHOUT DEDUCTING ANY SECURED CLAIM OR EXEMPTION
1. Cash on hand.				
2. Checking, savings or other financial accounts, certificates of deposit, or shares in banks, savings and loan, thrift, building and loan, and homestead associations, or credit unions, brokerage houses, or cooperatives.				
3. Security deposits with public utilities, telephone companies, landlords, and others.				
4. Household goods and furnishings, including audio, video, and computer equipment.				
5. Books; pictures and other art objects; antiques; stamp, coin, record, tape, compact disc, and other collections or collectibles.				
6. Wearing apparel.				
7. Furs and jewelry.				
8. Firearms and sports, photographic, and other hobby equipment.				
9. Interests in insurance policies. Name insurance company of each policy and itemize surrender or refund value of each.				
10. Annuities. Itemize and name each issuer.				

213

FORM B6B-Cont.
(10/89)

In re _____,   Case No. _____
            Debtor   (If known)

SCHEDULE B - PERSONAL PROPERTY
(Continuation Sheet)

TYPE OF PROPERTY	N O N E	DESCRIPTION AND LOCATION OF PROPERTY	HUSBAND, WIFE, JOINT, OR COMMUNITY	CURRENT MARKET VALUE OF DEBTOR'S INTEREST IN PROPERTY, WITHOUT DEDUCTING ANY SECURED CLAIM OR EXEMPTION
11. Interests in IRA, ERISA, Keogh, or other pension or profit sharing plans. Itemize.				
12. Stock and interests in incorporated and unincorporated businesses. Itemize.				
13. Interests in partnerships or joint ventures. Itemize.				
14. Government and corporate bonds and other negotiable and non-negotiable instruments.				
15. Accounts receivable.				
16. Alimony, maintenance, support, and property settlements to which the debtor is or may be entitled. Give particulars.				
17. Other liquidated debts owing debtor including tax refunds. Give particulars.				
18. Equitable or future interests, life estates, and rights or powers exercisable for the benefit of the debtor other than those listed in Schedule of Real Property.				
19. Contingent and noncontingent interests in estate of a decedent, death benefit plan, life insurance policy, or trust.				
20. Other contingent and unliquidated claims of every nature, including tax refunds, counterclaims of the debtor, and rights to setoff claims. Give estimated value of each.				
21. Patents, copyrights, and other intellectual property. Give particulars.				
22. Licenses, franchises, and other general intangibles. Give particulars.				

FORM B6B-cont.
(10/89)

In re _____ ,   Case No. _____
　　　　　　　Debtor　　　　　　　　　　　　　　　　　　　　　　　　　　　**(If known)**

SCHEDULE B -PERSONAL PROPERTY
(Continuation Sheet)

TYPE OF PROPERTY	N O N E	DESCRIPTION AND LOCATION OF PROPERTY	HUSBAND, WIFE, JOINT, OR COMMUNITY	CURRENT MARKET VALUE OF DEBTOR'S INTEREST IN PROPERTY, WITH-OUT DEDUCTING ANY SECURED CLAIM OR EXEMPTION
23. Automobiles, trucks, trailers, and other vehicles and accessories.				
24. Boats, motors, and accessories.				
25. Aircraft and accessories.				
26. Office equipment, furnishings, and supplies.				
27. Machinery, fixtures, equipment, and supplies used in business.				
28. Inventory.				
29. Animals.				
30. Crops - growing or harvested. Give particulars.				
31. Farming equipment and implements.				
32. Farm supplies, chemicals, and feed.				
33. Other personal property of any kind not already listed. Itemize.				

_____ continuation sheets attached　　　　Total ▶　| $

(Include amounts from any continuation
sheets attached. Report total also on
Summary of Schedules.)

215

FORM B6C
(6/90)

In re _____,   Case No. _____
          Debtor   **(If known)**

SCHEDULE C - PROPERTY CLAIMED AS EXEMPT

Debtor elects the exemptions to which debtor is entitled under:
(Check one box)

☐ 11 U.S.C. § 522(b)(1): Exemptions provided in 11 U.S.C. § 522(d). **Note: These exemptions are available only in certain states.**

☐ 11 U.S.C. § 522(b)(2): Exemptions available under applicable nonbankruptcy federal laws, state or local law where the debtor's domicile has been located for the 180 days immediately preceding the filing of the petition, or for a longer portion of the 180-day period than in any other place, and the debtor's interest as a tenant by the entirety or joint tenant to the extent the interest is exempt from process under applicable nonbankruptcy law.

DESCRIPTION OF PROPERTY	SPECIFY LAW PROVIDING EACH EXEMPTION	VALUE OF CLAIMED EXEMPTION	CURRENT MARKET VALUE OF PROPERTY WITHOUT DEDUCTING EXEMPTION

FORM B6D
(6/90)

In re _____,   Case No. _____
                    Debtor   **(If known)**

SCHEDULE D - CREDITORS HOLDING SECURED CLAIMS

   State the name, mailing address, including zip code, and account number, if any, of all entities holding claims secured by property of the debtor as of the date of filing of the petition. List creditors holding all types of secured interests such as judgment liens, garnishments, statutory liens, mortgages, deeds of trust, and other security interests. List creditors in alphabetical order to the extent practicable. If all secured creditors will not fit on this page, use the continuation sheet provided.

   If any entity other than a spouse in a joint case may be jointly liable on a claim, place an "X" in the column labeled "Codebtor," include the entity on the appropriate schedule of creditors, and complete Schedule H - Codebtors. If a joint petition is filed, state whether husband, wife, both of them, or the marital community may be liable on each claim by placing an "H," "W," "J," or "C" in the column labeled "Husband, Wife, Joint, or Community."

   If the claim is contingent, place an "X" in the column labeled "Contingent." If the claim is unliquidated, place an "X" in the column labeled "Unliquidated." If the claim is disputed, place an "X" in the column labeled "Disputed." (You may need to place an "X" in more than one of these three columns.)

   Report the total of all claims listed on this schedule in the box labeled "Total" on the last sheet of the completed schedule. Report this total also on the Summary of Schedules.

   ☐   Check this box if debtor has no creditors holding secured claims to report on this Schedule D.

CREDITOR'S NAME AND MAILING ADDRESS INCLUDING ZIP CODE	CODEBTOR	HUSBAND, WIFE, JOINT, OR COMMUNITY	DATE CLAIM WAS INCURRED, NATURE OF LIEN, AND DESCRIPTION AND MARKET VALUE OF PROPERTY SUBJECT TO LIEN	CONTINGENT	UNLIQUIDATED	DISPUTED	AMOUNT OF CLAIM WITHOUT DEDUCTING VALUE OF COLLATERAL	UNSECURED PORTION, IF ANY
ACCOUNT NO.								
			VALUE $					
ACCOUNT NO.								
			VALUE $					
ACCOUNT NO.								
			VALUE $					
ACCOUNT NO.								
			VALUE $					

_____ continuation sheets attached

Subtotal ▶ $ _____
(Total of this page)

Total ▶ $ _____
(Use only on last page)

(Report total also on Summary of Schedules)

217

FORM B6D - Cont.
(6/90)

In re _____,   Case No. _____
                        Debtor   (If known)

SCHEDULE D - CREDITORS HOLDING SECURED CLAIMS
(Continuation Sheet)

CREDITOR'S NAME AND MAILING ADDRESS INCLUDING ZIP CODE	CODEBTOR	HUSBAND, WIFE, JOINT, OR COMMUNITY	DATE CLAIM WAS INCURRED, NATURE OF LIEN, AND DESCRIPTION AND MARKET VALUE OF PROPERTY SUBJECT TO LIEN	CONTINGENT	UNLIQUIDATED	DISPUTED	AMOUNT OF CLAIM WITHOUT DEDUCTING VALUE OF COLLATERAL	UNSECURED PORTION, IF ANY
ACCOUNT NO.								
			VALUE $					
ACCOUNT NO.								
			VALUE $					
ACCOUNT NO.								
			VALUE $					
ACCOUNT NO.								
			VALUE $					
ACCOUNT NO.								
			VALUE $					

Sheet no. ___ of ___continuation sheets attached to Schedule of Creditors Holding Secured Claims   Subtotal▶ $ _____
                                                                                                    (Total of this page)
                                                                                        Total▶ | $ _____
                                                                              (Use only on last page)
                                                                  (Report total also on Summary of Schedules)

Form B6E
(Rev. 4/01)

In re _____,   Case No. _____
                    Debtor   (if known)

SCHEDULE E - CREDITORS HOLDING UNSECURED PRIORITY CLAIMS

A complete list of claims entitled to priority, listed separately by type of priority, is to be set forth on the sheets provided. Only holders of unsecured claims entitled to priority should be listed in this schedule. In the boxes provided on the attached sheets, state the name and mailing address, including zip code, and account number, if any, of all entities holding priority claims against the debtor or the property of the debtor, as of the date of the filing of the petition.

If any entity other than a spouse in a joint case may be jointly liable on a claim, place an "X" in the column labeled "Codebtor," include the entity on the appropriate schedule of creditors, and complete Schedule H-Codebtors. If a joint petition is filed, state whether husband, wife, both of them or the marital community may be liable on each claim by placing an "H,""W,""J," or "C" in the column labeled "Husband, Wife, Joint, or Community."

If the claim is contingent, place an "X" in the column labeled "Contingent." If the claim is unliquidated, place an "X" in the column labeled "Unliquidated." If the claim is disputed, place an "X" in the column labeled "Disputed." (You may need to place an "X" in more than one of these three columns.)

Report the total of claims listed on each sheet in the box labeled "Subtotal" on each sheet. Report the total of all claims listed on this Schedule E in the box labeled "Total" on the last sheet of the completed schedule. Repeat this total also on the Summary of Schedules.

☐ Check this box if debtor has no creditors holding unsecured priority claims to report on this Schedule E.

TYPES OF PRIORITY CLAIMS (Check the appropriate box(es) below if claims in that category are listed on the attached sheets)

☐ **Extensions of credit in an involuntary case**

Claims arising in the ordinary course of the debtor's business or financial affairs after the commencement of the case but before the earlier of the appointment of a trustee or the order for relief. 11 U.S.C. § 507(a)(2).

☐ **Wages, salaries, and commissions**

Wages, salaries, and commissions, including vacation, severance, and sick leave pay owing to employees and commissions owing to qualifying independent sales representatives up to $4,650* per person earned within 90 days immediately preceding the filing of the original petition, or the cessation of business, whichever occurred first, to the extent provided in 11 U.S.C. § 507(a)(3).

☐ **Contributions to employee benefit plans**

Money owed to employee benefit plans for services rendered within 180 days immediately preceding the filing of the original petition, or the cessation of business, whichever occurred first, to the extent provided in 11 U.S.C. § 507(a)(4).

☐ **Certain farmers and fishermen**

Claims of certain farmers and fishermen, up to $4,650* per farmer or fisherman, against the debtor, as provided in 11 U.S.C. § 507(a)(5).

☐ **Deposits by individuals**

Claims of individuals up to $2,100* for deposits for the purchase, lease, or rental of property or services for personal, family, or household use, that were not delivered or provided. 11 U.S.C. § 507(a)(6).

219

Form B6E
(Rev. 4/01)

In re _____ ,   Case No._____
                    Debtor   (if known)

☐ **Alimony, Maintenance, or Support**

Claims of a spouse, former spouse, or child of the debtor for alimony, maintenance, or support, to the extent provided in 11 U.S.C. § 507(a)(7).

☐ **Taxes and Certain Other Debts Owed to Governmental Units**

Taxes, customs duties, and penalties owing to federal, state, and local governmental units as set forth in 11 U.S.C. § 507(a)(8).

☐ **Commitments to Maintain the Capital of an Insured Depository Institution**

Claims based on commitments to the FDIC, RTC, Director of the Office of Thrift Supervision, Comptroller of the Currency, or Board of Governors of the Federal Reserve System, or their predecessors or successors, to maintain the capital of an insured depository institution. 11 U.S.C. § 507 (a)(9).

* Amounts are subject to adjustment on April 1, 2004, and every three years thereafter with respect to cases commenced on or after the date of adjustment.

_____ continuation sheets attached

FORM B6E - Cont.
(10/89)

In re _____,   Case No. _____
                    Debtor   **(If known)**

SCHEDULE E - CREDITORS HOLDING UNSECURED PRIORITY CLAIMS
(Continuation Sheet)

_____
TYPE OF PRIORITY

CREDITOR'S NAME AND MAILING ADDRESS INCLUDING ZIP CODE	CODEBTOR	HUSBAND, WIFE, JOINT, OR COMMUNITY	DATE CLAIM WAS INCURRED AND CONSIDERATION FOR CLAIM	CONTINGENT	UNLIQUIDATED	DISPUTED	TOTAL AMOUNT OF CLAIM	AMOUNT ENTITLED TO PRIORITY
ACCOUNT NO.								
ACCOUNT NO.								
ACCOUNT NO.								
ACCOUNT NO.								
ACCOUNT NO.								

Sheet no. ___ of ___ sheets attached to Schedule of Creditors
Holding Priority Claims

Subtotal▶ $
(Total of this page)
Total▶ $
(Use only on last page of the completed Schedule E.)
(Report total also on Summary of Schedules)

FORM B6F (Official Form 6F) (9/97)

In re _____,   Case No. _____
                 Debtor   **(If known)**

SCHEDULE F- CREDITORS HOLDING UNSECURED NONPRIORITY CLAIMS

State the name, mailing address, including zip code, and account number, if any, of all entities holding unsecured claims without priority against the debtor or the property of the debtor, as of the date of filing of the petition. Do not include claims listed in Schedules D and E. If all creditors will not fit on this page, use the continuation sheet provided.

If any entity other than a spouse in a joint case may be jointly liable on a claim, place an "X" in the column labeled "Codebtor," include the entity on the appropriate schedule of creditors, and complete Schedule H - Codebtors. If a joint petition is filed, state whether husband, wife, both of them, or the marital community maybe liable on each claim by placing an "H," "W," "J," or "C" in the column labeled "Husband, Wife, Joint, or Community."

If the claim is contingent, place an "X" in the column labeled "Contingent." If the claim is unliquidated, place an "X" in the column labeled "Unliquidated." If the claim is disputed, place an "X" in the column labeled "Disputed." (You may need to place an "X" in more than one of these three columns.)

Report total of all claims listed on this schedule in the box labeled "Total" on the last sheet of the completed schedule. Report this total also on the Summary of Schedules.

☐   Check this box if debtor has no creditors holding unsecured claims to report on this Schedule F.

CREDITOR'S NAME AND MAILING ADDRESS INCLUDING ZIP CODE	CODEBTOR	HUSBAND, WIFE, JOINT, OR COMMUNITY	DATE CLAIM WAS INCURRED AND CONSIDERATION FOR CLAIM. IF CLAIM IS SUBJECT TO SETOFF, SO STATE.	CONTINGENT	UNLIQUIDATED	DISPUTED	AMOUNT OF CLAIM
ACCOUNT NO.							
ACCOUNT NO.							
ACCOUNT NO.							
ACCOUNT NO.							

_____continuation sheets attached   Subtotal▶ | $ |

                                              Total ▶ | $ |
                                    (Report also on Summary of Schedules)

FORM B6F - Cont.
(10/89)

In re _____,   Case No. _____
                    Debtor   **(If known)**

SCHEDULE F - CREDITORS HOLDING UNSECURED NONPRIORITY CLAIMS
(Continuation Sheet)

CREDITOR'S NAME AND MAILING ADDRESS INCLUDING ZIP CODE	CODEBTOR	HUSBAND, WIFE, JOINT, OR COMMUNITY	DATE CLAIM WAS INCURRED, AND CONSIDERATION FOR CLAIM. IF CLAIM IS SUBJECT TO SETOFF, SO STATE.	CONTINGENT	UNLIQUIDATED	DISPUTED	AMOUNT OF CLAIM
ACCOUNT NO.							
ACCOUNT NO.							
ACCOUNT NO.							
ACCOUNT NO.							
ACCOUNT NO.							

Sheet no. ___ of ___ sheets attached to Schedule of
Creditors Holding Unsecured Nonpriority Claims

Subtotal ➤ $
(Total of this page)
Total ➤ $
(Use only on last page of the completed Schedule E.)
(Report total also on Summary of Schedules)

B6G
(10/89)

In re _____ ,   Case No._____
          Debtor   **(if known)**

SCHEDULE G - EXECUTORY CONTRACTS AND UNEXPIRED LEASES

    Describe all executory contracts of any nature and all unexpired leases of real or personal property. Include any timeshare interests.
    State nature of debtor's interest in contract, i.e., "Purchaser," "Agent," etc. State whether debtor is the lessor or lessee of a lease.
    Provide the names and complete mailing addresses of all other parties to each lease or contract described.

    NOTE: A party listed on this schedule will not receive notice of the filing of this case unless the party is also scheduled in the appropriate schedule of creditors.

☐ Check this box if debtor has no executory contracts or unexpired leases.

NAME AND MAILING ADDRESS, INCLUDING ZIP CODE, OF OTHER PARTIES TO LEASE OR CONTRACT.	DESCRIPTION OF CONTRACT OR LEASE AND NATURE OF DEBTOR'S INTEREST. STATE WHETHER LEASE IS FOR NONRESIDENTIAL REAL PROPERTY. STATE CONTRACT NUMBER OF ANY GOVERNMENT CONTRACT.

B6H
(6/90)

In re _____ ,   Case No. _____
                    Debtor   **(If known)**

SCHEDULE H - CODEBTORS

Provide the information requested concerning any person or entity, other than a spouse in a joint case, that is also liable on any debts listed by debtor in the schedules of creditors. Include all guarantors and co-signers. In community property states, a married debtor not filing a joint case should report the name and address of the nondebtor spouse on this schedule. Include all names used by the nondebtor spouse during the six years immediately preceding the commencement of this case.

☐ Check this box if debtor has no codebtors.

NAME AND ADDRESS OF CODEBTOR	NAME AND ADDRESS OF CREDITOR

FORM B6I
(6/90)

In re _____ ,   Case No._____
                    Debtor   **(if known)**

SCHEDULE I - CURRENT INCOME OF INDIVIDUAL DEBTOR(S)

The column labeled "Spouse" must be completed in all cases filed by joint debtors and by a married debtor in a chapter 12 or 13 case whether or not a joint petition is filed, unless the spouses are separated and a joint petition is not filed.

Debtor's Marital Status:	DEPENDENTS OF DEBTOR AND SPOUSE		
	NAMES	AGE	RELATIONSHIP

Employment:	DEBTOR	SPOUSE
Occupation		
Name of Employer		
How long employed		
Address of Employer		

	DEBTOR	SPOUSE
Income: (Estimate of average monthly income)		
Current monthly gross wages, salary, and commissions (pro rate if not paid monthly.)	$_____	$_____
Estimated monthly overtime	$_____	$_____
SUBTOTAL	$_____	$_____
LESS PAYROLL DEDUCTIONS		
a. Payroll taxes and social security	$_____	$_____
b. Insurance	$_____	$_____
c. Union dues	$_____	$_____
d. Other (Specify: _____)	$_____	$_____
SUBTOTAL OF PAYROLL DEDUCTIONS	$_____	$_____
TOTAL NET MONTHLY TAKE HOME PAY	$_____	$_____
Regular income from operation of business or profession or farm (attach detailed statement)	$_____	$_____
Income from real property	$_____	$_____
Interest and dividends	$_____	$_____
Alimony, maintenance or support payments payable to the debtor for the debtor's use or that of dependents listed above.	$_____	$_____
Social security or other government assistance (Specify) _____	$_____	$_____
Pension or retirement income	$_____	$_____
Other monthly income (Specify) _____	$_____	$_____
_____	$_____	$_____
TOTAL MONTHLY INCOME	$_____	$_____

TOTAL COMBINED MONTHLY INCOME $_____   (Report also on Summary of Schedules)

Describe any increase or decrease of more than 10% in any of the above categories anticipated to occur within the year following the filing of this document:

FORM B6J
(6/90)

In re _____ ,   Case No._____
                    Debtor   **(if known)**

SCHEDULE J - CURRENT EXPENDITURES OF INDIVIDUAL DEBTOR(S)

Complete this schedule by estimating the average monthly expenses of the debtor and the debtor's family. Pro rate any payments made bi-weekly, quarterly, semi-annually, or annually to show monthly rate.

☐   Check this box if a joint petition is filed and debtor's spouse maintains a separate household. Complete a separate schedule of expenditures labeled "Spouse."

Rent or home mortgage payment (include lot rented for mobile home)	$ _____
Are real estate taxes included? Yes _____ No _____	
Is property insurance included? Yes _____ No _____	
Utilities Electricity and heating fuel	$ _____
Water and sewer	$ _____
Telephone	$ _____
Other _____	$ _____
Home maintenance (repairs and upkeep)	$ _____
Food	$ _____
Clothing	$ _____
Laundry and dry cleaning	$ _____
Medical and dental expenses	$ _____
Transportation (not including car payments)	$ _____
Recreation, clubs and entertainment, newspapers, magazines, etc.	$ _____
Charitable contributions	$ _____
Insurance (not deducted from wages or included in home mortgage payments)	
Homeowner's or renter's	$ _____
Life	$ _____
Health	$ _____
Auto	$ _____
Other _____	$ _____
Taxes (not deducted from wages or included in home mortgage payments) (Specify) _____	$ _____
Installment payments: (In chapter 12 and 13 cases, do not list payments to be included in the plan)	
Auto	$ _____
Other _____	$ _____
Other _____	$ _____
Alimony, maintenance, and support paid to others	$ _____
Payments for support of additional dependents not living at your home	$ _____
Regular expenses from operation of business, profession, or farm (attach detailed statement)	$ _____
Other _____	$ _____
TOTAL MONTHLY EXPENSES (Report also on Summary of Schedules)	$_____

[FOR CHAPTER 12 AND 13 DEBTORS ONLY]
Provide the information requested below, including whether plan payments are to be made bi-weekly, monthly, annually, or at some other regular interval.

A. Total projected monthly income	$ _____
B. Total projected monthly expenses	$ _____
C. Excess income (A minus B)	$ _____
D. Total amount to be paid into plan each _____	$ _____
(interval)	

Form B6-Cont.
(12/94)

In re _____ ,   Case No. _____

        Debtor   (If known)

DECLARATION CONCERNING DEBTOR'S SCHEDULES

DECLARATION UNDER PENALTY OF PERJURY BY INDIVIDUAL DEBTOR

I declare under penalty of perjury that I have read the foregoing summary and schedules, consisting of _____
(Total shown on summary page plus 1.)

sheets, and that they are true and correct to the best of my knowledge, information, and belief.

Date _____   Signature: _____
                                                      Debtor

Date _____   Signature: _____
                                             (Joint Debtor, if any)

                          [If joint case, both spouses must sign.]

CERTIFICATION AND SIGNATURE OF NON-ATTORNEY BANKRUPTCY PETITION PREPARER (See 11 U.S.C. § 110)

I certify that I am a bankruptcy petition preparer as defined in 11 U.S.C. § 110, that I prepared this document for compensation, and that I have provided the debtor with a copy of this document.

_____   _____
Printed or Typed Name of Bankruptcy Petition Preparer   Social Security No.

_____

_____
Address

Names and Social Security numbers of all other individuals who prepared or assisted in preparing this document:

If more than one person prepared this document, attach additional signed sheets conforming to the appropriate Official Form for each person.

X _____   _____
   Signature of Bankruptcy Petition Preparer   Date

A bankruptcy petition preparer's failure to comply with the provisions of title 11 and the Federal Rules of Bankruptcy Procedure may result in fines or imprisonment or both. 11 U.S.C. § 110; 18 U.S.C. § 156.

DECLARATION UNDER PENALTY OF PERJURY ON BEHALF OF A CORPORATION OR PARTNERSHIP

I, the _____ [the president or other officer or an authorized agent of the corporation or a member or an authorized agent of the partnership] of the _____ [corporation or partnership] named as debtor in this case, declare under penalty of perjury that I have read the foregoing summary and schedules, consisting of _____ sheets, and that they are true and correct to the best of my knowledge, information, and belief.   *(Total shown on summary page plus 1.)*

Date _____

        Signature: _____

               _____
               [Print or type name of individual signing on behalf of debtor.]

[An individual signing on behalf of a partnership or corporation must indicate position or relationship to debtor.]

Penalty for making a false statement or concealing property: Fine of up to $500,000 or imprisonment for up to 5 years or both. 18 U.S.C. §§ 152 and 3571.

Form 7
(9/00)

FORM 7. STATEMENT OF FINANCIAL AFFAIRS

UNITED STATES BANKRUPTCY COURT

_____ **DISTRICT OF** _____

In re: _____,   Case No. _____
                (Name)   (if known)
                        Debtor

STATEMENT OF FINANCIAL AFFAIRS

This statement is to be completed by every debtor. Spouses filing a joint petition may file a single statement on which the information for both spouses is combined. If the case is filed under chapter 12 or chapter 13, a married debtor must furnish information for both spouses whether or not a joint petition is filed, unless the spouses are separated and a joint petition is not filed. An individual debtor engaged in business as a sole proprietor, partner, family farmer, or self-employed professional, should provide the information requested on this statement concerning all such activities as well as the individual's personal affairs.

Questions 1 - 18 are to be completed by all debtors. Debtors that are or have been in business, as defined below, also must complete Questions 19 - 25. **If the answer to an applicable question is "None," mark the box labeled "None."** If additional space is needed for the answer to any question, use and attach a separate sheet properly identified with the case name, case number (if known), and the number of the question.

DEFINITIONS

"In business." A debtor is "in business" for the purpose of this form if the debtor is a corporation or partnership. An individual debtor is "in business" for the purpose of this form if the debtor is or has been, within the six years immediately preceding the filing of this bankruptcy case, any of the following: an officer, director, managing executive, or owner of 5 percent or more of the voting or equity securities of a corporation; a partner, other than a limited partner, of a partnership; a sole proprietor or self-employed.

"Insider." The term "insider" includes but is not limited to: relatives of the debtor; general partners of the debtor and their relatives; corporations of which the debtor is an officer, director, or person in control; officers, directors, and any owner of 5 percent or more of the voting or equity securities of a corporate debtor and their relatives; affiliates of the debtor and insiders of such affiliates; any managing agent of the debtor. 11 U.S.C. § 101.

_____

1. **Income from employment or operation of business**

None
☐

State the gross amount of income the debtor has received from employment, trade, or profession, or from operation of the debtor's business from the beginning of this calendar year to the date this case was commenced. State also the gross amounts received during the **two years** immediately preceding this calendar year. (A debtor that maintains, or has maintained, financial records on the basis of a fiscal rather than a calendar year may report fiscal year income. Identify the beginning and ending dates of the debtor's fiscal year.) If a joint petition is filed, state income for each spouse separately. (Married debtors filing under chapter 12 or chapter 13 must state income of both spouses whether or not a joint petition is filed, unless the spouses are separated and a joint petition is not filed.)

AMOUNT   SOURCE (if more than one)

229

2. Income other than from employment or operation of business

None ☐ State the amount of income received by the debtor other than from employment, trade, profession, or operation of the debtor's business during the **two years** immediately preceding the commencement of this case. Give particulars. If a joint petition is filed, state income for each spouse separately. (Married debtors filing under chapter 12 or chapter 13 must state income for each spouse whether or not a joint petition is filed, unless the spouses are separated and a joint petition is not filed.)

AMOUNT	SOURCE

3. Payments to creditors

None ☐ a. List all payments on loans, installment purchases of goods or services, and other debts, aggregating more than $600 to any creditor, made within **90 days** immediately preceding the commencement of this case. (Married debtors filing under chapter 12 or chapter 13 must include payments by either or both spouses whether or not a joint petition is filed, unless the spouses are separated and a joint petition is not filed.)

NAME AND ADDRESS OF CREDITOR	DATES OF PAYMENTS	AMOUNT PAID	AMOUNT STILL OWING

None ☐ b. List all payments made within **one year** immediately preceding the commencement of this case to or for the benefit of creditors who are or were insiders. (Married debtors filing under chapter 12 or chapter 13 must include payments by either or both spouses whether or not a joint petition is filed, unless the spouses are separated and a joint petition is not filed.)

NAME AND ADDRESS OF CREDITOR AND RELATIONSHIP TO DEBTOR	DATE OF PAYMENT	AMOUNT PAID	AMOUNT STILL OWING

4. Suits and administrative proceedings, executions, garnishments and attachments

None ☐ a. List all suits and administrative proceedings to which the debtor is or was a party within **one year** immediately preceding the filing of this bankruptcy case. (Married debtors filing under chapter 12 or chapter 13 must include information concerning either or both spouses whether or not a joint petition is filed, unless the spouses are separated and a joint petition is not filed.)

CAPTION OF SUIT AND CASE NUMBER	NATURE OF PROCEEDING	COURT OR AGENCY AND LOCATION	STATUS OR DISPOSITION

None ☐   b.   Describe all property that has been attached, garnished or seized under any legal or equitable process within **one year** immediately preceding the commencement of this case. (Married debtors filing under chapter 12 or chapter 13 must include information concerning property of either or both spouses whether or not a joint petition is filed, unless the spouses are separated and a joint petition is not filed.)

NAME AND ADDRESS OF PERSON FOR WHOSE BENEFIT PROPERTY WAS SEIZED	DATE OF SEIZURE	DESCRIPTION AND VALUE OF PROPERTY

---

5.   Repossessions, foreclosures and returns

None ☐   List all property that has been repossessed by a creditor, sold at a foreclosure sale, transferred through a deed in lieu of foreclosure or returned to the seller, within **one year** immediately preceding the commencement of this case. (Married debtors filing under chapter 12 or chapter 13 must include information concerning property of either or both spouses whether or not a joint petition is filed, unless the spouses are separated and a joint petition is not filed.)

NAME AND ADDRESS OF CREDITOR OR SELLER	DATE OF REPOSSESSION, FORECLOSURE SALE, TRANSFER OR RETURN	DESCRIPTION AND VALUE OF PROPERTY

---

6.   Assignments and receiverships

None ☐   a.   Describe any assignment of property for the benefit of creditors made within **120 days** immediately preceding the commencement of this case. (Married debtors filing under chapter 12 or chapter 13 must include any assignment by either or both spouses whether or not a joint petition is filed, unless the spouses are separated and a joint petition is not filed.)

NAME AND ADDRESS OF ASSIGNEE	DATE OF ASSIGNMENT	TERMS OF ASSIGNMENT OR SETTLEMENT

None ☐   b.   List all property which has been in the hands of a custodian, receiver, or court-appointed official within **one year** immediately preceding the commencement of this case. (Married debtors filing under chapter 12 or chapter 13 must include information concerning property of either or both spouses whether or not a joint petition is filed, unless the spouses are separated and a joint petition is not filed.)

NAME AND ADDRESS OF CUSTODIAN	NAME AND LOCATION OF COURT CASE TITLE & NUMBER	DATE OF ORDER	DESCRIPTION AND VALUE OF PROPERTY

7. Gifts

None ☐ List all gifts or charitable contributions made within **one year** immediately preceding the commencement of this case except ordinary and usual gifts to family members aggregating less than $200 in value per individual family member and charitable contributions aggregating less than $100 per recipient. (Married debtors filing under chapter 12 or chapter 13 must include gifts or contributions by either or both spouses whether or not a joint petition is filed, unless the spouses are separated and a joint petition is not filed.)

NAME AND ADDRESS OF PERSON OR ORGANIZATION	RELATIONSHIP TO DEBTOR, IF ANY	DATE OF GIFT	DESCRIPTION AND VALUE OF GIFT

8. Losses

None ☐ List all losses from fire, theft, other casualty or gambling within **one year** immediately preceding the commencement of this case **or since the commencement of this case**. (Married debtors filing under chapter 12 or chapter 13 must include losses by either or both spouses whether or not a joint petition is filed, unless the spouses are separated and a joint petition is not filed.)

DESCRIPTION AND VALUE OF PROPERTY	DESCRIPTION OF CIRCUMSTANCES AND, IF LOSS WAS COVERED IN WHOLE OR IN PART BY INSURANCE, GIVE PARTICULARS	DATE OF LOSS

9. Payments related to debt counseling or bankruptcy

None ☐ List all payments made or property transferred by or on behalf of the debtor to any persons, including attorneys, for consultation concerning debt consolidation, relief under the bankruptcy law or preparation of a petition in bankruptcy within **one year** immediately preceding the commencement of this case.

NAME AND ADDRESS OF PAYEE	DATE OF PAYMENT, NAME OF PAYOR IF OTHER THAN DEBTOR	AMOUNT OF MONEY OR DESCRIPTION AND VALUE OF PROPERTY

10. Other transfers

None ☐ List all other property, other than property transferred in the ordinary course of the business or financial affairs of the debtor, transferred either absolutely or as security within **one year** immediately preceding the commencement of this case. (Married debtors filing under chapter 12 or chapter 13 must include transfers by either or both spouses whether or not a joint petition is filed, unless the spouses are separated and a joint petition is not filed.)

NAME AND ADDRESS OF TRANSFEREE, RELATIONSHIP TO DEBTOR	DATE	DESCRIBE PROPERTY TRANSFERRED AND VALUE RECEIVED

5

11. Closed financial accounts

None
☐

List all financial accounts and instruments held in the name of the debtor or for the benefit of the debtor which were closed, sold, or otherwise transferred within **one year** immediately preceding the commencement of this case. Include checking, savings, or other financial accounts, certificates of deposit, or other instruments; shares and share accounts held in banks, credit unions, pension funds, cooperatives, associations, brokerage houses and other financial institutions. (Married debtors filing under chapter 12 or chapter 13 must include information concerning accounts or instruments held by or for either or both spouses whether or not a joint petition is filed, unless the spouses are separated and a joint petition is not filed.)

NAME AND ADDRESS OF INSTITUTION	TYPE AND NUMBER OF ACCOUNT AND AMOUNT OF FINAL BALANCE	AMOUNT AND DATE OF SALE OR CLOSING

12. Safe deposit boxes

None
☐

List each safe deposit or other box or depository in which the debtor has or had securities, cash, or other valuables within **one year** immediately preceding the commencement of this case. (Married debtors filing under chapter 12 or chapter 13 must include boxes or depositories of either or both spouses whether or not a joint petition is filed, unless the spouses are separated and a joint petition is not filed.)

NAME AND ADDRESS OF BANK OR OTHER DEPOSITORY	NAMES AND ADDRESSES OF THOSE WITH ACCESS TO BOX OR DEPOSITORY	DESCRIPTION OF CONTENTS	DATE OF TRANSFER OR SURRENDER, IF ANY

13. Setoffs

None
☐

List all setoffs made by any creditor, including a bank, against a debt or deposit of the debtor within **90 days** preceding the commencement of this case. (Married debtors filing under chapter 12 or chapter 13 must include information concerning either or both spouses whether or not a joint petition is filed, unless the spouses are separated and a joint petition is not filed.)

NAME AND ADDRESS OF CREDITOR	DATE OF SETOFF	AMOUNT OF SETOFF

14. Property held for another person

None
☐

List all property owned by another person that the debtor holds or controls.

NAME AND ADDRESS OF OWNER	DESCRIPTION AND VALUE OF PROPERTY	LOCATION OF PROPERTY

233

15. Prior address of debtor

None ☐

If the debtor has moved within the **two years** immediately preceding the commencement of this case, list all premises which the debtor occupied during that period and vacated prior to the commencement of this case. If a joint petition is filed, report also any separate address of either spouse.

ADDRESS   NAME USED   DATES OF OCCUPANCY

16. Spouses and Former Spouses

None ☐

If the debtor resides or resided in a community property state, commonwealth, or territory (including Alaska, Arizona, California, Idaho, Louisiana, Nevada, New Mexico, Puerto Rico, Texas, Washington, or Wisconsin) within the **six-year period** immediately preceding the commencement of the case, identify the name of the debtor's spouse and of any former spouse who resides or resided with the debtor in the community property state.

NAME

17. Environmental Information.

For the purpose of this question, the following definitions apply:

"Environmental Law" means any federal, state, or local statute or regulation regulating pollution, contamination, releases of hazardous or toxic substances, wastes or material into the air, land, soil, surface water, groundwater, or other medium, including, but not limited to, statutes or regulations regulating the cleanup of these substances, wastes, or material.

"Site" means any location, facility, or property as defined under any Environmental Law, whether or not presently or formerly owned or operated by the debtor, including, but not limited to, disposal sites.

"Hazardous Material" means anything defined as a hazardous waste, hazardous substance, toxic substance, hazardous material, pollutant, or contaminant or similar term under an Environmental Law

None ☐

a. List the name and address of every site for which the debtor has received notice in writing by a governmental unit that it may be liable or potentially liable under or in violation of an Environmental Law. Indicate the governmental unit, the date of the notice, and, if known, the Environmental Law:

SITE NAME   NAME AND ADDRESS   DATE OF   ENVIRONMENTAL
AND ADDRESS   OF GOVERNMENTAL UNIT   NOTICE   LAW

None ☐

b. List the name and address of every site for which the debtor provided notice to a governmental unit of a release of Hazardous Material. Indicate the governmental unit to which the notice was sent and the date of the notice.

SITE NAME   NAME AND ADDRESS   DATE OF   ENVIRONMENTAL

AND ADDRESS   OF GOVERNMENTAL UNIT   NOTICE   LAW

None
☐

c.   List all judicial or administrative proceedings, including settlements or orders, under any Environmental Law with respect to which the debtor is or was a party. Indicate the name and address of the governmental unit that is or was a party to the proceeding, and the docket number.

NAME AND ADDRESS   DOCKET NUMBER   STATUS OR
OF GOVERNMENTAL UNIT   DISPOSITION

---

18 . Nature, location and name of business

None
☐

a.   If the debtor is an individual, list the names, addresses, taxpayer identification numbers, nature of the businesses, and beginning and ending dates of all businesses in which the debtor was an officer, director, partner, or managing executive of a corporation, partnership, sole proprietorship, or was a self-employed professional within the **six years** immediately preceding the commencement of this case, or in which the debtor owned 5 percent or more of the voting or equity securities within the **six years** immediately preceding the commencement of this case.

If the debtor is a partnership, list the names, addresses, taxpayer identification numbers, nature of the businesses, and beginning and ending dates of all businesses in which the debtor was a partner or owned 5 percent or more of the voting or equity securities, within the **six years** immediately preceding the commencement of this case.

If the debtor is a corporation, list the names, addresses, taxpayer identification numbers, nature of the businesses, and beginning and ending dates of all businesses in which the debtor was a partner or owned 5 percent or more of the voting or equity securities within the **six years** immediately preceding the commencement of this case.

NAME	TAXPAYER I.D. NUMBER	ADDRESS	NATURE OF BUSINESS	BEGINNING AND ENDING DATES

None
☐

b.   Identify any business listed in response to subdivision a., above, that is "single asset real estate" as defined in 11 U.S.C. § 101.

NAME   ADDRESS

The following questions are to be completed by every debtor that is a corporation or partnership and by any individual debtor who is or has been, within the **six years** immediately preceding the commencement of this case, any of the following: an officer, director, managing executive, or owner of more than 5 percent of the voting or equity securities of a corporation; a partner, other than a limited partner, of a partnership; a sole proprietor or otherwise self-employed.

*(An individual or joint debtor should complete this portion of the statement **only** if the debtor is or has been in business, as defined above, within the six years immediately preceding the commencement of this case. A debtor who has not been in business within those six years should go directly to the signature page.)*

8

19. Books, records and financial statements

None ☐   a.   List all bookkeepers and accountants who within the **two years** immediately preceding the filing of this bankruptcy case kept or supervised the keeping of books of account and records of the debtor.

NAME AND ADDRESS   DATES SERVICES RENDERED

None ☐   b.   List all firms or individuals who within the **two years** immediately preceding the filing of this bankruptcy case have audited the books of account and records, or prepared a financial statement of the debtor.

NAME   ADDRESS   DATES SERVICES RENDERED

None ☐   c.   List all firms or individuals who at the time of the commencement of this case were in possession of the books of account and records of the debtor. If any of the books of account and records are not available, explain.

NAME   ADDRESS

None ☐   d.   List all financial institutions, creditors and other parties, including mercantile and trade agencies, to whom a financial statement was issued within the **two years** immediately preceding the commencement of this case by the debtor.

NAME AND ADDRESS   DATE ISSUED

20. Inventories

None ☐   a.   List the dates of the last two inventories taken of your property, the name of the person who supervised the taking of each inventory, and the dollar amount and basis of each inventory.

                                        DOLLAR AMOUNT OF INVENTORY

DATE OF INVENTORY   INVENTORY SUPERVISOR   (Specify cost, market or other basis)

None ☐   b.   List the name and address of the person having possession of the records of each of the two inventories reported in a., above.

                                        NAME AND ADDRESSES OF CUSTODIAN

DATE OF INVENTORY   OF INVENTORY RECORDS

9

21 . Current Partners, Officers, Directors and Shareholders

None ☐   a.   If the debtor is a partnership, list the nature and percentage of partnership interest of each member of the partnership.

NAME AND ADDRESS   NATURE OF INTEREST   PERCENTAGE OF INTEREST

None ☐   b.   If the debtor is a corporation, list all officers and directors of the corporation, and each stockholder who directly or indirectly owns, controls, or holds 5 percent or more of the voting or equity securities of the corporation.

NAME AND ADDRESS   TITLE   NATURE AND PERCENTAGE
                                                         OF STOCK OWNERSHIP

22 . Former partners, officers, directors and shareholders

None ☐   a.   If the debtor is a partnership, list each member who withdrew from the partnership within **one year** immediately preceding the commencement of this case.

NAME   ADDRESS   DATE OF WITHDRAWAL

None ☐   b.   If the debtor is a corporation, list all officers, or directors whose relationship with the corporation terminated within **one year** immediately preceding the commencement of this case.

NAME AND ADDRESS   TITLE   DATE OF TERMINATION

23 . Withdrawals from a partnership or distributions by a corporation

None ☐   If the debtor is a partnership or corporation, list all withdrawals or distributions credited or given to an insider, including compensation in any form, bonuses, loans, stock redemptions, options exercised and any other perquisite during **one year** immediately preceding the commencement of this case.

NAME & ADDRESS   AMOUNT OF MONEY
OF RECIPIENT,   DATE AND PURPOSE   OR DESCRIPTION
RELATIONSHIP TO DEBTOR   OF WITHDRAWAL   AND VALUE OF PROPERTY

10

24. Tax Consolidation Group.

None
☐   If the debtor is a corporation, list the name and federal taxpayer identification number of the parent corporation of any consolidated group for tax purposes of which the debtor has been a member at any time within the **six-year period** immediately preceding the commencement of the case.

NAME OF PARENT CORPORATION   TAXPAYER IDENTIFICATION NUMBER

_____

25. Pension Funds.

None
☐   If the debtor is not an individual, list the name and federal taxpayer identification number of any pension fund to which the debtor, as an employer, has been responsible for contributing at any time within the **six-year period** immediately preceding the commencement of the case.

NAME OF PENSION FUND   TAXPAYER IDENTIFICATION NUMBER

_____

* * * * * *

[If completed by an individual or individual and spouse]

I declare under penalty of perjury that I have read the answers contained in the foregoing statement of financial affairs and any attachments thereto and that they are true and correct.

Date _____   Signature _____
                                      of Debtor

Date _____   Signature _____
                                      of Joint Debtor
                                      (if any)

_____

[If completed on behalf of a partnership or corporation]

I, declare under penalty of perjury that I have read the answers contained in the foregoing statement of financial affairs and any attachments thereto and that they are true and correct to the best of my knowledge, information and belief.

Date _____   Signature _____

                                      _____
                                      Print Name and Title

[An individual signing on behalf of a partnership or corporation must indicate position or relationship to debtor.]

_____ continuation sheets attached

Penalty for making a false statement: Fine of up to $500,000 or imprisonment for up to 5 years, or both. 18 U.S.C. § 152 and 3571

CERTIFICATION AND SIGNATURE OF NON-ATTORNEY BANKRUPTCY PETITION PREPARER (See 11 U.S.C. § 110)

I certify that I am a bankruptcy petition preparer as defined in 11 U.S.C. § 110, that I prepared this document for compensation, and that I have provided the debtor with a copy of this document.

_____   _____
Printed or Typed Name of Bankruptcy Petition Preparer   Social Security No.

_____
Address

Names and Social Security numbers of all other individuals who prepared or assisted in preparing this document:

If more than one person prepared this document, attach additional signed sheets conforming to the appropriate Official Form for each person.

X _____   _____
  Signature of Bankruptcy Petition Preparer   Date

A bankruptcy petition preparer's failure to comply with the provisions of title 11 and the Federal Rules of Bankruptcy Procedure may result in fines or imprisonment or both. 18 U.S.C. § 156.

114-1

239

Form B8 (Official Form 8)
(9/97)

Form 8. INDIVIDUAL DEBTOR'S STATEMENT OF INTENTION
[Caption as in Form 16B]

CHAPTER 7 INDIVIDUAL DEBTOR'S STATEMENT OF INTENTION

1. I have filed a schedule of assets and liabilities which includes consumer debts secured by property of the estate.

2. I intend to do the following with respect to the property of the estate which secures those consumer debts:

    a. *Property to Be Surrendered.*

Description of Property   **Creditor's name**

    b. *Property to Be Retained*   *[Check any applicable statement.]*

Description of Property	Creditor's Name	Property is claimed as exempt	Property will be redeemed pursuant to 11 U.S.C. § 722	Debt will be reaffirmed pursuant to 11 U.S.C. § 524(c)

Date: _____

_____
Signature of Debtor

CERTIFICATION OF NON-ATTORNEY BANKRUPTCY PETITION PREPARER (See 11 U.S.C. § 110)

I certify that I am a bankruptcy petition preparer as defined in 11 U.S.C. § 110, that I prepared this document for compensation, and that I have provided the debtor with a copy of this document.

_____   _____
Printed or Typed Name of Bankruptcy Petition Preparer   Social Security No.

_____

Address

Names and Social Security Numbers of all other individuals who prepared or assisted in preparing this document.

If more than one person prepared this document, attach additional signed sheets conforming to the appropriate Official Form for each person.

X_____   _____
Signature of Bankruptcy Petition Preparer   Date

A bankruptcy petition preparer's failure to comply with the provisions of title 11 and the Federal Rules of Bankruptcy Procedure may result in fines or imprisonment or both. 11 U.S.C. § 110; 18 U.S.C. § 156.

Form B9
(9/97)

FORM 9.   NOTICE OF COMMENCEMENT OF CASE UNDER THE
            BANKRUPTCY CODE, MEETING OF CREDITORS,
            AND DEADLINES

9A...........Chapter	7, Individual/Joint, No-Asset Case
9B...........Chapter	7, Corporation/Partnership, No-Asset Case
9C...........Chapter	7, Individual/Joint, Asset Case
9D...........Chapter	7, Corporation/Partnership, Asset Case
9E...........Chapter	11, Individual/Joint Case
9E(Alt.)..Chapter	11, Individual/Joint Case
9F...........Chapter	11, Corporation/Partnership Case
9F(Alt.)..Chapter	11, Corporation/Partnership Case
9G...........Chapter	12, Individual/Joint Case
9H...........Chapter	12, Corporation/Partnership Case
9I...........Chapter	13, Individual/Joint Case

FORM B9A (Chapter 7 Individual or Joint Debtor No Asset Case (9/97))

UNITED STATES BANKRUPTCY COURT _____ District of _____

Notice of
Chapter 7 Bankruptcy Case, Meeting of Creditors, & Deadlines

[A chapter 7 bankruptcy case concerning the debtor(s) listed below was filed on _____ (date).]

or [A bankruptcy case concerning the debtor(s) listed below was originally filed under chapter _____ on _____ (date) and was converted to a case under chapter 7 on_____.]

You may be a creditor of the debtor. **This notice lists important deadlines.** You may want to consult an attorney to protect your rights. All documents filed in the case may be inspected at the bankruptcy clerk's office at the address listed below. NOTE: The staff of the bankruptcy clerk's office cannot give legal advice.

See Reverse Side For Important Explanations.

Debtor(s) (name(s) and address):	Case Number:
	Social Security/Taxpayer ID Nos.:
Attorney for Debtor(s) (name and address):	Bankruptcy Trustee (name and address):
Telephone number:	Telephone number:

Meeting of Creditors:

Date: /   /   Time: (   ) A.M.   Location:
                                      (   ) P.M.

Deadlines:

Papers must be *received* by the bankruptcy clerk's office by the following deadlines:

Deadline to File a Complaint Objecting to Discharge of the Debtor *or* to Determine Dischargeability of Certain Debts:

Deadline to Object to Exemptions:
Thirty (30) days after the *conclusion* of the meeting of creditors.

Creditors May Not Take Certain Actions

The filing of the bankruptcy case automatically stays certain collection and other actions against the debtor and the debtor's property. If you attempt to collect a debt or take other action in violation of the Bankruptcy Code, you may be penalized.

Please Do Not File A Proof of Claim Unless You Receive a Notice To Do So.

Address of the Bankruptcy Clerk's Office:	For the Court:
	Clerk of the Bankruptcy Court:
Telephone number:	
Hours Open:	Date:

EXPLANATIONS

FORM B9A (9/97)

Filing of Chapter 7 Bankruptcy Case	A bankruptcy case under chapter 7 of the Bankruptcy Code (title 11, United States Code) has been filed in this court by or against the debtor(s) listed on the front side, and an order for relief has been entered.
Creditors May Not Take Certain Actions	Prohibited collection actions are listed in Bankruptcy Code § 362. Common examples of prohibited actions include contacting the debtor by telephone, mail or otherwise to demand repayment; taking actions to collect money or obtain property from the debtor; repossessing the debtor's property; starting or continuing lawsuits or foreclosures; and garnishing or deducting from the debtor's wages.
Meeting of Creditors	A meeting of creditors is scheduled for the date, time and location listed on the front side. *The debtor (both spouses in a joint case) must be present at the meeting to be questioned under oath by the trustee and by creditors.* Creditors are welcome to attend, but are not required to do so. The meeting may be continued and concluded at a later date without further notice.
Do Not File a Proof of Claim at This Time	There does not appear to be any property available to the trustee to pay creditors. *You therefore should not file a proof of claim at this time.* If it later appears that assets are available to pay creditors, you will be sent another notice telling you that you may file a proof of claim, and telling you the deadline for filing your proof of claim.
Discharge of Debts	The debtor is seeking a discharge of most debts, which may include your debt. A discharge means that you may never try to collect the debt from the debtor. If you believe that the debtor is not entitled to receive a discharge under Bankruptcy Code § 727(a) *or* that a debt owed to you is not dischargeable under Bankruptcy Code § 523(a)(2), (4), (6), or (15), you must start a lawsuit by filing a complaint in the bankruptcy clerk's office by the "Deadline to File a Complaint Objecting to Discharge of the Debtor or to Determine Dischargeability of Certain Debts" listed on the front side. The bankruptcy clerk's office must receive the complaint and the required filing fee by that Deadline.
Exempt Property	The debtor is permitted by law to keep certain property as exempt. Exempt property will not be sold and distributed to creditors. The debtor must file a list of all property claimed as exempt. You may inspect that list at the bankruptcy clerk's office. If you believe that an exemption claimed by the debtor is not authorized by law, you may file an objection to that exemption. The bankruptcy clerk's office must receive the objection by the "Deadline to Object to Exemptions" listed on the front side.
Bankruptcy Clerk's Office	Any paper that you file in this bankruptcy case should be filed at the bankruptcy clerk's office at the address listed on the front side. You may inspect all papers filed, including the list of the debtor's property and debts and the list of the property claimed as exempt, at the bankruptcy clerk's office.
Legal Advice	The staff of the bankruptcy clerk's office cannot give legal advice. You may want to consult an attorney to protect your rights.

—Refer To Other Side For Important Deadlines and Notices—

FORM B9B (Chapter 7 Corporation/Partnership No Asset Case) (9/97)

UNITED STATES BANKRUPTCY COURT	_____ District of _____

Notice of
Chapter 7 Bankruptcy Case, Meeting of Creditors, & Deadlines

[A chapter 7 bankruptcy case concerning the debtor(s) listed below was filed on _____ (date).]

or [A bankruptcy case concerning the debtor(s) listed below was originally filed under chapter _____ on _____ (date) and was converted to a case under chapter 7 on_____.]

You may be a creditor of the debtor. You may want to consult an attorney to protect your rights.

All documents filed in the case may be inspected at the bankruptcy clerk's office at the address listed below.

NOTE: The staff of the bankruptcy clerk's office cannot give legal advice.

See Reverse Side For Important Explanations.

Debtor (name(s) and address):	Case Number:
	Taxpayer ID Nos.:
Attorney for Debtor (name and address):	Bankruptcy Trustee (name and address):
Telephone number:	Telephone number:

Meeting of Creditors:

Date: /   /   Time: (   ) A.M.   Location:
                                       (   ) P.M.

Creditors May Not Take Certain Actions:

The filing of the bankruptcy case automatically stays certain collection and other actions against the debtor and the debtor's property. If you attempt to collect a debt or take other action in violation of the Bankruptcy Code, you may be penalized.

Please Do Not File A Proof of Claim Unless You Receive a Notice To Do So.

Address of the Bankruptcy Clerk's Office:	For the Court:
	Clerk of the Bankruptcy Court:
Telephone number:	
Hours Open:	Date:

EXPLANATIONS

FORM B9B (9/97)

Filing of Chapter 7 Bankruptcy Case	A bankruptcy case under chapter 7 of the Bankruptcy Code (title 11, United States Code) has been filed in this court by or against the debtor(s) listed on the front side, and an order for relief has been entered.
Creditors May Not Take Certain Actions	Prohibited collection actions are listed in Bankruptcy Code § 362. Common examples of prohibited actions include contacting the debtor by telephone, mail or otherwise to demand repayment; taking actions to collect money or obtain property from the debtor; repossessing the debtor's property; and starting or continuing lawsuits or foreclosures.
Meeting of Creditors	A meeting of creditors is scheduled for the date, time and location listed on the front side. *The debtor's representative must be present at the meeting to be questioned under oath by the trustee and by creditors.* Creditors are welcome to attend, but are not required to do so. The meeting may be continued and concluded at a later date without further notice.
Do Not File a Proof of Claim at This Time	There does not appear to be any property available to the trustee to pay creditors. *You therefore should not file a proof of claim at this time.* If it later appears that assets are available to pay creditors, you will be sent another notice telling you that you may file a proof of claim, and telling you the deadline for filing your proof of claim.
Bankruptcy Clerk's Office	Any paper that you file in this bankruptcy case should be filed at the bankruptcy clerk's office at the address listed on the front side. You may inspect all papers filed, including the list of the debtor's property and debts at the bankruptcy clerk's office.
Legal Advice	The staff of the bankruptcy clerk's office cannot give legal advice. You may want to consult an attorney to protect your rights.

—Refer To Other Side For Important Deadlines and Notices—

FORM B9C (Chapter 7 Individual or Joint Debtor Asset Case) (9/97)

UNITED STATES BANKRUPTCY COURT _____ District of_____

Notice of
Chapter 7 Bankruptcy Case, Meeting of Creditors, & Deadlines

[A chapter 7 bankruptcy case concerning the debtor(s) listed below was filed on _____ (date).]

or [A bankruptcy case concerning the debtor(s) listed below was originally filed under chapter _____ on _____ (date) and was converted to a case under chapter 7 on_____.]

You may be a creditor of the debtor. **This notice lists important deadlines.** You may want to consult an attorney to protect your rights. All documents filed in the case may be inspected at the bankruptcy clerk's office at the address listed below. NOTE: The staff of the bankruptcy clerk's office cannot give legal advice.

See Reverse Side For Important Explanations.

Debtor(s) (name(s) and address):	Case Number:
	Social Security/Taxpayer ID Nos.:
Attorney for Debtor(s) (name and address): Telephone number:	Bankruptcy Trustee (name and address): Telephone number:

Meeting of Creditors:

Date: / / Time: ( ) A.M. ( ) P.M.	Location:

Deadlines:

Papers must be *received* by the bankruptcy clerk's office by the following deadlines:

Deadline to File a Proof of Claim:

For all creditors (except a governmental unit):	For a governmental unit:

Deadline to File a Complaint Objecting to Discharge of the Debtor or to Determine Dischargeability of Certain Debts:

Deadline to Object to Exemptions:

Thirty (30) days after the *conclusion* of the meeting of creditors.

Creditors May Not Take Certain Actions:

The filing of the bankruptcy case automatically stays certain collection and other actions against the debtor and the debtor's property. If you attempt to collect a debt or take other action in violation of the Bankruptcy Code, you may be penalized.

Address of the Bankruptcy Clerk's Office:	For the Court:
	Clerk of the Bankruptcy Court:
Telephone number:	
Hours Open:	Date:

EXPLANATIONS

FORM B9C (9/97)

Filing of Chapter 7 Bankruptcy Case	A bankruptcy case under chapter 7 of the Bankruptcy Code (title 11, United States Code) has been filed in this court by or against the debtor(s) listed on the front side, and an order for relief has been entered.
Creditors May Not Take Certain Actions	Prohibited collection actions are listed in Bankruptcy Code § 362. Common examples of prohibited actions include contacting the debtor by telephone, mail or otherwise to demand repayment; taking actions to collect money or obtain property from the debtor; repossessing the debtor's property; starting or continuing lawsuits or foreclosures; and garnishing or deducting from the debtor's wages.
Meeting of Creditors	A meeting of creditors is scheduled for the date, time and location listed on the front side. *The debtor (both spouses in a joint case) must be present at the meeting to be questioned under oath by the trustee and by creditors.* Creditors are welcome to attend, but are not required to do so. The meeting may be continued and concluded at a later date without further notice.
Claims	A Proof of Claim is a signed statement describing a creditor's claim. If a Proof of Claim form is not included with this notice, you can obtain one at any bankruptcy clerk's office. If you do not file a Proof of Claim by the "Deadline to File a Proof of Claim" listed on the front side, you might not be paid any money on your claim against the debtor in the bankruptcy case. To be paid you must file a Proof of Claim even if your claim is listed in the schedules filed by the debtor.
Discharge of Debts	The debtor is seeking a discharge of most debts, which may include your debt. A discharge means that you may never try to collect the debt from the debtor. If you believe that the debtor is not entitled to receive a discharge under Bankruptcy Code § 727(a) *or* that a debt owed to you is not dischargeable under Bankruptcy Code § 523(a)(2), (4), (6), or (15), you must start a lawsuit by filing a complaint in the bankruptcy clerk's office by the "Deadline to File a Complaint Objecting to Discharge of the Debtor or to Determine Dischargeability of Certain Debts" listed on the front side. The bankruptcy clerk's office must receive the complaint and the required filing fee by that Deadline.
Exempt Property	The debtor is permitted by law to keep certain property as exempt. Exempt property will not be sold and distributed to creditors. The debtor must file a list of all property claimed as exempt. You may inspect that list at the bankruptcy clerk's office. If you believe that an exemption claimed by the debtor is not authorized by law, you may file an objection to that exemption. The bankruptcy clerk's office must receive the objection by the "Deadline to Object to Exemptions" listed on the front side.
Liquidation of the Debtor's Property and Payment of Creditors' Claims	The bankruptcy trustee listed on the front of this notice will collect and sell the debtor's property that is not exempt. If the trustee can collect enough money, creditors may be paid some or all of the debts owed to them, in the order specified by the Bankruptcy Code. To make sure you receive any share of that money, you must file a Proof of Claim, as described above.
Bankruptcy Clerk's Office	Any paper that you file in this bankruptcy case should be filed at the bankruptcy clerk's office at the address listed on the front side. You may inspect all papers filed, including the list of the debtor's property and debts and the list of the property claimed as exempt, at the bankruptcy clerk's office.
Legal Advice	The staff of the bankruptcy clerk's office cannot give legal advice. You may want to consult an attorney to protect your rights.

—Refer To Other Side For Important Deadlines and Notices—

FORM B9D (Chapter 7 Corporation/Partnership Asset Case) (9/97)

UNITED STATES BANKRUPTCY COURT _____ District of_____

Notice of
Chapter 7 Bankruptcy Case, Meeting of Creditors, & Deadlines

[A chapter 7 bankruptcy case concerning the debtor [corporation] *or* [partnership] listed below was filed on _____(date).]

or [A bankruptcy case concerning the debtor [corporation] *or* [partnership] listed below was originally filed under chapter ____

on

_____ (date) and was converted to a case under chapter 7 on_____.]

You may be a creditor of the debtor. **This notice lists important deadlines.** You may want to consult an attorney to protect your rights. All documents filed in the case may be inspected at the bankruptcy clerk's office at the address listed below. NOTE: The staff of the bankruptcy clerk's office cannot give legal advice.

See Reverse Side For Important Explanations.

Debtor (name(s) and address):	Case Number:
	Taxpayer ID Nos.:
Attorney for Debtor (name and address):	Bankruptcy Trustee (name and address):
Telephone number:	Telephone number:

Meeting of Creditors:

Date: /   /   Time: (   ) A.M.   Location:
                                      (   ) P.M.

Deadline to File a Proof of Claim

Proof of Claim must be *received* by the bankruptcy clerk's office by the following deadline:

For all creditors (except a governmental unit):	For a governmental unit:

Creditors May Not Take Certain Actions:

The filing of the bankruptcy case automatically stays certain collection and other actions against the debtor and the debtor's property. If you attempt to collect a debt or take other action in violation of the Bankruptcy Code, you may be penalized.

Address of the Bankruptcy Clerk's Office:	For the Court:
	Clerk of the Bankruptcy Court:
Telephone number:	
Hours Open:	Date:

EXPLANATIONS

FORM B9D (9/97)

Filing of Chapter 7 Bankruptcy Case	A bankruptcy case under chapter 7 of the Bankruptcy Code (title 11, United States Code) has been filed in this court by or against the debtor listed on the front side, and an order for relief has been entered.
Creditors May Not Take Certain Actions	Prohibited collection actions are listed in Bankruptcy Code § 362. Common examples of prohibited actions include contacting the debtor by telephone, mail or otherwise to demand repayment; taking actions to collect money or obtain property from the debtor; repossessing the debtor's property; and starting or continuing lawsuits or foreclosures.
Meeting of Creditors	A meeting of creditors is scheduled for the date, time and location listed on the front side. *The debtor's representative must be present at the meeting to be questioned under oath by the trustee and by creditors.* Creditors are welcome to attend, but are not required to do so. The meeting may be continued and concluded at a later date without further notice.
Claims	A Proof of Claim is a signed statement describing a creditor's claim. If a Proof of Claim form is not included with this notice, you can obtain one at any bankruptcy clerk's office. If you do not file a Proof of Claim by the "Deadline to File a Proof of Claim" listed on the front side, you might not be paid any money on your claim against the debtor in the bankruptcy case. To be paid you must file a Proof of Claim even if your claim is listed in the schedules filed by the debtor.
Liquidation of the Debtor's Property and Payment of Creditors' Claims	The bankruptcy trustee listed on the front of this notice will collect and sell the debtor's property. If the trustee can collect enough money, creditors may be paid some or all of the debts owed to them, in the order specified by the Bankruptcy Code. To make sure you receive any share of that money, you must file a Proof of Claim, as described above.
Bankruptcy Clerk's Office	Any paper that you file in this bankruptcy case should be filed at the bankruptcy clerk's office at the address listed on the front side. You may inspect all papers filed, including the list of the debtor's property and debts, at the bankruptcy clerk's office.
Legal Advice	The staff of the bankruptcy clerk's office cannot give legal advice. You may want to consult an attorney to protect your rights.

—Refer To Other Side For Important Deadlines and Notices—

FORM B9E (Chapter 11 Individual or Joint Debtor Case) (9/97)

UNITED STATES BANKRUPTCY COURT _____ District of _____

Notice of
Chapter 11 Bankruptcy Case, Meeting of Creditors, & Deadlines

[A chapter 11 bankruptcy case concerning the debtor(s) listed below was filed on _____ (date).]

or [A bankruptcy case concerning the debtor(s) listed below was originally filed under chapter _____ on _____ (date) and was converted to a case under chapter 11 on_____.]

You may be a creditor of the debtor. **This notice lists important deadlines.** You may want to consult an attorney to protect your rights. All documents filed in the case may be inspected at the bankruptcy clerk's office at the address listed below. NOTE: The staff of the bankruptcy clerk's office cannot give legal advice.

See Reverse Side For Important Explanations.

Debtor(s) (name(s) and address):	Case Number:
	Social Security/Taxpayer ID Nos.:
Attorney for Debtor(s) (name and address):	Telephone number:

Meeting of Creditors:

Date: /   /   Time: (   ) A.M.   Location:
                                 (   ) P.M.

Deadlines:

Papers must be *received* by the bankruptcy clerk's office by the following deadlines:

Deadline to File a Proof of Claim:

Notice of deadline will be sent at a later time.

Deadline to File a Complaint to Determine Dischargeability of Certain Debts:

Deadline to File a Complaint Objecting to Discharge of the Debtor:

First date set for hearing on confirmation of plan.
Notice of that date will be sent at a later time.

Deadline to Object to Exemptions:

Thirty (30) days after the *conclusion* of the meeting of creditors.

Creditors May Not Take Certain Actions:

The filing of the bankruptcy case automatically stays certain collection and other actions against the debtor and the debtor's property. If you attempt to collect a debt or take other action in violation of the Bankruptcy Code, you may be penalized.

Address of the Bankruptcy Clerk's Office:	For the Court:
	Clerk of the Bankruptcy Court:
Telephone number:	
Hours Open:	Date:

EXPLANATIONS

Filing of Chapter 11 Bankruptcy Case	A bankruptcy case under chapter 11 of the Bankruptcy Code (title 11, United States Code) has been filed in this court by or against the debtor(s) listed on the front side, and an order for relief has been entered. Chapter 11 allows a debtor to reorganize or liquidate pursuant to a plan. A plan is not effective unless confirmed by the court. You may be sent a copy of the plan and a disclosure statement telling you about the plan, and you might have the opportunity to vote on the plan. You will be sent notice of the date of the confirmation hearing, and you may object to confirmation of the plan and attend the confirmation hearing. Unless a trustee is serving, the debtor will remain in possession of the debtor's property and may continue to operate any business.
Creditors May Not Take Certain Actions	Prohibited collection actions are listed in Bankruptcy Code § 362. Common examples of prohibited actions include contacting the debtor by telephone, mail or otherwise to demand repayment; taking actions to collect money or obtain property from the debtor; repossessing the debtor's property; starting or continuing lawsuits or foreclosures; and garnishing or deducting from the debtor's wages.
Meeting of Creditors	A meeting of creditors is scheduled for the date, time and location listed on the front side. *The debtor (both spouses in a joint case) must be present at the meeting to be questioned under oath by the trustee and by creditors.* Creditors are welcome to attend, but are not required to do so. The meeting may be continued and concluded at a later date without further notice.
Claims	A Proof of Claim is a signed statement describing a creditor's claim. If a Proof of Claim form is not included with this notice, you can obtain one at any bankruptcy clerk's office. You may look at the schedules that have been or will be filed at the bankruptcy clerk's office. If your claim is scheduled and is *not* listed as disputed, contingent, or unliquidated, it will be allowed in the amount scheduled unless you file a Proof of Claim or you are sent further notice about the claim. Whether or not your claim is scheduled, you are permitted to file a Proof of Claim. If your claim is not listed at all *or* if your claim is listed as disputed, contingent, or unliquidated, then you must file a Proof of Claim or you might not be paid any money on your claim against the debtor in the bankruptcy case. The court has not yet set a deadline to file a Proof of Claim. If a deadline is set, you will be sent another notice.
Discharge of Debts	Confirmation of a chapter 11 plan may result in a discharge of debts, which may include all or part of your debt. See Bankruptcy Code § 1141(d). A discharge means that you may never try to collect the debt from the debtor except as provided in the plan. If you believe that a debt owed to you is not dischargeable under Bankruptcy Code § 523(a)(2), (4), (6), or (15), you must start a lawsuit by filing a complaint in the bankruptcy clerk's office by the "Deadline to File a Complaint to Determine Dischargeability of Certain Debts" listed on the front side. The bankruptcy clerk's office must receive the complaint and the required filing fee by that Deadline. If you believe that the debtor is not entitled to receive a discharge under Bankruptcy Code § 1141(d)(3), you must file a complaint with the required filing fee in the bankruptcy clerk's office not later than the first date set for the hearing on confirmation of the plan. You will be sent another notice informing you of that date.
Exempt Property	The debtor is permitted by law to keep certain property as exempt. Exempt property will not be sold and distributed to creditors, even if the debtor's case is converted to chapter 7. The debtor must file a list of all property claimed as exempt. You may inspect that list at the bankruptcy clerk's office. If you believe that an exemption claimed by the debtor is not authorized by law, you may file an objection to that exemption. The bankruptcy clerk's office must receive the objection by the "Deadline to Object to Exemptions" listed on the front side.
Bankruptcy Clerk's Office	Any paper that you file in this bankruptcy case should be filed at the bankruptcy clerk's office at the address listed on the front side. You may inspect all papers filed, including the list of the debtor's property and debts and the list of the property claimed as exempt, at the bankruptcy clerk's office.
Legal Advice	The staff of the bankruptcy clerk's office cannot give legal advice. You may want to consult an attorney to protect your rights.

—Refer To Other Side For Important Deadlines and Notices—

FORM B9E (ALT.) (Chapter 11 Individual or Joint Debtor Case) (9/97)

UNITED STATES BANKRUPTCY COURT _____ District of_____

Notice of
Chapter 11 Bankruptcy Case, Meeting of Creditors, & Deadlines

[A chapter 11 bankruptcy case concerning the debtor(s) listed below was filed on _____ (date).]

or [A bankruptcy case concerning the debtor(s) listed below was originally filed under chapter _____ on _____ (date) and was converted to a case under chapter 11 on_____.]

You may be a creditor of the debtor. **This notice lists important deadlines.** You may want to consult an attorney to protect your rights. All documents filed in the case may be inspected at the bankruptcy clerk's office at the address listed below. NOTE: The staff of the bankruptcy clerk's office cannot give legal advice.

See Reverse Side For Important Explanations.

Debtor(s) (name(s) and address):	Case Number:
	Social Security/Taxpayer ID Nos.:
Attorney for Debtor(s) (name and address):	Telephone number:

Meeting of Creditors:

Date: / / Time: ( ) A.M. Location:
( ) P.M.

Deadlines:

Papers must be *received* by the bankruptcy clerk's office by the following deadlines:

Deadline to File a Proof of Claim:

For all creditors (except a governmental unit):   For a governmental unit:

Deadline to File a Complaint to Determine Dischargeability of Certain Debts:

Deadline to File a Complaint Objecting to Discharge of the Debtor:

First date set for hearing on confirmation of plan.
Notice of that date will be sent at a later time.

Deadline to Object to Exemptions:

Thirty (30) days after the *conclusion* of the meeting of creditors.

Creditors May Not Take Certain Actions:

The filing of the bankruptcy case automatically stays certain collection and other actions against the debtor and the debtor's property. If you attempt to collect a debt or take other action in violation of the Bankruptcy Code, you may be penalized.

Address of the Bankruptcy Clerk's Office:	**For the Court:**
	Clerk of the Bankruptcy Court:
Telephone number:	
Hours Open:	Date:

EXPLANATIONS

FORM B9E (ALT.) (9/97)

Filing of Chapter 11 Bankruptcy Case	A bankruptcy case under chapter 11 of the Bankruptcy Code (title 11, United States Code) has been filed in this court by or against the debtor(s) listed on the front side, and an order for relief has been entered. Chapter 11 allows a debtor to reorganize or liquidate pursuant to a plan. A plan is not effective unless confirmed by the court. You may be sent a copy of the plan and a disclosure statement telling you about the plan, and you might have the opportunity to vote on the plan. You will be sent notice of the date of the confirmation hearing, and you may object to confirmation of the plan and attend the confirmation hearing. Unless a trustee is serving, the debtor will remain in possession of the debtor's property and may continue to operate any business.
Creditors May Not Take Certain Actions	Prohibited collection actions are listed in Bankruptcy Code § 362. Common examples of prohibited actions include contacting the debtor by telephone, mail or otherwise to demand repayment; taking actions to collect money or obtain property from the debtor; repossessing the debtor's property; starting or continuing lawsuits or foreclosures; and garnishing or deducting from the debtor's wages.
Meeting of Creditors	A meeting of creditors is scheduled for the date, time and location listed on the front side. *The debtor (both spouses in a joint case) must be present at the meeting to be questioned under oath by the trustee and by creditors.* Creditors are welcome to attend, but are not required to do so. The meeting may be continued and concluded at a later date without further notice.
Claims	A Proof of Claim is a signed statement describing a creditor's claim. If a Proof of Claim form is not included with this notice, you can obtain one at any bankruptcy clerk's office. You may look at the schedules that have been or will be filed at the bankruptcy clerk's office. If your claim is scheduled and is *not* listed as disputed, contingent, or unliquidated, it will be allowed in the amount scheduled unless you file a Proof of Claim or you are sent further notice about the claim. Whether or not your claim is scheduled, you are permitted to file a Proof of Claim. If your claim is not listed at all *or* if your claim is listed as disputed, contingent, or unliquidated, then you must file a Proof of Claim by the "Deadline to File a Proof of Claim" listed on the front side, or you might not be paid any money on your claim against the debtor in the bankruptcy case.
Discharge of Debts	Confirmation of a chapter 11 plan may result in a discharge of debts, which may include all or part of your debt. See Bankruptcy Code § 1141(d). A discharge means that you may never try to collect the debt from the debtor except as provided in the plan. If you believe that a debt owed to you is not dischargeable under Bankruptcy Code § 523(a)(2), (4), (6), or (15), you must start a lawsuit by filing a complaint in the bankruptcy clerk's office by the "Deadline to File a Complaint to Determine Dischargeability of Certain Debts" listed on the front side. The bankruptcy clerk's office must receive the complaint and the required filing fee by that Deadline. If you believe that the debtor is not entitled to receive a discharge under Bankruptcy Code § 1141(d)(3), you must file a complaint with the required filing fee in the bankruptcy clerk's office not later than the first date set for the hearing on confirmation of the plan. You will be sent another notice informing you of that date.
Exempt Property	The debtor is permitted by law to keep certain property as exempt. Exempt property will not be sold and distributed to creditors, even if the debtor's case is converted to chapter 7. The debtor must file a list of all property claimed as exempt. You may inspect that list at the bankruptcy clerk's office. If you believe that an exemption claimed by the debtor is not authorized by law, you may file an objection to that exemption. The bankruptcy clerk's office must receive the objection by the "Deadline to Object to Exemptions" listed on the front side.
Bankruptcy Clerk's Office	Any paper that you file in this bankruptcy case should be filed at the bankruptcy clerk's office at the address listed on the front side. You may inspect all papers filed, including the list of the debtor's property and debts and the list of the property claimed as exempt, at the bankruptcy clerk's office.
Legal Advice	The staff of the bankruptcy clerk's office cannot give legal advice. You may want to consult an attorney to protect your rights.

—Refer To Other Side For Important Deadlines and Notices—

FORM B9F (Chapter 11 Corporation/Partnership Asset Case) (9/97)

UNITED STATES BANKRUPTCY COURT	_____ District of _____

Notice of
Chapter 11 Bankruptcy Case, Meeting of Creditors, & Deadlines

[A chapter 11 bankruptcy case concerning the debtor [corporation] *or* [partnership] listed below was filed on _____ (date).] *or* [A bankruptcy case concerning the debtor [corporation] *or* [partnership] listed below was originally filed under chapter _____ on _____ (date) and was converted to a case under chapter 11 on_____.]

You may be a creditor of the debtor. **This notice lists important deadlines.** You may want to consult an attorney to protect your rights. All documents filed in the case may be inspected at the bankruptcy clerk's office at the address listed below. NOTE: The staff of the bankruptcy clerk's office cannot give legal advice.

See Reverse Side For Important Explanations.

Debtor (name(s) and address):	Case Number:
	Taxpayer ID Nos.:
Attorney for Debtor (name and address):	Telephone number:

Meeting of Creditors:

Date: /   /   Time: ( ) A.M.   Location:
                                ( ) P.M.

Deadline to File a Proof of Claim

Proof of Claim must be *received* by the bankruptcy clerk's office by the following deadline:
Notice of deadline will be sent at a later time.

Creditors May Not Take Certain Actions:

The filing of the bankruptcy case automatically stays certain collection and other actions against the debtor and the debtor's property. If you attempt to collect a debt or take other action in violation of the Bankruptcy Code, you may be penalized.

Address of the Bankruptcy Clerk's Office:	For the Court:
	Clerk of the Bankruptcy Court:
Telephone number:	
Hours Open:	Date:

EXPLANATIONS

FORM B9F (9/97)

Filing of Chapter 11 Bankruptcy Case	A bankruptcy case under chapter 11 of the Bankruptcy Code (title 11, United States Code) has been filed in this court by or against the debtor listed on the front side, and an order for relief has been entered. Chapter 11 allows a debtor to reorganize or liquidate pursuant to a plan. A plan is not effective unless confirmed by the court. You may be sent a copy of the plan and a disclosure statement telling you about the plan, and you might have the opportunity to vote on the plan. You will be sent notice of the date of the confirmation hearing, and you may object to confirmation of the plan and attend the confirmation hearing. Unless a trustee is serving, the debtor will remain in possession of the debtor's property and may continue to operate any business.
Creditors May Not Take Certain Actions	Prohibited collection actions are listed in Bankruptcy Code § 362. Common examples of prohibited actions include contacting the debtor by telephone, mail or otherwise to demand repayment; taking actions to collect money or obtain property from the debtor; repossessing the debtor's property; starting or continuing lawsuits or foreclosures.
Meeting of Creditors	A meeting of creditors is scheduled for the date, time and location listed on the front side. *The debtor's representative must be present at the meeting to be questioned under oath by the trustee and by creditors.* Creditors are welcome to attend, but are not required to do so. The meeting may be continued and concluded at a later date without further notice.
Claims	A Proof of Claim is a signed statement describing a creditor's claim. If a Proof of Claim form is not included with this notice, you can obtain one at any bankruptcy clerk's office. You may look at the schedules that have been or will be filed at the bankruptcy clerk's office. If your claim is scheduled and is *not* listed as disputed, contingent, or unliquidated, it will be allowed in the amount scheduled unless you file a Proof of Claim or you are sent further notice about the claim. Whether or not your claim is scheduled, you are permitted to file a Proof of Claim. If your claim is not listed at all *or* if your claim is listed as disputed, contingent, or unliquidated, then you must file a Proof of Claim or you might not be paid any money on your claim against the debtor in the bankruptcy case. The court has not yet set a deadline to file a Proof of Claim. If a deadline is set, you will be sent another notice.
Discharge of Debts	Confirmation of a chapter 11 plan may result in a discharge of debts, which may include all or part of your debt. See Bankruptcy Code § 1141(d). A discharge means that you may never try to collect the debt from the debtor, except as provided in the plan.
Bankruptcy Clerk's Office	Any paper that you file in this bankruptcy case should be filed at the bankruptcy clerk's office at the address listed on the front side. You may inspect all papers filed, including the list of the debtor's property and debts at the bankruptcy clerk's office.
Legal Advice	The staff of the bankruptcy clerk's office cannot give legal advice. You may want to consult an attorney to protect your rights.

—Refer To Other Side For Important Deadlines and Notices—

FORM B9F (ALT.) (Chapter 11 Corporation/Partnership Case) (9/97)

UNITED STATES BANKRUPTCY COURT _____ District of_____

Notice of
Chapter 11 Bankruptcy Case, Meeting of Creditors, & Deadlines

[A chapter 11 bankruptcy case concerning the debtor [corporation] *or* [partnership] listed below was filed on _____ (date).] *or* [A bankruptcy case concerning the debtor [corporation] *or* [partnership] listed below was originally filed under chapter _____ on _____ (date) and was converted to a case under chapter 11 on _____.]

You may be a creditor of the debtor. **This notice lists important deadlines.** You may want to consult an attorney to protect your rights. All documents filed in the case may be inspected at the bankruptcy clerk's office at the address listed below. NOTE: The staff of the bankruptcy clerk's office cannot give legal advice.

See Reverse Side For Important Explanations.

Debtor (name(s) and address):	Case Number:
	Taxpayer ID Nos.:
Attorney for Debtor (name and address):	Telephone number:

Meeting of Creditors:

Date: / / Time: ( ) A.M. ( ) P.M.	Location:

Deadlines to File a Proof of Claim

Proof of Claim must be *received* by the bankruptcy clerk's office by the following deadline:

For all creditors (except a governmental unit):	For a governmental unit:

Creditors May Not Take Certain Actions:

The filing of the bankruptcy case automatically stays certain collection and other actions against the debtor and the debtor's property. If you attempt to collect a debt or take other action in violation of the Bankruptcy Code, you may be penalized.

Address of the Bankruptcy Clerk's Office:	**For the Court:**
	Clerk of the Bankruptcy Court:
Telephone number:	
Hours Open:	Date:

EXPLANATIONS

FORM B9F (Alt.) (9/97)

Filing of Chapter 11 Bankruptcy Case	A bankruptcy case under chapter 11 of the Bankruptcy Code (title 11, United States Code) has been filed in this court by or against the debtor listed on the front side, and an order for relief has been entered. Chapter 11 allows a debtor to reorganize or liquidate pursuant to a plan. A plan is not effective unless confirmed by the court. You may be sent a copy of the plan and a disclosure statement telling you about the plan, and you might have the opportunity to vote on the plan. You will be sent notice of the date of the confirmation hearing, and you may object to confirmation of the plan and attend the confirmation hearing. Unless a trustee is serving, the debtor will remain in possession of the debtor's property and may continue to operate any business.
Creditors May Not Take Certain Actions	Prohibited collection actions are listed in Bankruptcy Code § 362. Common examples of prohibited actions include contacting the debtor by telephone, mail or otherwise to demand repayment; taking actions to collect money or obtain property from the debtor; repossessing the debtor's property; starting or continuing lawsuits or foreclosures.
Meeting of Creditors	A meeting of creditors is scheduled for the date, time and location listed on the front side. *The debtor's representative must be present at the meeting to be questioned under oath by the trustee and by creditors.* Creditors are welcome to attend, but are not required to do so. The meeting may be continued and concluded at a later date without further notice.
Claims	A Proof of Claim is a signed statement describing a creditor's claim. If a Proof of Claim form is not included with this notice, you can obtain one at any bankruptcy clerk's office. You may look at the schedules that have been or will be filed at the bankruptcy clerk's office. If your claim is scheduled and is *not* listed as disputed, contingent, or unliquidated, it will be allowed in the amount scheduled unless you file a Proof of Claim or you are sent further notice about the claim. Whether or not your claim is scheduled, you are permitted to file a Proof of Claim. If your claim is not listed at all *or* if your claim is listed as disputed, contingent, or unliquidated, then you must file a Proof of Claim by the "Deadline to File a Proof of Claim" listed on the front side, or you might not be paid any money on your claim against the debtor in the bankruptcy case.
Discharge of Debts	Confirmation of a chapter 11 plan may result in a discharge of debts, which may include all or part of your debt. See Bankruptcy Code § 1141(d). A discharge means that you may never try to collect the debt from the debtor, except as provided in the plan.
Bankruptcy Clerk's Office	Any paper that you file in this bankruptcy case should be filed at the bankruptcy clerk's office at the address listed on the front side. You may inspect all papers filed, including the list of the debtor's property and debts, at the bankruptcy clerk's office.
Legal Advice	The staff of the bankruptcy clerk's office cannot give legal advice. You may want to consult an attorney to protect your rights.

—Refer To Other Side For Important Deadlines and Notices—

FORM B9G (Chapter 12 Individual or Joint Debtor Family Farmer) (9/97)

UNITED STATES BANKRUPTCY COURT _____ District of_____

Notice of
Chapter 12 Bankruptcy Case, Meeting of Creditors, & Deadlines

[The debtor(s) listed below filed a chapter 12 bankruptcy case on _____ (date).]

or [A bankruptcy case concerning the debtor(s) listed below was originally filed under chapter _____ on _____ (date) and was converted to a case under chapter 12 on_____.]

You may be a creditor of the debtor. **This notice lists important deadlines.** You may want to consult an attorney to protect your rights. All documents filed in the case may be inspected at the bankruptcy clerk's office at the address listed below. NOTE: The staff of the bankruptcy clerk's office cannot give legal advice.

See Reverse Side For Important Explanations.

Debtor(s) (name(s) and address):	Case Number:
	Social Security/Taxpayer ID Nos.:
Attorney for Debtor(s) (name and address):	Bankruptcy Trustee (name and address):
Telephone number:	Telephone number:

Meeting of Creditors:

Date: /   /   Time: ( ) A.M.   Location:
                                    ( ) P.M.

Deadlines:

Papers must be *received* by the bankruptcy clerk's office by the following deadlines:

Deadline to File a Proof of Claim:

For all creditors (except a governmental unit):   For a governmental unit:

Deadline to File a Complaint to Determine Dischargeability of Certain Debts:

Deadline to Object to Exemptions:
Thirty (30) days after the *conclusion* of the meeting of creditors.

Filing of Plan, Hearing on Confirmation of Plan

[The debtor has filed a plan. The plan or a summary of the plan is enclosed. The hearing on confirmation will be held:
Date: _____ Time: _____ Location: _____]

or [The debtor has filed a plan. The plan or a summary of the plan and notice of confirmation hearing will be sent separately.]

or [The debtor has not filed a plan as of this date. You will be sent separate notice of the hearing on confirmation of the plan.]

Creditors May Not Take Certain Actions:

The filing of the bankruptcy case automatically stays certain collection and other actions against the debtor, the debtor's property, and certain codebtors. If you attempt to collect a debt or take other action in violation of the Bankruptcy Code, you may be penalized.

Address of the Bankruptcy Clerk's Office:	**For the Court:**
	Clerk of the Bankruptcy Court:
Telephone number:	
Hours Open:	Date:

EXPLANATIONS

FORM B9G (9/97)

Filing of Chapter 12 Bankruptcy Case	A bankruptcy case under chapter 12 of the Bankruptcy Code (title 11, United States Code) has been filed in this court by the debtor(s) listed on the front side, and an order for relief has been entered. Chapter 12 allows family farmers to adjust their debts pursuant to a plan. A plan is not effective unless confirmed by the court. You may object to confirmation of the plan and appear at the confirmation hearing. A copy or summary of the plan [is included with this notice] *or* [will be sent to you later], and [the confirmation hearing will be held on the date indicated on the front of this notice] *or* [you will be sent notice of the confirmation hearing]. The debtor will remain in possession of the debtor's property and may continue to operate the debtor's business unless the court orders otherwise.
Creditors May Not Take Certain Actions	Prohibited collection actions against the debtor and certain codebtors are listed in Bankruptcy Code § 362 and § 1201. Common examples of prohibited actions include contacting the debtor by telephone, mail or otherwise to demand repayment; taking actions to collect money or obtain property from the debtor; repossessing the debtor's property; starting or continuing lawsuits or foreclosures; and garnishing or deducting from the debtor's wages.
Meeting of Creditors	A meeting of creditors is scheduled for the date, time and location listed on the front side. *The debtor (both spouses in a joint case) must be present at the meeting to be questioned under oath by the trustee and by creditors.* Creditors are welcome to attend, but are not required to do so. The meeting may be continued and concluded at a later date without further notice.
Claims	A Proof of Claim is a signed statement describing a creditor's claim. If a Proof of Claim form is not included with this notice, you can obtain one at any bankruptcy clerk's office. If you do not file a Proof of Claim by the "Deadline to File a Proof of Claim" listed on the front side, you might not be paid any money on your claim against the debtor in the bankruptcy case. To be paid you must file a Proof of Claim even if your claim is listed in the schedules filed by the debtor.
Discharge of Debts	The debtor is seeking a discharge of most debts, which may include your debt. A discharge means that you may never try to collect the debt from the debtor. If you believe that a debt owed to you is not dischargeable under Bankruptcy Code § 523(a)(2), (4), (6), or (15), you must start a lawsuit by filing a complaint in the bankruptcy clerk's office by the "Deadline to File a Complaint to Determine Dischargeability of Certain Debts" listed on the front side. The bankruptcy clerk's office must receive the complaint and the required filing fee by that Deadline.
Exempt Property	The debtor is permitted by law to keep certain property as exempt. Exempt property will not be sold and distributed to creditors, even if the debtor's case is converted to chapter 7. The debtor must file a list of all property claimed as exempt. You may inspect that list at the bankruptcy clerk's office. If you believe that an exemption claimed by the debtor is not authorized by law, you may file an objection to that exemption. The bankruptcy clerk's office must receive the objection by the "Deadline to Object to Exemptions" listed on the front side.
Bankruptcy Clerk's Office	Any paper that you file in this bankruptcy case should be filed at the bankruptcy clerk's office at the address listed on the front side. You may inspect all papers filed, including the list of the debtor's property and debts and the list of the property claimed as exempt, at the bankruptcy clerk's office.
Legal Advice	The staff of the bankruptcy clerk's office cannot give legal advice. You may want to consult an attorney to protect your rights.

—Refer To Other Side For Important Deadlines and Notices—

FORM B9H (Chapter 12 Corporation/Partnership Family Farmer) (9/97)

UNITED STATES BANKRUPTCY COURT _____ District of _____

Notice of
Chapter 12 Bankruptcy Case, Meeting of Creditors, & Deadlines

[The debtor [corporation] *or* [partnership] listed below filed a chapter 12 bankruptcy case on _____(date).]
or [A bankruptcy case concerning the debtor [corporation] *or* [partnership] listed below was originally filed under chapter ____
on _____ (date) and was converted to a case under chapter 12 on_____.]

You may be a creditor of the debtor. **This notice lists important deadlines.** You may want to consult an attorney to protect your rights. All documents filed in the case may be inspected at the bankruptcy clerk's office at the address listed below. NOTE: The staff of the bankruptcy clerk's office cannot give legal advice.

See Reverse Side For Important Explanations.

Debtor (name(s) and address):	Case Number:
	Social Security/Taxpayer ID Nos.:
Attorney for Debtor (name and address):	Bankruptcy Trustee (name and address):
Telephone number:	Telephone number:

Meeting of Creditors:

Date: /   /   Time: (   ) A.M.   Location:
                                     (   ) P.M.

Deadlines:

Papers must be *received* by the bankruptcy clerk's office by the following deadlines:

Deadline to File a Proof of Claim:

For all creditors (except a governmental unit):	For a governmental unit:

Deadline to File a Complaint to Determine Dischargeability of Certain Debts:

Filing of Plan, Hearing on Confirmation of Plan

[The debtor has filed a plan. The plan or a summary of the plan is enclosed. The hearing on confirmation will be held:
Date: _____ Time: _____ Location: _____]
or [The debtor has filed a plan. The plan or a summary of the plan and notice of confirmation hearing will be sent separately.]
or [The debtor has not filed a plan as of this date. You will be sent separate notice of the hearing on confirmation of the plan.]

Creditors May Not Take Certain Actions:

The filing of the bankruptcy case automatically stays certain collection and other actions against the debtor, the debtor's property, and certain codebtors. If you attempt to collect a debt or take other action in violation of the Bankruptcy Code, you may be penalized.

Address of the Bankruptcy Clerk's Office:	**For the Court:**
	Clerk of the Bankruptcy Court:
Telephone number:	
Hours Open:	Date:

Filing of Chapter 12 Bankruptcy Case	A bankruptcy case under chapter 12 of the Bankruptcy Code (title 11, United States Code) has been filed in this court by the debtor listed on the front side, and an order for relief has been entered. Chapter 12 allows family farmers to adjust their debts pursuant to a plan. A plan is not effective unless confirmed by the court. You may object to confirmation of the plan and appear at the confirmation hearing. A copy or summary of the plan [is included with this notice] *or* [will be sent to you later], and [the confirmation hearing will be held on the date indicated on the front of this notice] *or* [you will be sent notice of the confirmation hearing]. The debtor will remain in possession of the debtor's property and may continue to operate the debtor's business unless the court orders otherwise.
Creditors May Not Take Certain Actions	Prohibited collection actions against the debtor and certain codebtors are listed in Bankruptcy Code § 362 and § 1201. Common examples of prohibited actions include contacting the debtor by telephone, mail or otherwise to demand repayment; taking actions to collect money or obtain property from the debtor; repossessing the debtor's property; and starting or continuing lawsuits or foreclosures.
Meeting of Creditors	A meeting of creditors is scheduled for the date, time and location listed on the front side. *The debtor's representative must be present at the meeting to be questioned under oath by the trustee and by creditors.* Creditors are welcome to attend, but are not required to do so. The meeting may be continued and concluded at a later date without further notice.
Claims	A Proof of Claim is a signed statement describing a creditor's claim. If a Proof of Claim form is not included with this notice, you can obtain one at any bankruptcy clerk's office. If you do not file a Proof of Claim by the "Deadline to File a Proof of Claim" listed on the front side, you might not be paid any money on your claim against the debtor in the bankruptcy case. To be paid you must file a Proof of Claim even if your claim is listed in the schedules filed by the debtor.
Discharge of Debts	The debtor is seeking a discharge of most debts, which may include your debt. A discharge means that you may never try to collect the debt from the debtor. If you believe that a debt owed to you is not dischargeable under Bankruptcy Code § 523(a)(2), (4), or (6), you must start a lawsuit by filing a complaint in the bankruptcy clerk's office by the "Deadline to File a Complaint to Determine Dischargeability of Certain Debts" listed on the front side. The bankruptcy clerk's office must receive the complaint and the required filing fee by that Deadline.
Bankruptcy Clerk's Office	Any paper that you file in this bankruptcy case should be filed at the bankruptcy clerk's office at the address listed on the front side. You may inspect all papers filed, including the list of the debtor's property and debts, at the bankruptcy clerk's office.
Legal Advice	The staff of the bankruptcy clerk's office cannot give legal advice. You may want to consult an attorney to protect your rights.

—Refer To Other Side For Important Deadlines and Notices—

FORM B9I (Chapter 13 Case) (9/97)

UNITED STATES BANKRUPTCY COURT _____ District of _____

Notice of
Chapter 13 Bankruptcy Case, Meeting of Creditors, & Deadlines

[The debtor(s) listed below filed a chapter 13 bankruptcy case on _____ (date).]

or [A bankruptcy case concerning the debtor(s) listed below was originally filed under chapter _____ on _____ (date) and was converted to a case under chapter 13 on_____.]

You may be a creditor of the debtor. **This notice lists important deadlines.** You may want to consult an attorney to protect your rights. All documents filed in the case may be inspected at the bankruptcy clerk's office at the address listed below. NOTE: The staff of the bankruptcy clerk's office cannot give legal advice.

See Reverse Side For Important Explanations.

Debtor(s) (name(s) and address):	Case Number:
	Social Security/Taxpayer ID Nos.:
Attorney for Debtor(s) (name and address):	Bankruptcy Trustee (name and address):
Telephone number:	Telephone number:

Meeting of Creditors:

Date: / / Time: ( ) A.M. ( ) P.M.	Location:

Deadlines:

Papers must be *received* by the bankruptcy clerk's office by the following deadlines:

Deadline to File a Proof of Claim:

For all creditors (except a governmental unit):	For a governmental unit:

Deadline to Object to Exemptions:

Thirty (30) days after the *conclusion* of the meeting of creditors.

Filing of Plan, Hearing on Confirmation of Plan

[The debtor has filed a plan. The plan or a summary of the plan is enclosed. The hearing on confirmation will be held:
Date: _____ Time: _____ Location: _____]

or [The debtor has filed a plan. The plan or a summary of the plan and notice of confirmation hearing will be sent separately.]

or [The debtor has not filed a plan as of this date. You will be sent separate notice of the hearing on confirmation of the plan.]

Creditors May Not Take Certain Actions:

The filing of the bankruptcy case automatically stays certain collection and other actions against the debtor, debtor's property, and certain codebtors. If you attempt to collect a debt or take other action in violation of the Bankruptcy Code, you may be penalized.

Address of the Bankruptcy Clerk's Office:	**For the Court:**
	Clerk of the Bankruptcy Court:
Telephone number:	
Hours Open:	Date:

EXPLANATIONS

FORM B9I (9/97)

Filing of Chapter 13 Bankruptcy Case	A bankruptcy case under chapter 13 of the Bankruptcy Code (title 11, United States Code) has been filed in this court by the debtor(s) listed on the front side, and an order for relief has been entered. Chapter 13 allows an individual with regular income and debts below a specified amount to adjust debts pursuant to a plan. A plan is not effective unless confirmed by the bankruptcy court. You may object to confirmation of the plan and appear at the confirmation hearing. A copy or summary of the plan [is included with this notice] *or* [will be sent to you later], and [the confirmation hearing will be held on the date indicated on the front of this notice] *or* [you will be sent notice of the confirmation hearing]. The debtor will remain in possession of the debtor's property and may continue to operate the debtor's business, if any, unless the court orders otherwise.
Creditors May Not Take Certain Actions	Prohibited collection actions against the debtor and certain codebtors are listed in Bankruptcy Code § 362 and § 1301. Common examples of prohibited actions include contacting the debtor by telephone, mail or otherwise to demand repayment; taking actions to collect money or obtain property from the debtor; repossessing the debtor's property; starting or continuing lawsuits or foreclosures; and garnishing or deducting from the debtor's wages.
Meeting of Creditors	A meeting of creditors is scheduled for the date, time and location listed on the front side. *The debtor (both spouses in a joint case) must be present at the meeting to be questioned under oath by the trustee and by creditors.* Creditors are welcome to attend, but are not required to do so. The meeting may be continued and concluded at a later date without further notice.
Claims	A Proof of Claim is a signed statement describing a creditor's claim. If a Proof of Claim form is not included with this notice, you can obtain one at any bankruptcy clerk's office. If you do not file a Proof of Claim by the "Deadline to File a Proof of Claim" listed on the front side, you might not be paid any money on your claim against the debtor in the bankruptcy case. To be paid you must file a Proof of Claim even if your claim is listed in the schedules filed by the debtor.
Discharge of Debts	The debtor is seeking a discharge of most debts, which may include your debt. A discharge means that you may never try to collect the debt from the debtor.
Exempt Property	The debtor is permitted by law to keep certain property as exempt. Exempt property will not be sold and distributed to creditors, even if the debtor's case is converted to chapter 7. The debtor must file a list of all property claimed as exempt. You may inspect that list at the bankruptcy clerk's office. If you believe that an exemption claimed by the debtor is not authorized by law, you may file an objection to that exemption. The bankruptcy clerk's office must receive the objection by the "Deadline to Object to Exemptions" listed on the front side.
Bankruptcy Clerk's Office	Any paper that you file in this bankruptcy case should be filed at the bankruptcy clerk's office at the address listed on the front side. You may inspect all papers filed, including the list of the debtor's property and debts and the list of property claimed as exempt, at the bankruptcy clerk's office.
Legal Advice	The staff of the bankruptcy clerk's office cannot give legal advice. You may want to consult an attorney to protect your rights.

—Refer To Other Side For Important Deadlines and Notices—

FORM B10 (Official Form 10) (4/01)

UNITED STATES BANKRUPTCY COURT _____ DISTRICT OF _____		PROOF OF CLAIM

Name of Debtor	Case Number

NOTE: This form should not be used to make a claim for an administrative expense arising after the commencement of the case. A "request" for payment of an administrative expense may be filed pursuant to 11 U.S.C. § 503.

Name of Creditor (The person or other entity to whom the debtor owes money or property):	☐ Check box if you are aware that anyone else has filed a proof of claim relating to your claim. Attach copy of statement giving particulars.	
Name and address where notices should be sent:	☐ Check box if you have never received any notices from the bankruptcy court in this case. ☐ Check box if the address differs from the address on the envelope sent to you by the court.	
Telephone number:		THIS SPACE IS FOR COURT USE ONLY

Account or other number by which creditor identifies debtor:	Check here if this claim ☐ replaces a previously filed claim, dated:_____ ☐ amends

1. Basis for Claim
- ☐ Goods sold
- ☐ Services performed
- ☐ Money loaned
- ☐ Personal injury/wrongful death
- ☐ Taxes
- ☐ Other _____

- ☐ Retiree benefits as defined in 11 U.S.C. § 1114(a)
- ☐ Wages, salaries, and compensation (fill out below)

Your SS #: _____ _____ _____

Unpaid compensation for services performed

from _____ to_____
 (date)   (date)

2. Date debt was incurred:	**3. If court judgment, date obtained:**

4. Total Amount of Claim at Time Case Filed: $ _____

If all or part of your claim is secured or entitled to priority, also complete Item 5 or 6 below.
☐ Check this box if claim includes interest or other charges in addition to the principal amount of the claim. Attach itemized statement of all interest or additional charges.

5. Secured Claim.
☐ Check this box if your claim is secured by collateral (including a right of setoff).
Brief Description of Collateral:
☐ Real Estate   ☐ Motor Vehicle
☐ Other_____
Value of Collateral: $_____

Amount of arrearage and other charges <u>at time case filed</u> included in secured claim, if any: $_____

6. Unsecured Priority Claim.
☐ Check this box if you have an unsecured priority claim
Amount entitled to priority $_____
Specify the priority of the claim:
☐ Wages, salaries, or commissions (up to $4,650),* earned within 90 days before filing of the bankruptcy petition or cessation of the debtor's business, whichever is earlier - 11 U.S.C. § 507(a)(3).
☐ Contributions to an employee benefit plan - 11 U.S.C. § 507(a)(4).
☐ Up to $2,100* of deposits toward purchase, lease, or rental of property or services for personal, family, or household use - 11 U.S.C. § 507(a)(6).
☐ Alimony, maintenance, or support owed to a spouse, former spouse, or child - 11 U.S.C. § 507(a)(7).
☐ Taxes or penalties owed to governmental units - 11 U.S.C. § 507(a)(8).
☐ Other - Specify applicable paragraph of 11 U.S.C. § 507(a)(___).
*Amounts are subject to adjustment on 4/1/04 and every 3 years thereafter with respect to cases commenced on or after the date of adjustment.

7. Credits: The amount of all payments on this claim has been credited and deducted for the purpose of making this proof of claim.

8. Supporting Documents: *Attach copies of supporting documents,* such as promissory notes, purchase orders, invoices, itemized statements of running accounts, contracts, court judgments, mortgages, security agreements, and evidence of perfection of lien. DO NOT SEND ORIGINAL DOCUMENTS. If the documents are not available, explain. If the documents are voluminous, attach a summary.

9. Date-Stamped Copy: To receive an acknowledgment of the filing of your claim, enclose a stamped, self-addressed envelope and copy of this proof of claim.

THIS SPACE IS FOR COURT USE ONLY

Date	Sign and print the name and title, if any, of the creditor or other person authorized to file this claim (attach copy of power of attorney, if any):

Penalty for presenting fraudulent claim: Fine of up to $500,000 or imprisonment for up to 5 years, or both. 18 U.S.C. §§ 152 and 3571.

FORM B10 (Official Form 10) (9/97)

INSTRUCTIONS FOR PROOF OF CLAIM FORM

The instructions and definitions below are general explanations of the law. In particular types of cases or circumstances, such as bankruptcy cases that are not filed voluntarily by a debtor, there may be exceptions to these general rules.

—— DEFINITIONS ——

Debtor

The person, corporation, or other entity that has filed a bankruptcy case is called the debtor.

Creditor

A creditor is any person, corporation, or other entity to whom the debtor owed a debt on the date that the bankruptcy case was filed.

Proof of Claim

A form telling the bankruptcy court how much the debtor owed a creditor at the time the bankruptcy case was filed (the amount of the creditor's claim). This form must be filed with the clerk of the bankruptcy court where the bankruptcy case was filed.

Secured Claim

A claim is a secured claim to the extent that the creditor has a lien on property of the debtor (collateral) that gives the creditor the right to be paid from that property before creditors who do not have liens on the property.

Examples of liens are a mortgage on real estate and a security interest in a car, truck, boat, television set, or other item of property. A lien may have been obtained through a court proceeding before the bankruptcy case began; in some states a court judgment is a lien. In addition, to the extent a creditor also owes money to the debtor (has a right of setoff), the creditor's claim may be a secured claim. (See also *Unsecured Claim*.)

Unsecured Claim

If a claim is not a secured claim it is an unsecured claim. A claim may be partly secured and partly unsecured if the property on which a creditor has a lien is not worth enough to pay the creditor in full.

Unsecured Priority Claim

Certain types of unsecured claims are given priority, so they are to be paid in bankruptcy cases before most other unsecured claims (if there is sufficient money or property available to pay these claims). The most common types of priority claims are listed on the proof of claim form. Unsecured claims that are not specifically given priority status by the bankruptcy laws are classified as *Unsecured Nonpriority Claims.*

Items to be completed in Proof of Claim form (if not already filled in)

Court, Name of Debtor, and Case Number:

Fill in the name of the federal judicial district where the bankruptcy case was filed (for example, Central District of California), the name of the debtor in the bankruptcy case, and the bankruptcy case number. If you received a notice of the case from the court, all of this information is near the top of the notice.

Information about Creditor:

Complete the section giving the name, address, and telephone number of the creditor to whom the debtor owes money or property, and the debtor's account number, if any. If anyone else has already filed a proof of claim relating to this debt, if you never received notices from the bankruptcy court about this case, if your address differs from that to which the court sent notice, or if this proof of claim replaces or changes a proof of claim that was already filed, check the appropriate box on the form.

1. Basis for Claim:

Check the type of debt for which the proof of claim is being filed. If the type of debt is not listed, check "Other" and briefly describe the type of debt. If you were an employee of the debtor, fill in your social security number and the dates of work for which you were not paid.

2. Date Debt Incurred:

Fill in the date when the debt first was owed by the debtor.

3. Court Judgments:

If you have a court judgment for this debt, state the date the court entered the judgment.

4. Total Amount of Claim at Time Case Filed:

Fill in the total amount of the entire claim. If interest or other charges in addition to the principal amount of the claim are included, check the appropriate place on the form and attach an itemization of the interest and charges.

5. Secured Claim:

Check the appropriate place if the claim is a secured claim. You must state the type and value of property that is collateral for the claim, attach copies of the documentation of your lien, and state the amount past due on the claim as of the date the bankruptcy case was filed. A claim may be partly secured and partly unsecured. (See DEFINITIONS, above).

6. Unsecured Priority Claim:

Check the appropriate place if you have an unsecured priority claim, and state the amount entitled to priority. (See DEFINITIONS, above). A claim may be partly priority and partly nonpriority if, for example, the claim is for more than the amount given priority by the law. Check the appropriate place to specify the type of priority claim.

7. Credits:

By signing this proof of claim, you are stating under oath that in calculating the amount of your claim you have given the debtor credit for all payments received from the debtor.

8. Supporting Documents:

You must attach to this proof of claim form copies of documents that show the debtor owes the debt claimed or, if the documents are too lengthy, a summary of those documents. If documents are not available, you must attach an explanation of why they are not available.

Form B11A
6/90

Form 11A. GENERAL POWER OF ATTORNEY

[Caption as in Form 16B]

GENERAL POWER OF ATTORNEY

To _____ of * _____ , and
_____ of * _____ .

    The undersigned claimant hereby authorizes you, or any one of you, as attorney in fact for the undersigned and with full power of substitution, to vote on any question that may be lawfully submitted to creditors of the debtor in the above-entitled case; *[if appropriate]* to vote for a trustee of the estate of the debtor and for a committee of creditors; to receive dividends; and in general to perform any act not constituting the practice of law for the undersigned in all matters arising in this case.

    Dated: _____

Signed: _____

By _____

as _____

Address: _____

_____

    [If executed by an individual] Acknowledged before me on _____ .

    [If executed on behalf of a partnership] Acknowledged before me on _____ , by _____ , who says that he [or she] is a member of the partnership named above and is authorized to execute this power of attorney in its behalf.

    [If executed on behalf of a corporation] Acknowledged before me on _____ , by _____ , who says that he [or she] is _____ of the corporation named above and is authorized to execute this power of attorney in its behalf.

_____

_____

[Official character.]

* State mailing address.

266

Form B11B
6/90

Form 11B. SPECIAL POWER OF ATTORNEY

[Caption as in Form 16B]

SPECIAL POWER OF ATTORNEY

To _____ of * _____ , and
_____ of * _____ .

    The undersigned claimant hereby authorizes you, or any one of you, as attorney in fact for the undersigned *[if desired: and with full power of substitution,]* to attend the meeting of creditors of the debtor or any adjournment thereof, and to vote in my behalf on any question that may be lawfully submitted to creditors at such meeting or adjourned meeting, and for a trustee or trustees of the estate of the debtor.

    Dated: _____

                  Signed: _____

                  By _____

                  as _____

                  Address: _____

                      _____

[If executed by an individual] Acknowledged before me on _____ .

[If executed on behalf of a partnership] Acknowledged before me _____ , by _____ , who says that he *[or she]* is a member of the partnership named above and is authorized to execute this power of attorney in its behalf.

[If executed on behalf of a corporation] Acknowledged before me on _____ , by _____ , who says that he *[or she]* is _____ of the corporation named above and is authorized to execute this power of attorney in its behalf.

                  _____

                  _____

                    [Official character.]

* State mailing address.

Form B12
6/90

Form 12. ORDER AND NOTICE FOR HEARING
ON DISCLOSURE STATEMENT

[Caption as in Form 16A]

ORDER AND NOTICE FOR HEARING
ON DISCLOSURE STATEMENT

To the debtor, its creditors, and other parties in interest:

A disclosure statement and a plan under chapter 11 [br chapter 9] of the Bankruptcy Code having been filed by _____ on _____, IT IS ORDERED and notice is hereby given, that:

    1.   The hearing to consider the approval of the disclosure statement shall be held at: _____, on _____, at _____ o'clock __.m.

    2. _____ is fixed as the last day for filing and serving in accordance with Fed. R. Bankr. P. 3017(a) written objections to the disclosure statement.

    3. Within _____ days after entry of this order, the disclosure statement and plan shall be distributed in accordance with Fed. R. Bankr. P. 3017(a).

    4. Requests for copies of the disclosure statement and plan shall be mailed to the debtor in possession *or* trustee *or* debtor *or* _____] at * _____.

Dated: _____

BY THE COURT

_____
United States Bankruptcy Judge

* State mailing address

Form B13
6/90

Form 13. ORDER APPROVING DISCLOSURE STATEMENT AND FIXING TIME FOR FILING ACCEPTANCES OR REJECTIONS OF PLAN, COMBINED WITH NOTICE THEREOF

[Caption as in Form 16A]

ORDER APPROVING DISCLOSURE STATEMENT AND FIXING TIME FOR FILING ACCEPTANCES OR REJECTIONS OF PLAN, COMBINED WITH NOTICE THEREOF

A disclosure statement under chapter 11 of the Bankruptcy Code having been filed by _____, on _____ *if[appropriate,* and by _____, on _____], referring to a plan under chapter 11 of the Code filed by _____, on _____*if[appropriate,* and by _____, on _____ respectively*][appropriate,* as modified by a modification filed on _____]; and

It having been determined after hearing on notice that the disclosure statement[or statements] contains[s] adequate information:

IT IS ORDERED, and notice is hereby given, that:

A. The disclosure statement filed by _____ dated _____*if[appropriate,* and by _____, dated _____ is [are] approved.

B. _____ is fixed as the last day for filing written acceptances or rejections of the plan [or plans] referred to above.

C. Within _____ days after the entry of this order, the plan[or plans] *or* a summary *or* summaries thereof approved by the court, [and [*if appropriate]* a summary approved by the court of its opinion, if any, dated _____, approving the disclosure statement [or statements]], the disclosure statement [or statements], and a ballot conforming to Official Form 14 shall be mailed to creditors, equity security holders, and other parties in interest, and shall be transmitted to the United States trustee, as provided in Fed. R. Bankr. P. 3017(d).

D. If acceptances are filed for more than one plan, preferences among the plans so accepted may be indicated.

E. *[If appropriate]* _____ is fixed for the hearing on confirmation of the plan [or plans].

F. *[If appropriate]* _____ is fixed as the last day for filing and serving pursuant to Fed. R. Bankr. P. 3020(b)(1) written objections to confirmation of the plan.

Dated: _____

BY THE COURT

_____
United States Bankruptcy Judge

[If the court directs that a copy of the opinion should be transmitted in lieu of or in addition to the summary thereof, the appropriate change should be made in paragraph C of this order.]

269

Form B14 (Official Form 14)
(9/97)

Form 14. BALLOT FOR ACCEPTING OR REJECTING A PLAN

[Caption as in Form 16A]

CLASS [   ] BALLOT FOR ACCEPTING OR REJECTING
PLAN OF REORGANIZATION

[Proponent] filed a plan of reorganization dated *[Date]* (the "Plan") for the Debtor in this case. The Court has *[conditionally]* approved a disclosure statement with respect to the Plan (the "Disclosure Statement"). The Disclosure Statement provides information to assist you in deciding how to vote your ballot. If you do not have a Disclosure Statement, you may obtain a copy from *[name, address, telephone number and telecopy number of proponent/proponent's attorney.]* Court approval of the disclosure statement does not indicate approval of the Plan by the Court.

You should review the Disclosure Statement and the Plan before you vote. You may wish to seek legal advice concerning the Plan and your classification and treatment under the Plan. Your *[claim] [equity interest]* has been placed in class [   ] under the Plan. If you hold claims or equity interests in more than one class, you will receive a ballot for each class in which you are entitled to vote.

If your ballot is not received by *[name and address of proponent's attorney or other appropriate address]* on or before *[date]*, and such deadline is not extended, your vote will not count as either an acceptance or rejection of the Plan.

If the Plan is confirmed by the Bankruptcy Court it will be binding on you whether or not you vote.

ACCEPTANCE OR REJECTION OF THE PLAN

[At this point the ballot should provide for voting by the particular class of creditors or equity holders receiving the ballot using one of the following alternatives;]

[If the voter is the holder of a secured, priority, or unsecured nonpriority claim:]

The undersigned, the holder of a Class [   ] claim against the Debtor in the unpaid amount of
            Dollars ($)

[or, if the voter is the holder of a bond, debenture, or other debt security:]

The undersigned, the holder of a Class [   ] claim against the Debtor, consisting of Dollars ($) principal amount of *[describe bond, debenture, or other debt security]* of the Debtor (For purposes of this Ballot, it is not necessary and you should not adjust the principal amount for any accrued or unmatured interest.)

Form B14 continued
(9/97)

[or, if the voter is the holder of an equity interest:]

The undersigned, the holder of Class *[   ]* equity interest in the Debtor, consisting of _ shares or other interests of *[describe equity interest]* in the Debtor

[In each case, the following language should be included:]

(Check one box only)

[ ] ACCEPTS THE PLAN   [ ] REJECTS THE PLAN

Dated: _____

Print or type name: _____

Signature: _____

Title (if corporation or partnership) _____

Address: _____

                  _____

RETURN THIS BALLOT TO:

[Name and address of proponent's attorney or other appropriate address]

Form B15
6/90

Form 15. ORDER CONFIRMING PLAN

[Caption as in Form 16A]

ORDER CONFIRMING PLAN

The plan under chapter 11 of the Bankruptcy Code filed by _____, on
_____ [*if applicable*, as modified by a modification filed on _____,] or a summary
thereof, having been transmitted to creditors and equity security holders; and

It having been determined after hearing on notice that the requirements for confirmation set forth in 11 U.S.C.
§ 1129(a) [*or, if appropriate,* 11 U.S.C. § 1129(b)] have been satisfied;

IT IS ORDERED that:

The plan filed by _____, on _____, *[If*
appropriate, include dates and any other pertinent details of modifications to the plan] is confirmed.
A copy of the confirmed plan is attached.

Dated: _____

BY THE COURT

_____
United States Bankruptcy Judge.

Form B16A
11/94

Form 16A. CAPTION (FULL)

UNITED STATES BANKRUPTCY COURT
_____**DISTRICT OF**_____

In re _____,   )
    Set forth here all names including married,   )
    maiden, and trade names used by debtor within   )
    last 6 years.]   )
                  Debtor   )   Case No. _____

)
)
Address _____   )
)

    _____   )   Chapter _____
)
Social Security No(s). _____ and all   )
Employer's Tax Identification No(s). *[if any]*_____   )
_____   )

[Designation of Character of Paper]

Form B16B
12/94

FORM 16B. CAPTION (SHORT TITLE)

(May be used if 11 U.S.C. § 342(c) is not applicable)

UNITED STATES BANKRUPTCY COURT
_____ DISTRICT OF _____

In re _____,
                        Debtor

                                    Case No. _____

                                    Chapter _____

[Designation of Character of Paper]

Form 16C
12/94

FORM 16C. CAPTION OF COMPLAINT IN ADVERSARY PROCEEDING FILED BY A DEBTOR

UNITED STATES BANKRUPTCY COURT
_____ DISTRICT OF _____

In re _____,   )   Case No. _____
                            Debtor   )
)
)
Address _____   )   Chapter _____
)
_____   )
)
Social Security No(s). _____ or   )
Employer's Tax Identification No(s). *[if any]*_____   )
_____   )
)
)
_____,   )
                          Plaintiff   )
)
             v.   )
)
_____,   )   Adv. Proc. No. _____
                          Defendant   )

COMPLAINT

Form B16D
12/94

Form 16D. CAPTION FOR USE IN ADVERSARY PROCEEDING OTHER THAN FOR A COMPLAINT FILED BY A DEBTOR

UNITED STATES BANKRUPTCY COURT
_____ **DISTRICT OF** _____

In re _____,)
          Debtor) Case No. _____
)
_____,) Chapter _____
          Plaintiff)
)
     v.)
)
_____,) Adv. Proc. No. _____
         Defendant)

COMPLAINT [*or* other Designation]

[If used in a Notice of Appeal (see Form 17) or other notice filed and served by a debtor, this caption must be altered to include the debtor's address and Employer's Tax Identification Number(s) or Social Security Number(s) as in Form 16C.]

Form B17 (Official Form 17)
(9/97)

FORM 17. NOTICE OF APPEAL UNDER 28 U.S.C. § 158(a) or (b) FROM A JUDGMENT, ORDER, OR DECREE OF A BANKRUPTCY JUDGE

[Caption as in Form 16A, 16B, or 16D, as appropriate]

NOTICE OF APPEAL

_____, the plaintiff [*or* defendant *or* other party] appeals under 28 U.S.C. § 158(a) or (b) from the judgment, order, or decree of the bankruptcy judge (describe) entered in this adversary proceeding [*or other proceeding, describe type*] on the _____ day of _____, (year) .

The names of all parties to the judgment, order, or decree appealed from and the names, addresses, and telephone numbers of their respective attorneys are as follows:

Dated: _____

Signed: _____
Attorney for Appellant (or Appellant, if not represented by an Attorney)

Attorney Name: _____

Address: _____

_____

Telephone No: _____

If a Bankruptcy Appellate Panel Service is authorized to hear this appeal, each party has a right to have the appeal heard by the district court. The appellant may exercise this right only by filing a separate statement of election at the time of the filing of this notice of appeal. Any other party may elect, within the time provided in 28 U.S.C. § 158(c), to have the appeal heard by the district court.

Form B18 (Official Form 18)
(9/97)

Form 18. DISCHARGE OF DEBTOR

IN A CHAPTER 7 CASE

[Caption as in Form 16A]

DISCHARGE OF DEBTOR

It appearing that the debtor is entitled to a discharge, **IT IS ORDERED:** The debtor is granted a discharge under section 727 of title 11, United States Code, (the Bankruptcy Code).

Dated: _____

BY THE COURT

_____
United States Bankruptcy Judge

SEE THE BACK OF THIS ORDER FOR IMPORTANT INFORMATION.

Form B18 continued
(9/97)

EXPLANATION OF BANKRUPTCY DISCHARGE
IN A CHAPTER 7 CASE

This court order grants a discharge to the person named as the debtor. It is not a dismissal of the case and it does not determine how much money, if any, the trustee will pay to creditors.

Collection of Discharged Debts Prohibited

The discharge prohibits any attempt to collect from the debtor a debt that has been discharged. For example, a creditor is not permitted to contact a debtor by mail, phone, or otherwise, to file or continue a lawsuit, to attach wages or other property, or to take any other action to collect a discharged debt from the debtor. *[In a case involving community property:]* [There are also special rules that protect certain community property owned by the debtor's spouse, even if that spouse did not file a bankruptcy case.] A creditor who violates this order can be required to pay damages and attorney's fees to the debtor.

However, a creditor may have the right to enforce a valid lien, such as a mortgage or security interest, against the debtor's property after the bankruptcy, if that lien was not avoided or eliminated in the bankruptcy case. Also, a debtor may voluntarily pay any debt that has been discharged.

Debts That are Discharged

The chapter 7 discharge order eliminates a debtor's legal obligation to pay a debt that is discharged. Most, but not all, types of debts are discharged if the debt existed on the date the bankruptcy case was filed. (If this case was begun under a different chapter of the Bankruptcy Code and converted to chapter 7, the discharge applies to debts owed when the bankruptcy case was converted.)

Debts that are Not Discharged.

Some of the common types of debts which are not discharged in a chapter 7 bankruptcy case are:

a. Debts for most taxes;

b. Debts that are in the nature of alimony, maintenance, or support;

c. Debts for most student loans;

d. Debts for most fines, penalties, forfeitures, or criminal restitution obligations;

e. Debts for personal injuries or death caused by the debtor's operation of a motor vehicle while intoxicated;

f. Some debts which were not properly listed by the debtor;

g. Debts that the bankruptcy court specifically has decided or will decide in this bankruptcy case are not discharged;

h. Debts for which the debtor has given up the discharge protections by signing a reaffirmation agreement in compliance with the Bankruptcy Code requirements for reaffirmation of debts.

This information is only a general summary of the bankruptcy discharge. There are exceptions to these general rules. Because the law is complicated, you may want to consult an attorney to determine the exact effect of the discharge in this case.

Form B19
12/94

Form 19. CERTIFICATION AND SIGNATURE OF NON-ATTORNEY BANKRUPTCY PETITION PREPARER (See 11 U.S.C. § 110)

[Caption as in Form 16B.]

CERTIFICATION AND SIGNATURE OF NON-ATTORNEY BANKRUPTCY PETITION PREPARER (See 11 U.S.C. § 110)

I certify that I am a bankruptcy petition preparer as defined in 11 U.S.C. § 110, that I prepared this document for compensation, and that I have provided the debtor with a copy of this document.

_____

Printed or Typed Name of Bankruptcy Petition Preparer

_____

Social Security No.

_____

_____

Address

Names and Social Security numbers of all other individuals who prepared or assisted in preparing this document:

If more than one person prepared this document, attach additional signed sheets conforming to the appropriate Official Form for each person.

X _____   _____

   Signature of Bankruptcy Petition Preparer   Date

A bankruptcy petition preparer's failure to comply with the provisions of title 11 and the Federal Rules of Bankruptcy Procedure may result in fines or imprisonment or both. 11 U.S.C. § 110; 18 U.S.C. § 156.

Form B20A (Official Form 20A)
(9/97)

Form 20A. Notice of Motion or Objection

[Caption as in Form 16A.]

NOTICE OF [MOTION TO   ] [OBJECTION TO   ]

_____has filed papers with the court to [relief sought in motion or objection].

<u>Your rights may be affected.</u> You should read these papers carefully and discuss them with your attorney, if you have one in this bankruptcy case. (If you do not have an attorney, you may wish to consult one.)

If you do not want the court to [relief sought in motion or objection], or if you want the court to consider your views on the [motion] [objection], then on or before _(date)_, you or your attorney must:

[File with the court a written request for a hearing {*or, if the court requires a written response*, an answer, explaining your position} at:

{address of the bankruptcy clerk's office}

If you mail your {request}{response} to the court for filing, you must mail it early enough so the court will **receive** it on or before the date stated above.

You must also mail a copy to:

{movant's attorney's name and address}

{names and addresses of others to be served}]

[Attend the hearing scheduled to be held on __(date)__, _(year)_, at ___ a.m./p.m. in Courtroom ____, United States Bankruptcy Court, {address}.]

[Other steps required to oppose a motion or objection under local rule or court order.]

If you or your attorney do not take these steps, the court may decide that you do not oppose the relief sought in the motion or objection and may enter an order granting that relief.

Date: _____   Signature: _____
                                                    Name:
                                                    Address:

Form B20B (Official Form 20B)
(9/97)

Form 20B. Notice of Objection to Claim

[Caption as in Form 16A.]

NOTICE OF OBJECTION TO CLAIM

_____ has filed an objection to your claim in this bankruptcy case.

Your claim may be reduced, modified, or eliminated. You should read these papers carefully and discuss them with your attorney, if you have one.

If you do not want the court to eliminate or change your claim, then on or before ___(date)___ , you or your lawyer must:

> {If required by local rule or court order.}

> [File with the court a written response to the objection, explaining your position, at:

>> {address of the bankruptcy clerk's office}

> If you mail your response to the court for filing, you must mail it early enough so that the court will **receive** it on or before the date stated above.

> You must also mail a copy to:

>> {objector's attorney's name and address}

>> {names and addresses of others to be served}]

> Attend the hearing on the objection, scheduled to be held on (date),
> (year) , at _____a.m./p.m. in Courtroom ____, United States Bankruptcy Court, {address}.

If you or your attorney do not take these steps, the court may decide that you do not oppose the objection to your claim.

Date: _____   Signature: _____
                                 Name:
                                 Address: